GOLDEN TALES OF
NEW ENGLAND

Selected and

with an Introduction

by

MAY LAMBERTON BECKER

Decorations by

LOIS LENSKI

BONANZA BOOKS

NEW YORK

ACKNOWLEDGMENTS

The gratitude of the editor goes not only to these collaborating authors and publishers but to the staff of the New York Public Library, whose reading-room at Forty-second street extended countless courtesies and to the Nantucket Public Library and the Lowell Public Library, for valuable information.

A LOCAL COLORIST by Annie Trumbull Slosson
From *A Local Colorist and Other Stories*
(This selection is used by permission of the publishers, Charles Scribner's Sons, New York.)

THE GUESTS OF MRS. TIMMS by Sarah Orne Jewett
From *The Life of Nancy*
(This selection is used by permission of, and by arrangement with, Houghton Mifflin Company, the authorized publishers.)

THE PARING-BEE by Rowland Robinson
From *Danvis Folks*
(This selection is used by permission of, and by arrangement with, Houghton Mifflin Company, the authorized publishers.)

A TOWN MOUSE AND A COUNTRY MOUSE by Rose Terry Cooke
From *Huckleberries from New England Hills* (1892)

"THERE SHE BLOWS!" by William Hussey Macy From *There She Blows!* (1877)

OLD ESTHER DUDLEY by Nathaniel Hawthorne
From *Twice Told Tales* (1837)

THE WELLFLEET OYSTERMAN by Henry D. Thoreau
From *Cape Cod* (1865)

THE EVENT OF THE SEASON by Oliver Wendell Holmes
From *Elsie Venner* (1861)

HOW WE KEPT THANKSGIVING AT OLDTOWN by Harriet Beecher Stowe
From *Old Town Folks* (1869)

"LIFE IS ONE DARN THING AFTER ANOTHER" by Henry A. Shute
From *Plupy* (1910)

LIFE-EVERLASTIN' by Mary E. Wilkins
From *A New England Nun*
(Copyrighted by Harper and Brothers. This selection is reprinted by permission of the publishers.)

OLD MAN WARNER by Dorothy Canfield
From *Raw Material*
(This selection is used by permission of the publishers, Harcourt, Brace and Company, New York.)

BY THE COMMITTEE by Bliss Perry
From *Scribner's Magazine*

FROM REYKJAVIK TO GLOUCESTER by James Brendan Connolly
From *Out of Gloucester*
(This selection is used by permission of the publishers, Charles Scribner's Sons, New York.)

This 1985 edition is published by Bonanza Books, distributed by Crown Publishers, Inc.,
by arrangement with Dodd, Mead & Company, Inc.

Manufactured in the United States of America

Library of Congress Cataloging in Publication Data
Main entry under title:

Golden tales of New England.

1. American literature — New England.   2. Short stories, American — New England.   3. New England — Literary collections.   4. New England — Fiction.   5. New England — Addresses, essays, lectures.   I. Becker, May Lamberton, 1873-1958.
PS541.G64   1985   813'.01' 08974   84-24296
ISBN: 0-517-467917

h g f e d c b a

CONTENTS

CONTENTS

FOREWORD

The preface to this collection will be found scattered through its pages, in the introductory notes to the stories. In other words, there will be seventeen curtain-raisers and no overture. All there will be at this point is a statement of its purpose: to bring back—living, breathing, talking—some part of an America that has ceased to be, but only in the sense that it has disappeared from our everyday experience to become part of our national consciousness.

New England has always been known as a good place to go away from, and from the earlier days of her history her sons have left her for every part of our country. I have seen hanging from clotheslines in a Missouri village as fine a collection of hand-pieced ancestral bedquilts as ever I found in Vermont. Travelling in Wisconsin the trainman telephoned ahead for my luncheon to be brought aboard and a market-basket was handed in with a New England boiled dinner complete in every detail, as savory and succulent as those of my Massachusetts great-grandmother, and she could compile and edit a boiled dinner in her ninetieth year. Wherever that strong stock was transplanted it struck root and went on vigorously growing. But the sap was the idealism of an earlier day. In this deepest sense, old New England lives in the veins of American history and national character.

It is the fond hope of the editor that some of these stories will make someone homesick. It may be for a particular farm-house, barn or village street, or it may be that more subtle nostalgia, homesickness for a home one has never seen. For old New England, that "plantation of God in the wilderness," was for many a formative year in our history such a spiritual home of American idealism. Hamlin Garland, at the climax of his pilgrimage to Boston as a youth from the Middle Border, stood on the hallowed Common and looked about him as one revisiting a spiritual inheritance. Vachel Lindsay's "rocky mountain cat" explained in "So Much the Worse for Boston" what Boston meant to the hopes of the West. To the American of to-day the dreams of New England remain as a spiritual heritage.

New York City, 1931.   MAY LAMBERTON BECKER

ANNIE TRUMBULL SLOSSON
(1838–1926)

If some kind fairy could lift a homesick New Englander sleeping far away, and set him down in bed in the kitchen chamber of the old farmhouse, he would know he was in New England before he opened his eyes. Of course there would be in summer the scent of cinnamon roses and barn hay through the open window, or in winter the rich whiff from butt'ry or sullerway through the half-closed door, but besides there would somewhere be someone talking. There would be a tone in the voices, a blend of *timbre* and *tempo* that we call a "twang" because, like a plucked string, the last note lingers—but as the awakening exile came up to the surface of consciousness he would realize—and with what a throb of recognition!—that he was once more listening to people who savored speech and came of an ancestry that had for generations admired and respected words.

Language, like costume, tends to become standardized throughout the United States; the radio is the mail-order catalogue of speech. Only in hill country or along lonesome roads the old speech lingers in New England, and only old people really speak it even there. The cultured already were "collecting" examples of it eighty years ago. Fur-bearing seals must have been more confiding in the forties, when James Russell Lowell listened enchanted to the talk of two farm-boys watching a pair of them that had made their way as far as the wharves near Boston, and were disporting off shore. "Wal, neaow," asked one, "be them kind o' critters common up this way, do ye suppose? Be they— or be they?" and the other replied, "Wal, dunno's they be and dunno ez they be." Repeat this to one who claims New England ancestry—making sure to put the right tune to the words—and see if he does not take a sort of personal pride in that bit of dialogue: T. W. Higginson called it "this perfect flower of New England speech, twin blossoms on one stem." It was Higginson's brother who brought home a lovely turn of phrase from a lonely farmhouse where he had stopped for dinner when he was helping to lay out the Old Colony Railroad, and where he had regretfully declined a second portion of mince. "Consult your feelings, sir, about the meat pie," said his host. Whoever he was, he had the sense of words.

One of the reasons why this story has been placed out of its chronological order in a collection where, let us admit, chronology will be often set aside, is that it gives the reader not only an unrivalled collection of ancient and characteristic forms and turns of speech, but something even more important, an understanding of the habit of mind that makes it possible for this speech to survive. It must be more than respected if it is to go on living; it must be taken for granted as the really right way of talking, and above all, it must never be laughed at.

Annie Trumbull, who married Edward Slosson of New York in 1867, was born in Connecticut of a family learned in politics, war and science, and lived a long time in the high country in which this action takes place. She was a naturalist devoted especially to botany, and to be a botanist north of Boston is to be on the way to an understanding of some apparent contradictions of character. No one could be taken quite by surprise at finding strange contrasts between human nature and its environment who has searched out arbutus, or Indian pipes, or the incongruous beauty of the moccasin-flower, or has parted pine-branches and come upon the tropic blaze of the red lily, bright in a clearing.

In "Fishin' Jimmy," "Seven Dreamers," and "Dumb Foxglove" she wrote—at the height of the renascence of the New England short story—about characters often "a little touched," kind souls on terms too good with solitude. But in this, the title story of a collection published in 1912, the heroine is quite as kind and completely clear-headed.

A LOCAL COLORIST

By ANNIE TRUMBULL SLOSSON

WHEN I was a mite of a child, I was always sayin' that I'd
be a book-writer when I growed up. I rec'lect lots of times
folks askin' me—as they're always doin' with young ones,
you know—what I was goin' to be when I got a woman
grown, and my sayin' every time I should be a great author.
Sometimes I'd make it more partic'lar and say a poet or a
story-writer, or again I'd have it an editor or some kind of
newspaper-maker, but most gen'rally 'twas just a plain
author, no partic'lar sort. So, feelin' that way from the very
beginnin', 'twas queer that I never did write for print as
the years went by. I was forever thinkin' about it, plannin'
for it, surmisin' just how 'twould feel when my own
makin's-up was printed out and read all over the airth, and
I never for one single minute give up bein' certain sure that
before I died—and long afterward, too—I should be
known and spoke of as a great, a dreadful great, authoress.
But I never seemed to get at it. You see, I was so busy. I
never had to work for my livin', but I was oldest of five
and had lots to do helpin' ma with the little ones and the
housework.

Then there was school and lessons till I was nigh seventeen, and after that beaux, and pretty soon one beau in partic'lar—Mr. Kidder, you know. You can't write much in
courtin' days, nor in marryin'-time neither, and 'course

4

when little Nathan come and then Fanny Ann and Prudence, my hands were too full for authorin'. But I kep' on lottin' on doin' it some day, knowin' I should manage it somehow.

It wa'n't till I was left all alone by myself two year ago that I felt I could really begin. I set the day quite a spell aforehand. It was to be the 28th of May. The spring cleanin' would be through by that time, and the preservin' and cannin' and puttin' up jell and pickles not begun. Only a few summer boarders gen'rally come as early as that, so there wouldn't be much goin' on outside to watch from the windows and take off my mind. Altogether it seemed just the right time. Of course there had to be a set day in case my writin's turned out pop'lar and talked about, and I was pretty certain they would. Folks always want to know all about great writers, and I kep' sayin' over to myself words from the newspaper accounts: "It was only a few years ago, on the 28th of May, that this interestin' "—or "thrillin'," or "beautiful," or somethin', as the case might be—"authoress began her first and perchance her greatest book."

I laid in my writin' things, a new bottle of ink, some pens, and a quire of paper, and fixed my table in a good light. That was in March, for I was always forehanded. I was beginnin' to be a mite impatient, wantin' to have the worst over, when one day a new idee come into my head. Up to that cold March mornin', if you'll believe it, I never once thought what kind of writin' I should begin with; verses or prose pieces, narr'tives or what-all, I hadn't decided on any of 'em. It didn't take very long, though. I was dreadful fond of story-books, and I never cared no

great for poetry or lives of folks or travellin' adventur's.
I'd write stories, just one first off, and then a lot of 'em
"by the authoress of ———." My! I hadn't fixed on a name.
But that could come later when I knew what kind of a story
it was. Then come the hardest of all—what it should be
about. I couldn't make up my mind about that. I won't go
over all the different plans I had; to write about lords and
earls or lay it in heathen lands or in *Mayflower* days
among the Pilgrims, or in the Civil War, or among
pirates and Captain Kidd, or early Christian martyrs.
I went over all them and lots more, but wasn't a
bit nearer decidin', when Mary Dowd passed through
here on her way to Hall. She'd writ me aforehand, and
I went over to the depot to see her. There was only about
half an hour between trains, and we had a great deal to
say. She is real smart, you know—had the Dayville School
three terms, and is a great book-reader, so I wanted her
advice. But she was all for my tellin' her first how my
rhubarb pies was made; then she branched off into pie
crust gen'rally, and how hers never had that light short-
ness mine always had, and it was only a few minutes before train-time that I got a chance to put my case. She was
real interested, and she says right off quick, without havin'
to think it over, "Oh," she says, "write a dialect story;
that's the only thing that takes these days." "What in
creation's that?" I says, and she looked most sorry for me.
But she's real kind-hearted, and she begun to explain.
Before I could get much idee of the thing the train whistled and she started to pick up her bag. Near as I could
understand, dialect—I didn't know just how to spell it or

speak it then, but I got it right afterward—dialect was any kind of queer, outlandish talk folks in any deestrict use, the queerer the better. The more you put in your story and the worse 'twas spelt and the harder to understand, why, as I gathered from what she said as she climbed up the steps—bag in one hand and umbrella in the other and a book under each arm, so't she couldn't help steppin' on her skirt in front every step—why, the better your story was and the bigger pay it fetched. "But where'll I get this derelict talk?" I says, not gettin' the right word first off, and knowin' the other from Captain Gates, who'd followed the sea. "Go 'round till you find it," she says, as she went into the car, and tripped on the sill so's she most fell over, "and then write it out." "How'll I know how to spell it?" I calls out as she settles into her seat and begins to fix her things. "You don't have to know," says she through the window; "don't make any difference how it's spelt; that's why it's so easy." Just as the train started she put her face down to the open part of the window—it was only up a little way and was wedged there as they always be in cars—and called out, "And be sure you put in lots of local color." "What color?" I hollered out as loud as I could. I see her mouth open, but I couldn't for the life of me catch a word, and in a jiffy she was out of sight. Well, I wrote to her for more partic'lars, and she sent me a whole sheetful of explainin's. She said dialect was most everywheres, but different in different places. I'd find it nigh me or further away. But when I'd got it I mustn't only take it down lit'ral, but I must put in the color she'd spoke of, which meant the sort of folks that talked the dialect, how they looked and acted and all about the place and the scenery, and partic'lar the weather. There must be dark, lowerin' clouds, or an azure sky or wailin' winds or lurid sunsets or something similar. That was all called local color, she said, and it was a most important—in fact, a necessary—ingredjent. "Like lard in pie crust," I says to myself, for that word ingredjent sounded like receipt-book talk, and the last part of her letter was about my rhubarb pies again.

Well, 'course I had to begin now, first thing, to hunt up folks that talked dialects, and it wasn't any easy job I tell you. Mary'd said it might be found right 'round you or further away. 'Twas certain sure it couldn't be 'round me, for I lived then, just as I do now, here in the mountains, though it was in Francony those days instead of here in Lisbon, and there wasn't a thing of the kind in the whole place. I knew every single soul for miles 'round, and they all talked good, plain, sensible talk like everybody else, nothin' queer or what you might call dialectic. But I was set on bein' fair and correct, and not leavin' any stone unturned, as the sayin' is, without turnin' it up. So I went over in my mind all the folks there and what languages they used. I didn't seem to find anything sing'lar, but thinks I, I'll go 'round amongst the people a little and talk with 'em and take partic'lar notice of what they say. It didn't come to anythin'. Even the old aged folks that might have fetched down from past generations some strange lingo or other, they talked the right kind of talk we all of us use. I didn't tell 'em what I was at, but sort of drawed 'em out on different subjects and watched sharp for any dialects. But not a sign of 'em turned up. Even Gran'sir Peckham, more'n eighty year old, didn't show a mite of it. I talked about the weather with him as he stood at the gate one time; asked him if he thought 'twould be a nice day, and so on. He said just what anybody anywheres that had took notice of the clouds would say, that it was goin' to be catchin' weather like the day afore, when he got soppin' wet over to the medder lot, and he cal'lated 'twould keep on thataway till the moon fulled. " 'T any rate," he says, "it's growthy weather for grass." Nobody could have talked sensibler nor more like other folks nor with scurser dialect. And Aunt Drusilly Bowles, born and raised right there on the Butter Hill road, she was just the same. A mite of a body she is, you know, lookin' as if you could blow her over with one breath, but tough and rugged. She was carryin' two pails of water, one in each hand, as I went by, and I called out to her, "Ain't they heavy?" I says. "Not a mite—that is, for me," says she. "I could heft twice as much." She come out to the road, still a-carryin' the pails, and went on talkin'. "I don't see," says she, "but I'm jest as spry and up-and-doin' as I was twenty year back. The Priests, our branch—mother's side, ye know—they're a long-lived tribe and peart and chirky to the last. Ma herself was dreadful poor, never weighed ninety pound in all her born days, but she was powerful strong, all bone and sinner to the last. There wa'n't never a peakid or pindlin' Priest I ever heerd tell on," she says, straightenin' up, sort o' proud like. And it was all like that, plain, nat'ral language like anybody's, not a sign of dialection, as you might call it. So I traipsed 'round that town till my feet ached lookin' for what I knowed aforehand wasn't there. I wouldn't go anywheres else till I'd tried every chance to home.

When I was sure there wasn't a speck of real dialect in Francony nor for miles 'round there, I took the cars for Haverhill, where my niece's son, Eben Reynolds, lived. Ridin' in the stage over to Bethlehem for the mornin' train, I couldn't get this thing out o' my head. You're somethin' of a writer yourself, ma'am, and must know how it kind o' spiles things havin' to think how they'd look in print. I know I heerd Leonard Colby say once—he used to write pieces for the paper, you know—that he couldn't even say good night to his girl when he was keepin' company with Ellen Peabody without thinkin' to himself how 'twould be called in print "a yearnin' embrace" or somethin'; said it took part of the int'rest out of it. So 'twas with me that time. 'Twas a real nice mornin', a spring feelin' in the air, the trees not exactly budded out, but showin' they were goin' to be pretty soon, a kind of live purplish gray all over 'em, and the sky a pictur'. But I couldn't just set still and let it all soak into me without act'ally thinkin' about it, as I used to, no more'n these new folks that call theirselves natur'-lovers can really love natur'. They're after book names for what they see, examples of amazin' smartness in birds or creatur's like what Professor Thingamy or Doctor Thisorthat writ about. And I was huntin' for the dialect way of tellin' what I see that day. I looked up to the sky, such a pretty blue, and the little soft white woolly clouds strimmered all over it, and

I wondered if there was any dialectic word that answered to strimmer. Seems 's if there couldn't be one that pictur'd out the real thing so good. For them clouds was strimmered and nothin' else. I thought as I see the apple trees with their spranglin', crooked, knotty branches showin' a'ready signs of the spring life, thinks I, "They'll be pink with blowth afore we know it." And then 'stead of just being comfortable and pleased over that idee I went and begun guessin' if there was any other word in any part of the world that stood for "blowth." Certain sure there couldn't be a word that described things so plain. Why, you can't only see the posies as you're sayin' it, but you can act'ally smell 'em. "Oh, how glad I be," I says to myself, "that I don't have to talk dialect or any other outlandish languages started, I daresay, in Babel times when folks got so mixed up and confused." 'Course I'm always kind to foreigners and make allowances for 'em. Look at it one way, it ain't their fault their talkin' that way. But I feel to rejoice, as they say in prayer-meetin', that I wasn't born or raised one. Sometimes seems 's if, even if I had been, I'd have broke away when I growed up and sensed things. I can't pictur' anybody with a drop of Spooner blood in 'em talkin' such lingo as Dutch Peter over to Lisbon or Mary Bodoe on Wallace Hill keep jabberin' all the time. However and wherewithal, as Deacon Lamb used to say in meetin's, thankful as I might be that I talked good New Hampshire, I was bound to find the other kind afore May 28th, when my book was to begin.

But I hadn't any more luck Haverhill way than 'round home. It made me feel real mean, too, visitin' as I was

and folks showin' me so much attention, and me spyin' on
'em, as you might say, and prickin' up my ears in hopes of
hearin' some queer dialecty talk to use in my writin's.
Served me right that I didn't hear a speck. Eben's folks
come from our way, and o' course they talked good Fran-
cony-American, and their neighbors done the same. When
I went over the river to Bradford I was in Vermont, you
know. I thought mebbe they'd speak different over there,
but they didn't. They conversed jest our way, only more
so, if anything. For some of the old folks kep' up words
I had 'most forgot, but good, sensible, straight-meanin'
words, with nothin' outlandish or dialectical about 'em.
Grandma Quimby, raised in Whitefield, but marryin' a
Bradford man and livin' there thirty year, she says when
I asked her how her little granddaughter Dorry was,
"Little?" say she. "Why, you'd ought to see her; she's
a great big gormin' girl now." That "gormin'" did bring
back old times and pa. He always applied that term to me
when I was growin' up, and it's a scrumtious word. I do
lot on words that pictur' things out like that. And her
daughter, Aunt Meeny Tucker, she puts in: "And Cyrus's
gettin' a big boy too. It's all his pa can do to manage him.
He's got the Dodge grit, and he's real masterful, runs all
over the town without leave, the kitin'est boy." Exactly
what ma used to say about Dan'l. Oh, I do so set by the
good, plain, meanin' talk! By this time I see I must go
further away if I expected to get hold of anything to use in
my writin's, and I decided to go to Nashaway to Jane
Webster's, and if I didn't get it there to keep on as fur as
Brown's Corners, 'cross the Massachusetts line. "If I don't

find it there," I says to myself, "I'll give up. I can't go to Injy's coral strands, not even to find ingredjents for my book-writin'."

'Twas the same story at Nashaway, no dialects at all, not the least taste, though I visited 'round, in all classes, as they say. Then I went to Massachusetts. But, dear land! Brown's Corners wasn't a mite different from Francony or Lisbon, Haverhill or Bradford. Common talk full o' common sense, both of 'em common to all New England, f'r aught I know. I didn't know anybody at the Corners but Mis' Harris Spooner, own cousin to Mr. Kidder's first wife, and I put up with her. She'd always lived in Massachusetts, born there, and I sort of hoped I could pick up something sing'lar in her conversation worth puttin' into my story. But 'twas no good; seems even there so nigh to Boston their languages is same as ourn. She didn't talk of anything scursely but about Viletty—Mr. Kidder's first, you know, my predecessor, 's they say—and how pious and sickly she was. Told me all about her last days, how white and meechin' she looked, and how dreadful poor and skinny, and yet how she hung on, hung on till seemed 's if she never'd pass away. And she dwelt on Mr. Kidder's sorrer and how he kind o' clung to Viletty 's if he couldn't part with her, and how mebbe that was the reason she hung on, hung on so long. She said some folks think if you hold on too tight to them you set by when they're sick and ready to go, they can't break loose, somethin' seems to draw 'em back and pin 'em down. And she told how she says to him frequent, "Reuben, Reuben," says she, "let her go home, loose your hold and let her depart." Well, seems he did. 'T any rate she did depart, or else o' course I wouldn't have been Mis' Reuben Kidder now. 'Twas real interestin' and nigh about all news to me, for Mr. Kidder wasn't no great of a talker. Anyway, men folks never seem to talk about things as well as women, do they? Leave out the little trimmin's that set it off so and stick to main facts, the last thing we care about. He'd never once mentioned all the time we lived together how Viletty had hung on, hung on, and it's bein' thought likely 'twas because of his tight hold on her. You'd think he'd a-known it would be entertainin' to me, takin' Viletty's place as I had. The whole narr'tive was spoke in as good plain talk as any I could have put it in myself, down to the very end, Viletty's dyin' words, the layin' out, the wreaths and crowns and pillers from the neighbors, and the funeral exercises. She said she'd take me out to the buryin'-ground afore I left, a dreadful sightly place on Dodd's Hill, to see the grave. I'd have admired to go, but it rained the whole endurin' time, and I didn't get a chance.

Well, here 'twas the 24th of May, and no dialections to put into that story that was to be started on the 28th. I was dreadful upset and put out. Seemed certain sure that I couldn't do the kind of book that was most in the fashion that time, and so must set to work at something different. As for the local color, if that only meant sceneries and weather and actin's and doin's, why, I could fix them all right, but, as I understood Mary Dowd to say, that wasn't no use without a lot o' this dialect, and that I couldn't find high nor low. Up to that time I hadn't told a single

creatur' what I was at. But that day, as I was goin' along
in the train, who should get in at Greenfield station but
Abby Matthews on her way home from visitin' with
Ephraim's folks. I was so glad to see her, and so filled
up with all I'd been through and wanted to go through,
that I spilled over and emptied out my whole heart. I told
her every single thing, how I'd always been set on bein'
an authoress and what Mary Dowd said and how I'd
traipsed all over the airth lookin' for dialects and couldn't
find a speck, and me only four days from the date I'd set
for beginnin' my great, prob'ly my greatest, work. She
was real interested and pleased too, said 'twould be a great
thing for Francony and for Grafton County—in fact, for
the whole State o' New Hampshire—to have an authoress
of their own. As for this dialect, she said she'd heerd of it
as bein' all the go nowadays in storybook writin', but to the
best of her rememberin' she hadn't never seen a case of it
herself. It was some kind of queer-soundin' talk when you
heerd it, and queerer-lookin' when you read it, and the
spellin' was every which way, no reg'lar rule. As for her,
says she, she never conceited folks did talk just that way in
any deestrict on the airth; she'd always held that the story-
writers made it up as they went along, and she'd advise
me to do so myself. As for "local color," she never'd heerd
of such a thing, and I'd better not have anything to do
with it. "Tell your story plain and straight, and put everything down in black and white and steer clear o' any other
colors, local or be-they-who-they-be," she says. "But I
can't make up a thing I don't know anything about," says
I. "If I only could see a sample of this dialectical talk or

hear somebody speak a mite of it, I'd see where I was standin', but I can't make a start afore I know more about it; that's the thing of it. I'm every bit as sot as you can be, Abby Matthews, on beginnin' this great work. All is, I must have a mite of a hint or a help to start me, and then I can go on like a house afire." She see the sense of that, and just then the train slowed up comin' into Bath, where she was goin' to get out, and in a minute I was left by myself again.

"Well, Abby ain't been of much use in one way," thinks I, "but she gave me sympathy, and 'twas a sight of comfort to talk things over with her. And, after all, I guess sympathy's worth more'n dialect in the long run, and sometimes seems 's if 'twas nigh about as scurse." I just gave up hope that night, yet 'twas only next day that I found what I was lookin' for—dialect and plenty of it.

I'm afraid you won't hardly understand, and mebbe 'll think it dreadful when I tell you 'twas in answer to prayer. I've always been in the habit of askin' the Lord for what I wanted, even if I wasn't sure 'twas a right thing to want. I left it to Him to decide that and to show me if I'd made a mistake. He give the gift of tongues one time, you know, and He promises to put the very words into your mouth that you'd ought to speak in tryin' times, so why'd this thing be so dreadful different? Anyway, I tried it, and I told Him the whole story that night. And I says if there wasn't any harm in my bein' an authoress—and lots of real Christians followed that business, as He well knew—and if I couldn't be a real fav'rite without puttin' in this thing, would He p'int out to me where to find it and how I'd

ought to make use of it and, if 'twas possible, to do good
with it. I got up real comforted and went to bed easier in
my mind than I had for a long spell. I was 'round the
house next forenoon doin' the work, and I stepped to the
window to shake out my dust-cloth. I see some one goin'
along the road; a stranger I knew 'twas right off. 'Twas
a young lady, real nice-lookin', and I guessed she must be
an early summer boarder. I didn't want to be seen starin'
at her, and was just goin' to step back out o' sight, when
she looked up and smiled in a real pretty, friendly way.
'Course I smiled back, and she come closer and says
"Good morning." I slat the dust-cloth down and come
'round to the front door, and in five minutes we was talkin'
away like old cronies. Seems she was stayin' over to Mis'
Nichols's—I'd heerd they was expectin' a boarder—only
come night before, and she was lookin' 'round the place.
Well, I hadn't heerd her say a dozen words 'fore I see
she talked different from the folks 'round there, different
from anybody I'd heerd anywheres. Now I can't show you
just how 'twas different. I never could act out things and
show how folks did 'em, copyin' their talk and ways. I
always broke down and sp'iled the dialogues at school ex-
hibition if they give me a part. But I can tell you some of
the things that made this talk so dreadful queer and give
me, right at the very beginnin', what they call in prayer-
meetin' a tremblin' hope that I was findin' what I'd looked
for so long.

First place, everything she said sounded like readin' out
of a book. Now you know 'most everybody has two kinds
of talk, one for speakin' and the other for writin' and

readin'. Talk-talk and book-talk, as you might put it. But my! you couldn't see any difference here; any of it might have been read off from a book or a paper. And then such queer, long stretched-out words, some of 'em span new to me and some I'd seen in books or heerd in sermons or lectur's. She had a way of stoppin' short 'twixt her words that I couldn't make out or get used to, like this: When she wanted to say she didn't like winter 's well as summer she said she "did not like it at," then a kind of stop before she put in "all." First off I thought it was an accident and she'd stopped to swaller or get her breath or something. But she done it again and kep' doin' it, and I see 'twas a habit—part of her dialects. "At—all" says she every single time 'stead of "atall," as everybody else says. Then the most musical thing—I almost laughed every time she said it—when she asked me if I'd ever been somewheres or done something partic'lar she'd say "Did—you" this or that, with a stop between the words long enough for a swaller, or a stutter, or a gap, or a hiccup. "Did—you" she'd always say, 'stead of "didjer," as other folks say. And when she wanted to put in "ever" she'd stop the same way 'twixt you and ever. "Did-you-ever" she says, 'stead of the right way, "Didjever," like other folks. She was int'rested in all I said and real friendly, wanted to keep me talkin', and hoped she wasn't inconveniencin' me, and so on. And when I said I wasn't partic'lar busy, only just potterin' 'round she says, "Potterin'! Such a delightful term!" she says; "it reminds me of Keerammix" whoever he was—"and the plastic art. Potterin'!" she says over again, laughin', as if 'twas some uncommon, foreignish word or other. Where *did* she come from? Why, that word's used all over the airth, far's I know. I did hear a woman one time from down Connecticut way say putterin' 'stead of potterin', but I guess that was only her way of pronouncin' it. When I says of Joel Butts, settin' on his door-step 'cross the street, that he was "shif'less as a cow blackbird," she claspt her hands and says, "Delicious! and shows such a fa-mil-i-ar-i-ty with nature and a certain knowledge of orni—something." (I writ that down as quick as she went away.) 'Course I didn't let her see I was usin' her for a copy; she didn't suspicion it. She ast lots of questions and listened sharp to what I said. But I guess she see pretty quick there wa'n't nothin' queer about my languages. The commonest things, the talk used by all sensible folks the world over, seemed to strike her most and stir her all up. Times I thought she wasn't exactly polite, what we'd call, for she'd repeat over somethin' I'd said and laugh, but as she always ended by praisin' it up I didn't mind. And I was so tickled at findin' a case of genuin' dialects. There was a chiny posy-holder in my window with some dried grass in it from last year, just a common one, had belonged to ma. She didn't seem to know what 'twas 'tall; asked if it was an "antic" or a "airloom"; and again she spoke of it as a "varze." When I told her over again and louder, conceitin' she might be a mite hard o' hearin', that 'twas only a old crock'ry posy-holder, she hollered out, "Posy-holder—how dear!" And I hadn't said a word about the price. I didn't want to sell it, anyway. "Posy," says she, "the quaint old word of the poets, Old English," she says. But I told her no, 'twas Chinee, I guessed, fetched over by ma's brother, Uncle Elam, who follered the sea.

That started her off again, and she says it after me: "Follered the sea! How expressive and vivid, suggestin' the call of the ocean to its lovers," and such queer crazy-soundin' talk. I had to write it down quick, makin' an excuse to go into the other room. Another thing queer was her 'pologizin' the whole 'durin' time for goodness knows what and beggin' me to forgive her for somethin' or 'nother. If she didn't sense what I said and wanted to hear it over again, she'd ask me to excuse her dumbness by sayin' "Beg pardon." Time and again she says that when she hadn't done a thing, and when I answered polite every time, "Don't mention it," I see she was still expectin' somethin' and waitin' for me to say over again what I'd said afore. Then I see 'twas dialect for "What say?" and I put it down on my list. She had lots of those dialectics. When she was surprised at anything I'd tell her, she'd say, kind o' drawlin' like, "Fancy!" the fan part sort o' spread out, and I found that meant "Do tell" or "You don't say." And over 'n' over when I fetched in some common sayin', a weather sign about thunder in the mornin', farmers take warnin', or how turnin' back some o' your clothes you'd put on wrong side afore was bad luck, or any such well-known things, she'd say a real queer word. "Foclore," most 's if she was swearin', as Uncle Ben Knapp used to say "C'rinthians!" when he got excited.

One time I fetched her out a glass of milk and some hot gingerbread I'd just baked, and I fixed her in the rocker under the big ellum. She was real tickled, and give me to understand that it made her think of somebody named Al Fresscoe. I s'pose he most gen'rally et outdoors. She always had some queer remark to make about everything. When Si Little's ox team was standin' out in the road one day she went out and looked right into the creatur's' faces, and she says over some lingo about Juno and oxides; or mebbe 'twas ox-hides. And when I was tellin' her about Elbert Hill and how climbin' he was, how he'd come up from a poor boy, and now took in partner with Knight Brothers and aimin' to be a selectman some day, she was real struck and says, "Excelsior!" I think 'twas that; 'twas some kind o' stuffin' material, anyway. Even the commonest things like sayin' Jabez Goss was the well-to-doist man in Littleton, which everybody knows he is, she'd appear so struck or tickled over. I'd wonder every minute what fur-off ign'rant country she come from. Once I was tellin' her about Jesse Baker to Sugar Hill and how he could make verses on anything in the heavens or airth or the waters under the airth, f'r aught I know. I said nobody ever learnt him how to do it, he just took to it soon's he could speak; 'twas natur', I guessed. And she says some of her queer outlandish jabber about poets bein' nasty and not fit. She didn't say for what. Wonder if she'd say that about Watts and the rest o' the hymn-makers. 'Course this I'm tellin' you didn't all take place in that first meetin'. It wanted four days then to the 28th, the time I was to become an authoress, and I contrived to see Miss Mandeville (I'd found out her name) lots. I'd run out in the front yard whenever I see her comin' by, and I'd happen into the store if she went in. She was more'n willin' to talk with me, and I got together a whole mess of dialections and writ 'em down careful, though I didn't worry about the spellin', as I'd heerd that wasn't no great matter. She come into my house two or three times and was real int'rested in my things and talked dialect about 'em like a streak all the time. She looked at my old clock on the mantel-shelf that was grandma's and asked about it. It had stopped, as it had a way of doin' frequent, and I told her it didn't keep reg'lar time like my new one in the kitchen, but I said I liked it better than that one because it had been in our family so long and I'd seen it since I was a speck of a young one, and she says, "That goes without sayin'," says she. I hadn't an idee what she meant, for it don't go at all most times whether you say anything or not.

She was lookin' over my photograph album and she come to a likeness of Timothy Banks that used to keep store to Whitefield and moved down East. She turned it over to look on the back for his name, I s'pose, and she says, "Oh, Parree!" 'Twas one of her by-words, I guess, for there wa'n't any name there, only the man that took the pictur' down in Paris, Maine, where the Bankses live. Oh, she had some outlandish word for everything under the sun. What do you think she called goin' anywheres to stay over Sabbath day? You'd never guess. Wee Kend! 'Pears to be dialect for visitin' from Saturday to Monday —bakin'-day to wash-day, you know. But I can't tell you half; 'twould take a month o' Sundays.

She had out-o'-the-wayest words for everything. Speakin' o' Lyman Waters and how he'd fell away from his religion and now didn't even believe there was any God at all, what do you think she called him? An agg nostick! That was her dialection for a plain, common infidel that says in his heart there is no God. The Bible just calls him a fool, you know. And them different ways folks get into by spells, catchin' ways, you know, that runs through a deestrict, she spoke of as fads. Asked me one time if I'd took up this new fad of mas-ti-catin' my food a long time as recommended by Whitcher, or Belcher, or some one or other. But I told her no, I just chewed my victuals before swallowin', 's I always had.

I was so tickled by findin' all these dialects for my story that I 'most forgot I hadn't got a mite of local color to spread over 'em. How could I get it, not knowin' anything of the kind of local'ty she come from, her folks, and her bringin' up? Mebbe, thinks I, that will come out after a spell, and I can put it on last thing, like the third coat o' paint 'Lias Davis is puttin' on his house 'cross the road there. Sing'lar, I says to myself, to speak o' writin' 's if 'twas different colors. Though, come to think of it, I've heard of blue laws and blue books and yellow newspapers, red letters and black lists. But I never knew anything till lately of this local colorin' matter to stories, and I haven't got an idee how to put it on, just plain and thick all over, or strimmered about and different in spots. 'Course I could describe Miss Mandeville and all her colors—reddish hair, and indiger blue eyes, and pale-complected, and all. I could put in the weather, too; there's more in Francony than most deestricts, and it's all colors, too, probably local 's well as the rest, though I hadn't got yet a real clear idee what that was. But that way-off, sing'lar land she come from, where her folks lived, and everybody talked dialect talk, why, I hadn't no more idee how to paint it out than—than anything.

Well, come May 28th, I waked up 'fore sunrise full o' my story. I got breakfast out o' the way and washed up the dishes bright and early and done the housework so's to be all ready to set down to my writin'. My list o' dialec- tions, all took from this queer boarder's talk, was real lengthy now, plenty to begin with, anyway. As for the colorin', I could put in some weather and scenery—Mary Dowd said that was part of it—and touch it up bime-by with another shade or so as I got some more information. I'm sot on havin' lots of that color 'tany rate, thinks I, so if it runs or fades there'll be enough left to show. I'd tried my pen and found it went all right, and took a clean sheet o' paper to begin, when all of a sudden I rec'lected that I hadn't said my prayers that mornin'. I was dreadful ashamed. But it's bein' the great anniversary I'd looked ahead to so long and me so excited and nerved up and all, I'd clean forgot my duty and my religion. Land's sake, how small I felt! Down went my pen and I shoved back my chair and went up-chamber's quick as I could go.

It's well I done it. And yet it fetched me the biggest disapp'intment of my whole life long and as good as changed all my futur', my line o' business, my hopes, my everything. I was kneelin' by my bed, dreadful ashamed and just beginnin' to tell the Lord about it, when—before you could say Jack Robinson—a queer feelin' come all over me, and I was seein' things in a terrible different light. What had I been doin' these last few days? What was I lookin' ahead to doin' the days to come? I most heerd them questions asked out loud by some one, and I hid my face in the patchwork quilt and wished it could cover me up soul and body I was that ashamed. A poor young creatur', a stranger within our gates, had come to my door, come friendly and well-meanin'. And how had I acted to her? I had drawed her out, spied on her, took notice of her mistakes, set down on paper her dialections, rejoicin' over her stumblin' speech that I might set it out in print for the world to laugh over. And all that I, Abigail Jane Kidder, might be a great authoress. Do you wonder I was so ashamed I could a-crawled under that bed if 'twould a-hid me from every human bein'. That poor young creatur'! I thinks. Was it her fault she used that form o' speech, that "lispin', stammerin' tongue," as the hymn says? Didn't most likely her own folks use it, or similar, in that fur-off land from whence she come? Mightn't I, raised 's I'd been in a civilized c'mmunity, amongst plain-speakin' folks, have got into that kind o' dialectics if my relations and neighbors had all talked it in my comp'ny? Likely enough, for language is dreadful catchin'.

Well, never mind about that next hour. That's between me and some One else. But when I got up off my knees, brushed off my skirt, and smoothed out the quilt, I knew as well as I know it this very minute that I wasn't ever goin' to be a dialectical story-writer. I'd left off that habit afore 'twas too strong to break.

I won't deny I was disappointed. I own 'twas kind o' hard, one way, to think that the 28th of May, looked ahead to so long as the day of my beginnin' to be a great authoress, was, after all, the day of my leavin' off bein' one. But I knew my duty and I meant to do it. You might think I could a-took up some other kind of writin' that wouldn't ask one to draw out sing'lar folks and make fun of 'em. But somehow the sad turnin' out of this experiment kind o' set me agin' literary things, and I couldn't scursely look at that new pen and the clean white foolscap without feelin' qualmy. So I ain't an authoress, after all, and I guess I never will be now.

It come out after Miss Mandeville went away—I forgot to say she'd gone that very day afore I see her again, called home sudden—it come out she was from Boston way, not so dreadful fur off, after all, and was some kind of a writin' person. Some folks had it she was lookin' up dialectics herself to make pieces out of, but that couldn't be, I guess, or she wouldn't a-come here. Though mebbe she'd been misinformed, and so, after she met me and the other folks and heerd us talk, she found out she'd come to the wrong local'ty and went off. But I think of her frequent, and sometimes I find myself hopin' that though she wa'n't here long she may a-profited a mite by what she heerd, and left off some of her own talk and took on some o' ourn. As I said, afore, language is real catchin', and we never know what little word o'ourn, dropped in season, as they say, may spring up and bear fruit—yea. a hundred-fold. And mebbe even dialect, if it ain't been too long standin', may be broke up and helped—or mebbe clean cured, take it in time and afore you're too old and sot in your ways.

SARAH ORNE JEWETT
(1849–1909)

Even a motorist bent on making mileage is likely to pause at Portsmouth, New Hampshire, if only to look at some of the doorways for which that charming town is famous. I never saw lovelier save perhaps in Dublin, city of fair portals, and Portsmouth's have the advantage that passing through them you do not come, as too often through eighteenth-century Dublin doorways, into the squalor of tenement life. The portals of Portsmouth lead to dwellings that still retain much of their former dignity, though less of their former state. For this was a rich town early in its long history, knowing how to spend its money in elegances as well as comforts, and how to entertain with dignity as well as mirth. For those mansions bricks were brought from Holland, wallpaper from England, porcelain from France, and from the seven seas curios that gave drawing-rooms an exotic touch; there were formal dinners and stately receptions and on moonlight nights river-parties with music, up the Piscataqua as far as Berwick, where there were other noble houses with balustraded roofs. On one of these water-parties the grandmother of Sarah Orne Jewett made a romantic impression on a French prisoner-of-war, but she married a New Englander of wealth and family. Maine has its "Brahmin caste"; indeed Mr. Langdon in "Elsie Venner," offered as a typical young Brahmin of that period, is supposed to have come from Portland or Newburyport, or from Portsmouth. In a fine old house in North Berwick, the year that Poe died, Sarah Orne Jewett was born.

It held by that time the office of a country doctor, though Dr. Jewett was not only a general practitioner but professor in the medical department of Bowdoin. He is gratefully portrayed in Miss Jewett's "A Country Doctor," and he undoubtedly laid the foundation of her literary career. For he took his daughter with him on those occasions when shams are laid aside—the calls of a doctor who knows all about the patient and his family before him, in time of serious illness or the inescapable realities of birth and death. The young girl, whose health was somewhat delicate, went along for the ride, kept him company on the way, and on occasion listened to his patients or stayed to help them. It was a chance to see New England character with its defenses down, and it is to the credit of the characters not only of the countryside but of Miss Jewett, that the more she saw the more she seemed to respect her townspeople and the people of her state.

So when she began to write she had her purpose in hand; to interpret this character to an outside world whose experience as summer-boarders had been too much for illusion and not enough for understanding. She told only what she chose to tell, but this she told honestly and completely. Moreover, she gave her stories a sure clear definiteness of outline that lifted them clean out of the field of reporting. Just how she did this she was herself scarcely aware. "Good heavens!" she wrote to Mrs. Fields, "what a wonderful kind of chemistry it is that evolves all the details of a story and writes them presently in one flash of time! For two weeks I have been noticing a certain string of things and having hints of character, etc., and day before yesterday the plan of the story comes into my mind, and in half an hour I have put all the little words and ways into their places and can read it off to myself like print. Who does it? For I grow more and more sure that I don't!"

The ladies who set out on their precarious expedition in this story show in their speech the same respect for the spoken word to which we have already called attention, but they prefer "nice" words, as they prefer to take nice steps. Out of the richness of Miss Jewett's short-story collections—volume after volume from which to choose—I chose this one because it presents New England hospitality, obliquely to be sure, but so as to see it in more than one characteristic aspect. Visiting is a feature of life in the country: before the telephone it was likely to be visitation. How various types took to it—and practised it—is shown by example in this story.

THE GUESTS OF MRS. TIMMS

By SARAH ORNE JEWETT

MRS. PERSIS FLAGG stood in her front doorway taking leave of Miss Cynthia Pickett, who had been making a long call. They were not intimate friends. Miss Pickett always came formally to the front door and rang when she paid her visits, but, the week before, they had met at the county conference, and happened to be sent to the same house for entertainment, and so had deepened and renewed the pleasures of acquaintance.

It was an afternoon in early June; the syringa-bushes were tall and green on each side of the stone doorsteps, and were covered with their lovely white and golden flowers. Miss Pickett broke off the nearest twig, and held it before her prim face as she talked. She had a pretty childlike smile that came and went suddenly, but her face was not one that bore the marks of many pleasures. Mrs. Flagg was a tall, commanding sort of person, with an air of satisfaction and authority.

"Oh, yes, gather all you want," she said stiffly, as Miss Pickett took the syringa without having asked beforehand; but she had an amiable expression, and just now her large countenance was lighted up by pleasant anticipation.

"We can tell early what sort of a day it's goin' to be," she said eagerly. "There ain't a cloud in the sky now. I'll stop for you as I come along, or if there should be anything unforeseen to detain me, I'll send you word. I don't expect you'd want to go if it wa'n't so that I could?"

"Oh my sakes, no!" answered Miss Pickett discreetly, with a timid flush. "You feel certain that Mis' Timms won't be put out? I shouldn't feel free to go unless I went 'long o' you."

"Why nothin' could be plainer than her words," said Mrs. Flagg in a tone of reproval. "You saw how she urged me, an' had over all that talk about how we used to see each other often when we both lived to Longport, and told how she'd been thinkin' of writin', and askin' if it wa'n't so I should be able to come over and stop three or four days as soon as settled weather come, because she couldn't make no fire in her best chamber on account of the chimbley smokin' if the wind wa'n't just right. You see how she felt toward me, kissin' of me comin' and goin'? Why, she even asked me who I employed to do over my bonnet, Miss Pickett, just as interested as if she was a sister; an' she remarked she should look for us any pleasant day after we all got home, an' were settled after the conference."

Miss Pickett smiled, but did not speak, as if she expected more arguments still.

"An' she seemed just about as much gratified to meet with you again. She seemed to desire to meet you again very particular," continued Mrs. Flagg. "She really urged us to come together an' have a real good day talkin' over old times—there, don't le' 's go all over it again! I've always heard she'd made that old house of her aunt Bascoms' where she lives look real handsome. I once heard her best parlor carpet described as being an elegant carpet, different from any there was round here. Why, nobody couldn't be more cordial, Miss Pickett; you ain't goin' to give out just at the last?"

"Oh, no!" answered the visitor hastily; "no, 'm! I want to go full as much as you do, Mis' Flagg, but you see I never was so well acquainted with Mis' Cap'n Timms, an' I always seem to dread putting myself for'ard. She certain was very urgent, an' she said plain enough to come any day next week, an' here 't is Wednesday, though of course she wouldn't look for us either Monday or Tuesday. 'T will be a real pleasant occasion, an' now we've been to the conference it don't seem near so much effort to start."

"Why, I don't think nothin' of it," said Mrs. Flagg proudly. "We shall have a grand good time, goin' together an' all, I feel sure."

Miss Pickett still played with her syringa flower, tapping her thin cheek, and twirling the stem with her fingers. She looked as if she were going to say something more, but after a moment's hesitation she turned away.

"Good-afternoon, Mis' Flagg," she said formally, looking up with a quick little smile; "I enjoyed my call; I hope I ain't kep' you too late; I don't know but what it's 'most tea-time. Well, I shall look for you in the mornin'."

"Good-afternoon, Miss Pickett; I'm glad I was in when you came. Call again, won't you?" said Mrs. Flagg. "Yes; you may expect me in good season," and so they parted. Miss Pickett went out at the neat clicking gate in the white fence, and Mrs. Flagg a moment later looked out of her sitting-room window to see if the gate were latched, and felt the least bit disappointed to find that it was. She sometimes went out after the departure of a guest, and fastened the gate herself with a loud, rebuking sound. Both of these Woodville women lived alone, and were very precise in their way of doing things.

II

The next morning dawned clear and bright, and Miss Pickett rose even earlier than usual. She found it most difficult to decide which of her dresses would be best to wear. Summer was still so young that the day had all the freshness of spring, but when the two friends walked away together along the shady street, with a chorus of golden robins singing high overhead in the elms, Miss Pickett decided that she had made a wise choice of her second-best black silk gown, which she had just turned again and freshened. It was neither too warm for the season nor too cool, nor did it look overdressed. She wore her large cameo pin, and this, with a long watch-chain, gave an air of proper mural decoration. She was a straight, flat little person, as if, when not in use, she kept herself, silk dress and all, between the leaves of a book. She carried a noticeable parasol with a fringe, and a small shawl, with a pretty border, neatly folded over her left arm. Mrs. Flagg always dressed in black cashmere, and looked, to hasty observers, much the same one day as another; but her companion recognized the fact that this was the best black cashmere of all, and for a moment quailed at the thought that Mrs. Flagg was paying such extreme deference to their prospective hostess. The visit turned for a moment into an unexpectedly solemn formality, and pleasure seemed to wane before Cynthia Pickett's eyes, yet with great courage she never slackened a single step. Mrs. Flagg carried a somewhat worn black leather hand-bag, which Miss Pickett regretted; it did not give the visit that casual and unpremeditated air which she felt to be more elegant.

"Sha'n't I carry your bag for you?" she asked timidly. Mrs. Flagg was the older and more important person.

"Oh, dear me, no," answered Mrs. Flagg. "My pocket's so remote, in case I should desire to sneeze or anything, that I thought 't would be convenient for carrying my handkerchief and pocketbook; an' then I just tucked in a couple o' glasses o' my crabapple jelly for Mis' Timms. She used to be a great hand for preserves of every sort, an' I thought 't would be a kind of an attention, an' give rise to conversation. I know she used to make excellent drop-cakes when we was both residin' to Longport; folks used to say she never would give the right receipt, but if I get a real good chance, I mean to ask her. Or why can't you, if I start talkin' about receipts—why can't you say, sort of innocent, that I have always spoken frequently of her drop-cakes, an' ask for the rule? She would be very sensible to the compliment, and could pass it off if she didn't feel to indulge us. There, I do so wish you would!"

"Yes, 'm," said Miss Pickett doubtfully; "I'll try to make the opportunity. I'm very partial to drop-cakes. Was they flour or rye, Mis' Flagg?"

"They was flour, dear," replied Mrs. Flagg approvingly; "crisp an' light as any you ever see."

"I wish I had thought to carry somethin' to make it

pleasant," said Miss Pickett, after they had walked a little farther; "but there, I don't know's 't would look just right, this first visit, to offer anything to such a person as Mis' Timms. In case I ever go over to Baxter again I won't forget to make her some little present, as nice as I've got. 'T was certain very polite of her to urge me to come with you. I did feel very doubtful at first. I didn't know but she thought it behooved her, because I was in your company at the conference, and she wanted to save my feelin's, and yet expected I would decline. I never was well acquainted with her; our folks wasn't well off when I first knew her; 't was before uncle Cap'n Dyer passed away an' remembered mother an' me in his will. We couldn't make no han'some companies in them days, so we didn't go to none, an' kep' to ourselves; but in my grandmother's time, mother always said, the families was very friendly. I shouldn't feel like goin' over to pass the day with Mis' Timms if I didn't mean to ask her to return the visit. Some don't think o' these things, but mother was very set about not being done for when she couldn't make no return."

" 'When it rains porridge hold up your dish,' " said Mrs. Flagg; but Miss Pickett made no response beyond a feeble "Yes, 'm," which somehow got caught in her pale-green bonnet-strings.

"There, 't ain't no use to fuss too much over all them things," proclaimed Mrs. Flagg, walking along at a good pace with a fine sway of skirts, and carrying her head high. "Folks walks right by an' forgits all about you; folks can't always be going through with just so much. You'd had a good deal better time, you an' your ma, if you'd been freer in your ways; now don't you s'pose you would? 'T ain't what you give folks to eat so much as 't is makin' 'em feel welcome. Now there's Mis' Timms; when we was to Longport she was dreadful methodical. She wouldn't let Cap'n Timms fetch nobody home to dinner without lettin' of her know, same's other cap'ns' wives had to submit to. I was thinkin', when she was so cordial over to Danby, how she'd softened with time. Years do learn folks somethin'! She did seem very pleasant an' desirous. There, I am so glad we got started; if she'd gone an' got up a real good dinner to-day, an' then not had us come till to-morrow, 't would have been real too bad. Where anybody lives alone such a thing is very tryin'."

"Oh, so 't is!" said Miss Pickett. "There, I'd like to tell you what I went through with year before last. They come an' asked me one Saturday night to entertain the minister, that time we was having candidates—"

"I guess we'd better step along faster," said Mrs. Flagg suddenly. "Why, Miss Pickett, there's the stage comin' now! It's dreadful prompt, seems to me. Quick! there's folks awaitin', an' I sha'n't get to Baxter in no state to visit Mis' Cap'n Timms if I have to ride all the way there backward!"

III

The stage was not full inside. The group before the store proved to be made up of spectators, except one man, who climbed at once to a vacant seat by the driver. Inside there was only one person, after two passengers got out, and she preferred to sit with her back to the horses, so that Mrs. Flagg and Miss Pickett settled themselves comfortably in the coveted corners of the back seat. At first they took no notice of their companion, and spoke to each other in low tones, but presently something attracted the attention of all three and engaged them in conversation.

"I never was over this road before," said the stranger. "I s'pose you ladies are well acquainted all along."

"We have often traveled it in past years. We was over this part of it last week goin' and comin' from the county conference," said Mrs. Flagg in a dignified manner.

"What persuasion?" inquired the fellow-traveler, with interest.

"Orthodox," said Miss Pickett quickly, before Mrs. Flagg could speak. "It was a very interestin' occasion; this other lady an' me stayed through all the meetin's."

"I ain't Orthodox," announced the stranger, waiving any interest in personalities. "I was brought up amongst the Freewill Baptists."

"We're well acquainted with several of that denomination in our place," said Mrs. Flagg, not without an air of patronage. "They've never built 'em no church; there ain't but a scattered few."

"They prevail where I come from," said the traveler. "I'm goin' now to visit with a Freewill lady. We was to a conference together once, same's you an' your friend, but 't was a state conference. She asked me to come some time an' make her a good visit, and I'm on my way now. I didn't seem to have nothin' to keep me to home."

"We're all goin' visitin' to-day, ain't we?" said Mrs.

Flagg sociably; but no one carried on the conversation.

The day was growing very warm; there was dust in the sandy road, but the fields of grass and young growing crops looked fresh and fair. There was a light haze over the hills, and birds were thick in the air. When the stage-horses stopped to walk, you could hear the crows caw, and the bobolinks singing, in the meadows. All the farmers were busy in their fields.

"It don't seem but little ways to Baxter, does it?" said Miss Pickett, after a while. "I felt we should pass a good deal o' time on the road, but we must be pretty near half-way there a'ready."

"Why, more'n half!" exclaimed Mrs. Flagg. "Yes; there's Beckett's Corner right ahead, an' the old Beckett house. I haven't been on this part of the road for so long that I feel kind of strange. I used to visit over here when I was a girl. There's a nephew's widow owns the place now. Old Miss Susan Beckett willed it to him, an' he died; but she resides there an' carries on the farm, an unusual smart woman, everybody says. Ain't it pleasant here, right out among the farms!"

"Mis' Beckett's place, did you observe?" said the stranger, leaning forward to listen to what her companions said. "I expect that's where I'm goin'—Mis' Ezra Beckett's?"

"That's the one," said Miss Pickett and Mrs. Flagg together, and they both looked out eagerly as the coach drew up to the front door of a large old yellow house that stood close upon the green turf of the roadside.

The passenger looked pleased and eager, and made

haste to leave the stage with her many bundles and bags. While she stood impatiently tapping at the brass knocker, the stage-driver landed a large trunk, and dragged it toward the door across the grass. Just then a busy-looking middle-aged woman made her appearance, with floury hands and a look as if she were prepared to be somewhat on the defensive.

"Why, how do you do, Mis' Beckett?" exclaimed the guest. "Well, here I be at last. I didn't know's you thought I was ever comin'. Why, I do declare, I believe you don't recognize me, Mis' Beckett."

"I believe I don't," said the self-possessed hostess. "Ain't you made some mistake, ma'am?"

"Why, don't you recollect we was together that time to the state conference, an' you said you should be pleased to have me come an' make you a visit some time, an' I said I would certain? There, I expect I look more natural to you now."

Mrs. Beckett appeared to be making the best possible effort, and gave a bewildered glance, first at her unexpected visitor, and then at the trunk. The stage-driver, who watched this encounter with evident delight, turned away with reluctance. "I can't wait all day to see how they settle it," he said, and mounted briskly to the box, and the stage rolled on.

"He might have waited just a minute to see," said Miss Pickett indignantly, but Mrs. Flagg's head and shoulders were already far out of the stage window—the house was on her side. "She ain't got in yet," she told Miss Pickett triumphantly. "I could see 'em quite a spell. With that trunk, too! I do declare, how inconsiderate some folks is!"

"'Twas pushin' an acquaintance most too far, wa'n't it?" agreed Miss Pickett. "There, 'twill be somethin' laughable to tell Mis' Timms. I never see anything more divertin'. I shall kind of pity that woman if we have to stop an' git her as we go back this afternoon."

"Oh, don't let's forget to watch for her," exclaimed Mrs. Flagg, beginning to brush off the dust of travel. "There, I feel an excellent appetite, don't you? And we ain't got more'n three or four miles to go, if we have that. I wonder what Mis' Timms is likely to give us for dinner; she spoke of makin' a good many chicken-pies, an' I happened to remark how partial I was to 'em. She felt above most of the things we had provided for us over to the conference. I know she was always counted the best o' cooks when I knew her so well to Longport. Now, don't you forget, if there's a suitable opportunity, to inquire about the drop-cakes"; and Miss Pickett, a little less doubtful than before, renewed her promise.

IV

"My gracious, won't Mis' Timms be pleased to see us! It's just exactly the day to have company. And ain't Baxter a sweet pretty place?" said Mrs. Flagg, as they walked up the main street. "Cynthy Pickett, now ain't you proper glad you come? I felt sort o' calm about it part o' the time yesterday, but I ain't felt so like a girl for a good while. I do believe I'm goin' to have a splendid time."

Miss Pickett glowed with equal pleasure as she paced

along. She was less expansive and enthusiastic than her companion, but now that they were fairly in Baxter, she lent herself generously to the occasion. The social distinction of going away to spend a day in company with Mrs. Flagg was by no means small. She arranged the folds of her shawl more carefully over her arm so as to show the pretty palm-leaf border, and then looked up with great approval to the row of great maples that shaded the broad sidewalk. "I wonder if we can't contrive to make time to go an' see old Miss Nancy Fell?" she ventured to ask Mrs. Flagg. "There ain't a great deal o' time before the stage goes at four o'clock; 'twill pass quickly, but I should hate to have her feel hurt. If she was one we had visited often at home, I shouldn't care so much, but such folks feel any little slight. She was a member of our church; I think a good deal of that."

"Well, I hardly know what to say," faltered Mrs. Flagg coldly. "We might just look in a minute; I shouldn't want her to feel hurt."

"She was one that always did her part, too," said Miss Pickett, more boldly. "Mr. Cronin used to say that she was more generous with her little than many was with their much. If she hadn't lived in a poor part of the town, and so been occupied with a different kind of people from us, 'twould have made a difference. They say she's got a comfortable little home over here, an' keeps house for a nephew. You know she was to our meeting one Sunday last winter, and 'peared dreadful glad to get back; folks seemed glad to see her, too. I don't know as you were out."

"She always wore a friendly look," said Mrs. Flagg indulgently. "There, now, there's Mis' Timms's residence; it's handsome, ain't it, with them big spruce-trees? I expect she may be at the window now, an' see us as we come along. Is my bonnet on straight, an' everything? The blinds looks open in the room this way; I guess she's to home fast enough."

The friends quickened their steps, and with shining eyes and beating hearts hastened forward. The slightest mists of uncertainty were now cleared away; they gazed at the house with deepest pleasure; the visit was about to begin.

They opened the front gate and went up the short walk, noticing the pretty herring-bone pattern of the bricks, and as they stood on the high steps Cynthia Pickett wondered whether she ought not to have worn her best dress, even though there was lace at the neck and sleeves, and she usually kept it for the most formal of tea-parties and exceptional parish festivals. In her heart she commended Mrs. Flagg for that familiarity with the ways of a wider social world which had led her to wear the very best among her black cashmeres.

"She's a good while coming to the door," whispered Mrs. Flagg presently. "Either she didn't see us, or else she's slipped upstairs to make some change, an' is just goin' to let us ring again. I've done it myself sometimes. I'm glad we come right over after her urgin' us so; it seems more cordial than to keep her expectin' us. I expect she'll urge us terribly to remain with her over-night."

"Oh, I ain't prepared," began Miss Pickett, but she looked pleased. At that moment there was a slow withdrawal of the bolt inside, and a key was turned, the front door opened, and Mrs. Timms stood before them with a smile. Nobody stopped to think at that moment what kind of smile it was.

"Why, if it ain't Mis' Flagg," she exclaimed politely, "an' Miss Pickett too! I am surprised!"

The front entry behind her looked well furnished, but not exactly hospitable; the stairs with their brass rods looked so clean and bright that it did not seem as if anybody had ever gone up or come down. A cat came purring out, but Mrs. Timms pushed her back with a determined foot, and hastily closed the sitting-room door. Then Miss Pickett let Mrs. Flagg precede her, as was becoming, and they went into a darkened parlor, and found their way to some chairs, and seated themselves solemnly.

" 'Tis a beautiful day, ain't it?" said Mrs. Flagg, speaking first. "I don't know's I ever enjoyed the ride more. We've been having a good deal of rain since we saw you at the conference, and the country looks beautiful."

"Did you leave Woodville this morning? I thought I hadn't heard you was in town," replied Mrs. Timms formally. She was seated just a little too far away to make things seem exactly pleasant. The darkness of the best room seemed to retreat somewhat and Miss Pickett looked over by the door, where there was a pale gleam from the sidelights in the hall, to try to see the pattern of the carpet; but her effort failed.

"Yes, 'm," replied Mrs. Flagg to the question. "We left Woodville about half past eight, but it is quite a ways from where we live to where you take the stage. The stage does come slow, but you don't seem to mind it such a beautiful day."

"Why, you must have come right to see me first!" said Mrs. Timms, warming a little as the visit went on. "I hope you're going to make some stop in town. I'm sure it was very polite of you to come right an' see me; well, it's very pleasant, I declare. I wish you'd been in Baxter last Sabbath; our minister did give us an elegant sermon on faith an' works. He spoke of the conference, and gave his views on some o' the questions that came up, at Friday evenin' meetin'; but I felt tired after getting home, an' so I wasn't out. We feel very much favored to have such a man amon'st us. He's building up the parish very considerable. I understand the pew-rents come to thirty-six dollars more this quarter than they did last."

"We also feel grateful in Woodville for our pastor's efforts," said Miss Pickett; but Mrs. Timms turned her head away sharply, as if the speech had been untimely, and trembling Miss Pickett had interrupted.

"They're thinking here of raisin' Mr. Barlow's salary another year," the hostess added; "a good many of the old parishioners have died off, but every one feels to do what they can. Is there much interest among the young people in Woodville, Mis' Flagg?"

"Considerable at this time, ma'am," answered Mrs. Flagg, without enthusiasm, and she listened with unusual silence to the subsequent fluent remarks of Mrs. Timms.

The parlor seemed to be undergoing the slow processes of a winter dawn. After a while the three women could

begin to see one another's faces, which aided them somewhat in carrying on a serious and impersonal conversation.
There were a good many subjects to be touched upon, and
Mrs. Timms said everything that she should have said,
except to invite her visitors to walk upstairs and take off
their bonnets. Mrs. Flagg sat her parlor-chair as if it were
a throne, and carried her banner of self-possession as high
as she knew how, but toward the end of the call even she
began to feel hurried.

"Won't you ladies take a glass of wine an' a piece of
cake after your ride?" inquired Mrs. Timms, with an air
of hospitality that almost concealed the fact that neither
cake nor wine was anywhere to be seen; but the ladies
bowed and declined with particular elegance. Altogether it
was a visit of extreme propriety on both sides, and Mrs.
Timms was very pressing in her invitation that her guests
should stay longer.

"Thank you, but we ought to be going," answered Mrs.
Flagg, with a little show of ostentation, and looking over
her shoulder to be sure that Miss Pickett had risen too.
"We've got some little ways to go," she added with dignity. "We should be pleased to have you call an' see us
in case you have occasion to come to Woodville," and Miss
Pickett faintly seconded the invitation. It was in her heart
to add, "Come any day next week," but her courage did
not rise so high as to make the words audible. She looked
as if she were ready to cry; her usual smile had burnt itself out into gray ashes; there was a white, appealing look
about her mouth. As they emerged from the dim parlor
and stood at the open front door, the bright June day,

the golden-green trees, almost blinded their eyes. Mrs. Timms was more smiling and cordial than ever.

"There, I ought to have thought to offer you fans; I am afraid you was warm after walking," she exclaimed, as if to leave no stone of courtesy unturned. "I have so enjoyed meeting you again, I wish it was so you could stop longer. Why, Mis' Flagg, we haven't said one word about old times when we lived to Longport. I've had news from there, too, since I saw you; my brother's daughter-in-law was here to pass the Sabbath after I returned."

Mrs. Flagg did not turn back to ask any questions as she stepped stiffly away down the brick walk. Miss Pickett followed her, raising the fringed parasol; they both made ceremonious little bows as they shut the high white gate behind them. "Good-by," said Mrs. Timms finally, as she stood in the door with her set smile; and as they departed she came out and began to fasten up a rose-bush that climbed a narrow white ladder by the steps.

"Oh, my goodness alive!" exclaimed Mrs. Flagg, after they had gone some distance in aggrieved silence, "if I haven't gone and forgotten my bag! I ain't goin' back, whatever happens. I expect she'll trip over it in that dark room and break her neck!"

"I brought it; I noticed you'd forgotten it," said Miss Pickett timidly, as if she hated to deprive her companion of even that slight consolation.

"There, I'll tell you what we'd better do," said Mrs. Flagg gallantly; "we'll go right over an' see poor old Miss Nancy Fell; 't will please her about to death. We can say we felt like goin' somewhere to-day, an' 'twas a good many years since either one of us had seen Baxter, so we come just for the ride, an' to make a few calls. She'll like to hear all about the conference; Miss Fell was always one that took a real interest in religious matters."

Miss Pickett brightened, and they quickened their step. It was nearly twelve o'clock, they had breakfasted early, and now felt as if they had eaten nothing since they were grown up. An awful feeling of tiredness and uncertainty settled down upon their once buoyant spirits.

"I can forgive a person," said Mrs. Flagg, once, as if she were speaking to herself; "I can forgive a person, but when I'm done with 'em, I'm done."

V

"I do declare, 'twas like a scene in Scriptur' to see that poor good-hearted Nancy Fell run down her walk to open the gate for us!" said Mrs. Persis Flagg later that afternoon, when she and Miss Pickett were going home in the stage. Miss Pickett nodded her head approvingly.

"I had a good sight better time with her than I should have had at the other place," she said with fearless honesty. "If I'd been Mis' Cap'n Timms, I'd made some apology or just passed us the compliment. If it wa'n't convenient, why couldn't she just tell us so after all her urgin' and sayin' how she should expect us?"

"I thought then she'd altered from what she used to be," said Mrs. Flagg. "She seemed real sincere an' open away from home. If she wa'n't prepared to-day, 'twas easy enough to say so; we was reasonable folks, an' should have gone away with none but friendly feelin's. We did have a grand time with Nancy. She was as happy to see us as if we'd been queens."

" 'T was a real nice little dinner," said Miss Pickett gratefully. "I thought I was goin' to faint away just before we got to the house, and I didn't know how I should hold out if she undertook to do anything extra, and keep us a-waitin'; but there, she just made us welcome, simple-hearted, to what she had. I never tasted such dandelion greens; an' that nice little piece o' pork and new biscuit, why, they was just splendid. She must have an excellent good cellar, if 'tis such a small house. Her potatoes was truly remarkable for this time o' year. I myself don't deem it necessary to cook potatoes when I'm goin' to have dandelion greens. Now, didn't it put you in mind of that verse in the Bible that says, 'Better is a dinner of herbs where love is'? An' how desirous she'd been to see somebody that could tell her some particulars about the conference!"

"She'll enjoy tellin' folks about our comin' over to see her. Yes, I'm glad we went; 'twill be of advantage every way, an' our bein' of the same church an' all, to Woodville. If Mis' Timms hears of our bein' there, she'll see we had reason, an' knew of a place to go. Well, I needn't have brought this old bag!"

Miss Pickett gave her companion a quick resentful glance, which was followed by one of triumph directed at the dust that was collecting on the shoulders of the best black cashmere; then she looked at the bag on the front seat, and suddenly felt illuminated with the suspicion that

Mrs. Flagg had secretly made preparations to pass the night in Baxter. The bag looked plump, as if it held much more than the pocketbook and the jelly.

Mrs. Flagg looked up with unusual humility. "I did think about that jelly," she said, as if Miss Pickett had openly reproached her. "I was afraid it might look as if I was tryin' to pay Nancy for her kindness."

"Well, I don't know," said Cynthia; "I guess she'd been pleased. She'd thought you just brought her over a little present: but I do' know as 't would been any good to her after all; she'd thought so much of it, comin' from you, that she'd kep' it till 'twas all candied." But Mrs. Flagg didn't look exactly pleased by this unexpected compliment, and her fellow-traveler colored with confusion and a sudden feeling that she had shown undue forwardness.

Presently they remembered the Beckett house, to their great relief, and, as they approached, Mrs. Flagg reached over and moved her hand-bag from the front seat to make room for another passenger. But nobody came out to stop the stage, and they saw the unexpected guest sitting by one of the front windows comfortably swaying a palm-leaf fan, and rocking to and fro in calm content. They shrank back into their corners, and tried not to be seen. Mrs. Flagg's face grew very red.

"She got in, didn't she?" said Miss Pickett, snipping her words angrily, as if her lips were scissors. Then she heard a call, and bent forward to see Mrs. Beckett herself appear in the front doorway, very smiling and eager to stop the stage.

The driver was only too ready to stop his horses. "Got a passenger for me to carry back, ain't ye?" said he facetiously. "Them's the kind I like; carry both ways, make somethin' on a double trip," and he gave Mrs. Flagg and Miss Pickett a friendly wink as he stepped down over the wheel. Then he hurried toward the house, evidently in a hurry to put the baggage on; but the expected passenger still sat rocking and fanning at the window.

"No, sir; I ain't got any passengers," exclaimed Mrs. Beckett, advancing a step or two to meet him, and speaking very loud in her pleasant excitement. "This lady that come this morning wants her large trunk with her summer things that she left to the depot in Woodville. She's very desirous to git into it, so don't you go an' forgit; ain't you got a book or somethin', Mr. Ma'sh? Don't you forgit to make a note of it; here's her check, an' we've kep' the number in case you should mislay it or anything. There's things in the trunk she needs; you know you overlooked stoppin' to the milliner's for my bunnit last week."

"Other folks disremembers things as well's me," grumbled Mr. Marsh. He turned to give the passengers another wink more familiar than the first, but they wore an offended air, and were looking the other way. The horses had backed a few steps, and the guest at the front window had ceased the steady motion of her fan to make them a handsome bow, and been puzzled at the lofty manner of their acknowledgment.

"Go 'long with your foolish jokes, John Ma'sh!" Mrs. Beckett said cheerfully, as she turned away. She was a comfortable, hearty person, whose appearance adjusted the beauties of hospitality. The driver climbed to his seat, chuckling, and drove away with the dust flying after the wheels.

"Now, she's a friendly sort of a woman, that Mis' Beckett," said Mrs. Flagg unexpectedly, after a few moments of silence, when she and her friend had been unable to look at each other. "I really ought to call over an' see her some o' these days, knowing her husband's folks as well as I used to, an' visitin' of 'em when I was a girl." But Miss Pickett made no answer.

"I expect it was all for the best, that woman's comin'," suggested Mrs. Flagg again hopefully. "She looked like a willing person who would take right hold. I guess Mis' Beckett knows what she's about, and must have had her reasons. Perhaps she thought she'd chance it for a couple o' weeks anyway after the lady'd come so fur, an' bein' one of her own denomination. Hayin'-time'll be here before we know it. I think myself, gen'rally speakin', 'tis just as well to let anybody know you're comin'."

"Them seemed to be Mis' Cap'n Timms's views," said Miss Pickett in a low tone; but the stage rattled a good deal, and Mrs. Flagg looked up inquiringly, as if she had not heard.

ROWLAND ROBINSON
(1833–1900)

Other forms of entertainment will be chronicled in this book,
but it would surely be incomplete without some sort of "bee."
There are several good ones in our literature, but the best of all
I know takes place in "Danvis Folks," when Uncle Lisha, hero
of an earlier volume, comes back from trying to live in the West
and joyfully takes up the dropped threads of Vermont living.

Throughout New England the bee was not only a social occasion in the days before cold storage; it began as an economic
necessity arising from the tendency of harvest to ripen all at once
and the consequent call on all hands for salvage. Old Vermont
may have been considered by Connecticut clergymen as a field
for missionary endeavor, but her spirit was Puritan enough to
need some reasonable and preferably economic excuse for having
a thoroughly good time. One of these reasons is the custom of
apples to grow squshy without warning. The advantages and dis-
advantages of giving a bee are set forth in the conversation of the
women, but when they refer the decision to Uncle Lisha the prospect of a jollification tips the scale. Out go the invitations, and the
fun is on.

However, economic reasons were not always entirely absent
even from the invitations; Tom Hamlin in this story is asked together with his parin'-machine, "for one hain't no good withaout

the other." These machines had an important place in kitchen furniture, especially in large families; the Beechers managed with the aid of one to maintain a sort of self-contained literary society. Harriet Beecher Stowe says in her early reminiscences of Litchfield: "I have the image of my father still, as he sat working the apple-peeler. 'Come, George,' he said, 'I'll tell you what we'll do to make the evening go off. You and I'll take turns, and see who'll tell the most out of Scott's novels.' And so they took them, novel by novel, reciting scenes and incidents, which kept the eyes of the children wide open, and made the work go on without flagging."

Rowland Robinson was well on in years before he wrote these sketches, as yet unsurpassed in their own field, of life in "Danvis" in the thirties: some say it was Lincoln, Vermont: he himself lived at Ferrisburg. Also he was quite blind before he wrote them, and it may well be that this sharpened his sense of sound; certainly he gave us some of the most faithful descriptions of spoken mountainese that we have in print. He was a naturalist and an artist before his eyes failed, writing and illustrating for *Forest and Stream*, and even after that he went fishing, or tramped with his son through his beloved woods. His stories are source-books of northern nature and of human nature as it developed among the hills.

It is not really necessary to have the notes of Uncle Lisha's dancing-song. The effect will be produced if one bears in mind that it should be roared, that there are heavy bumps on the *lums* and *hums,* and that the voice should be fully let out on the last *law.* Thus performed, almost anyone could dance to it.

THE PARING-BEE

By Rowland Robinson

Next morning Uncle Lisha laid aside his holiday attire with a sense of great relief from the constraint and care which their wearing had imposed upon him, and put on his ordinary garb with the comfortable feeling of being rehabilitated in his real self. Making such haste with his breakfast that Aunt Jerusha said he was "in a bigger hurry 'n a boy a-goin' a-fishin'," he put on his leather apron and set about the odd jobs of mending for the family.

Sam and his father went out to their husking, and the door between the kitchen and the shop being opened, that the old man might have the companionship of the women folks, the house presently rang with the merry thud of the hammer on his lapstone.

Huldah was paring apples with a worn-out shoe knife discarded from Uncle Lisha's kit, and Aunt Jerusha quartered and cored them with frugal care that the least possible share should go to the pigs, while the baby made frequent excursions on all fours between the two great objects of interest presented by the two industries.

Now he brought a chubby fistful of stolen shoe pegs to his mother's knee, then made restitution to the owner with a slice of apple, begrimed by repeated contact with the floor during its transportation.

"Why, yes, bub," said the old man, beaming down a

kindly glance through his round glasses upon the upturned baby face as he took the proffered gift and laid it on the bench beside him, "it's turrible nice, but Uncle Lisher don't 'pear tu feel like eatin' on 't jest naow. He hain't apple hungry; guess he eat tew much breakfus' er suthin'. Ta' keer. Don't put his leetle hanny ont' the lapstun. Git it smashed finer 'n a barn. No, bubby, couldn't hev the wax. Gaum him all up so 't mammy 'd hafter nigh abaout skin him tu git him clean ag'in; an' haow she would scold both on us, an' haow we would cry, wouldn't we? Here, take a pooty paig to Aunt Jerushy an' ask her 'f she ever see sech a cur'osity. Clipper, naow."

"Thank ye, a thaousan' times, you darlin' creetur," cried Aunt Jerusha, when the child had scrambled to her with his gift. "I never see a neater paig an' I'm a-goin' tu keep it tu hev me a shoe made. These 'ere apples seems ef they was gittin' turrible meller, Huldy, an' wa'n't a-goin' tu keep no gret spell."

"I know it," said Huldah, putting a thin slice between her lips and meditatively munching it. "There's lots an' sacks on 'em that's all squ'sh, an' ef we save many of 'em we've got tu hev a parin'-bee ef you an' Uncle Lisher could stan' the rumpus."

"Stan' it! Law sakes. I could stan' a leetle o' the young folkses catousin, an' he'd enj'y it jest as much as any on 'em, furzino. But apple cuts is turrible wasteful an' mussin' an' gin'ally cost more 'n they come tu."

"But we'd get the apples worked off an' the young folks'd have a good time. I wonder if father Lovel would care?"

"Law sakes alive," said Aunt Jerusha, "if he c'd stan' S'manthy twenty year, I guess he c'n stan' one evenin's catousin. But hear me talk, an' she an ol' neighbor an' your mother-in-law ef she was a-livin'. Lisher!" she called, "du you s'pose you an' Timerthy could stan' it, ef we had a apple cut?" and she shook her knife at Huldah while they paused in their work to hear his answer.

"A apple cut? A parin'-bee? Good airth an' seas! You jest try it an' see. I bate ye, me an' him'll shake our hommels wi' the spryest on em."

"What 'd I tell ye?" Aunt Jerusha whispered triumphantly.

When the subject was broached to them at dinner, Sam and his father made no objections, and it was settled that the entertainment should be given as soon as the necessary preparations could be made.

A whole day was spent in bountiful if not elaborate cooking; the frying of at least a bushel of doughnuts and the making and baking of pumpkin pies, whose crowded ranks filled half the pantry shelves. Then the rooms were put in cleanly order, which Aunt Jerusha declared, while giving her best efforts to it, "A useless work, a-scrubbin' an' puttin' tu rights jest tu hev 'em mussed an' cluttered intu jest a hoorah's nest."

Meantime invitations were issued, not on perfumed paper, but by hearty word of mouth, and given pretty generally yet discreetly.

"Don't ye gin no invite tu none o' them Forge fellers," said Huldah as Sam lingered on the threshold in indecision between the various routes. "They're such a rantankerous passel o' critters, allers fer raisin' a rumpus. An' don't ye forgit tu gin Tom Hamlin a bid, an' his parin'-machine, both on 'em, for one hain't no good withaout t' other. An' come raound by Joel Bartlett's an' git ten paound o' his best cheese, but don't let him know what ye want on 't. He wouldn't knowingly let his cheese git mixed up wi' no sech worl' people's fryvolity."

"Sho, I guess his screuples hain't wuth more 'n seven cents a paound," said Sam irreverently.

"An' I hope you'll make it a pint tu give Peltier a bid tu the apple cut," Uncle Lisha called from the shop; "he needs chirkin' up wust of any on us, the poor love-cracked creetur. Ef Danvis gals is pooty 's they was when aour womern was gals, Samwill, the' 'll be some here pooty enough tu take his mind off 'm that lake shore gill flirt, maremaid, I d' know but she is. Did he find her in the lake, Samwill? An' ef ye can scare up a fiddler, git him. What's come o' that leetle hump-backed feller 'at, when he sot in the corner a-fiddlin', you couldn't see nothin' on, behind his fiddle? But good airth an' seas, he'd saw that fiddle all up into tunes. He'd be ekernomical for a kitchen tunk, gitten' intu a corner so, aout 'n the way."

Sam hurried away before he should be burdened with further instructions, lamenting as he went the loss of so fine a hunting morning.

On the evening appointed for the entertainment the full moon was seen, but as a pale and dimly defined blotch behind the gray veil of cloud that overspread the sky and blended with the vague rim of the horizon.

There was a dull, sullen chill in the air, which was motionless in the expectancy wherewith nature so often awaits her changes. The night was jarred by the rumble of wagons jolting over the frozen roads and pierced by the merry voices of coming guests.

Some of these were occupants of the wagons, above whose rumble and clatter they strove to make one another hear between abrupt breaks of the thread of conversation when a wheel struck a stone or dropped into a rut. Some were coming across the fields on foot in couples and squads, but it was noticeable that the couples emerged from the half gloom before their voices were heard, while the gabble and laughter of the groups ran far before them to herald their coming.

Beams of light shone hospitably forth from every window of the kitchen and square room, and the heavy latch clanked and the door slammed announcement of the frequent arrivals.

The women folks came from the bedroom, where they had bestowed their hoods and shawls and cloaks on Huldah's bed, each with an apron shielding the front of her tidy calico or homespun woolen gown. The men hung their coats on the pegs of the kitchen wall and became comfortable in their accustomed indoor shirt-sleeves.

Soon pans and knives were brought forth, bushel baskets of apples lugged in, chairs drawn into convenient groups, and the business of the evening began.

Tom Hamlin and another almost as famous an apple parer bestrode their machines, placed on the seats of high-backed chairs, and entered upon such a strife for the championship that the clattering din of their clumsily geared machines was almost incessant, and the parings spurting from their knives in curved jets were scarcely broken in the quick shifting of the apples on the forks. Presently a dozen pairs of hands were busy quartering the peeled apples, as many more were coring them, while others strung them with wire needles on long strings of pack thread, for drying.

Every one except Tom Hamlin and his rival was talking, and almost every voice strove to make itself heard above every other and the deafening clatter of the machines. Some couples with heads close together utilized the uproar to say things meant for no other ears.

In the centre of an interesting group, Uncle Lisha, splitting apples with his shoe knife, roared like a lion concerning the wonders of the West, and to as interested a feminine audience, Aunt Jerusha quavered shrilly of the discomforts of Western life while she industriously strung the quarters of apples in her pan.

"Fifty an' a hunderd acres in one field o' wheat an' the hull on 't as level as the Forge Pawnd," Uncle Lisha shouted.

"Ten miles tu the nighest store," shrieked his wife to her group of listeners, "an' when you got to 't, the tea an' snuff they kept wa'n't wuth a-kerryin' hum, though goodness knows they ast enough for 'em. Land sakes! how be I goin't to git a pinch o' snuff, wi' both my han's in these 'ere apples?"

"Jest look o' Mandy Varney," cried a buxom damsel to those around her. "She hain't done nothin' only chank every identicle quarter she's cored, an' listen to that Jim Putman, sence she soddaown. Wonder ef she thinks it's a sparkin'-bee steaddy a parin'-bee?"

"What s'pose the reason is, the' hain't none o' Cap'n Peck's folks come?" inquired another high-keyed voice; to which a middle-aged matron answered, with a backward toss of the head, while she kept her eyes rigidly fixed upon her apple and knife, "Proberbly they're 'bove goin' to such common duins, naow 't he's sot in the leegislatur. Ef 't was 'fore 'lection the' 'd all ha' come fast 'nough."

"They du say 'at on the stren'th on 't she's ben tu V'gennes an' bought a hull set o' flowin' blue dishes. Clapham hadn't nothin' quite good enough for a member o' the leegislatur's wife," cried another.

"Highty tighty," said the elder matron, "an' there be them 'at hain't so turrible old that remember when the hull fam'ly eat the' puddin' an' milk aouten braown airthenware bowls, an' glad 'nough to get 'em." Even Danvis was not without its social jealousies.

"Suthin ben a-ketchin' Joel Bartlett's sheep," announced one of a knot of married men, who, assembled apart from their wives, were not laboring very assiduously. "Some thinks it's dawgs an' some thinks it's a animil."

" 'Tain't no ways likely it's a bear," another remarked; "the time o' the year's ag'in' that. But it might be a painter."

"Wal, no, I don't favor the idee, 'cause the' was ten or a dozen sheep 't was killed aout an' aout; jest the' thrut cut. A painter wouldn't ha' killed more'n one or tew, an' sat'fied hisself a-eatin' the meat. Hain't that so, Samwill?" appealing to their host, who had come within call as he moved from group to group to see that each was properly provided for.

"I cal'late it's a wolf," he said, "from what I've hearn tell o' their duins. More'n all that, I've consaited all the fall 'at the' was one a-hangin' raound, fer I've seen signs 'at I couldn't lay to no other critter. But ef he don't make himself sca'ce 'fore many hours, I reckon we'll have a chance to find aout what he is, fer ef it don't snow before mornin' I miss my guess."

"I'm a-goin' aout tu take a look o' the weather jest fer greens," said one of the party, rising with a sigh of relief and dropping his pan in his chair. After an absence which must have enabled him to make a thorough study of the weather, he reentered the kitchen so powdered with snow that he did not need to proclaim that "it was snowin' like fun."

Many of the company needed further ocular proof of his report, and hastened forth to obtain it, while others were content to cool their noses against the window panes and stare out upon the landscape grown more obscure behind the veil of falling snow, all dull and lifeless, but for the candles' weird reflections—unreal lights by which, perhaps, witches were holding carnival. Perhaps it was the hope of beholding them that so long kept some fair cheeks in close proximity to bearded ones.

"If it holds up by mornin' I'll take a rantomscoot up back o' Joel's and see what tracks I c'n find," Sam said, and hurried away as Tom Hamlin, tossing away the last apple and kicking over the empty basket, shouted, "Fetch on your apples ef you want 'em skinned."

So with unflagging zeal and unabated clamor of voices, and clatter of implements and machines, the work went on till half a dozen bushels of apples were on the strings and ready to festoon the kitchen walls and poles that hung from hooks in the ceiling, and the welcome announcement was made that the labor of the evening was over.

"Naow, then," said Sam, making his way with careful steps across the floor slippery with scattered skins and cores, "we'll clear up the thickest o' this mess and then we'll see ef aour womern folks has saved any cold victuals fer us. I believe I saw some cold 'taters in the buttry an' I do' know but the' 's some o' Drive's johnny-cake left."

But before the floor was cleaned, a dozen girls must try for their lover's initials with apple parings whirled thrice above their heads and cast over the right shoulder to the floor behind them.

"Wal! fer all the world," cried Amanda Varney, blushing as red as the apple peeling she had just cast behind her, and was now regarding with surprised delight, "ef it hain't a perfect P."

"It might be most anything," said Mary Ann Jones, who in the early evening had called attention to Amanda's flirtation.

" 'Twould be good enough ef you'd ha' made it," said Amanda; "I'll leave it tu Uncle Lisher ef 'tain't a good P," as the old man drew near the circle widening to admit him.

"Yes," he said, after adjusting his spectacles and critically examining the initial. "It's julluk handwritin'. But it don't stan' fer Putman ner fer Peggs. It's tew long and lank. Guess it stands fer Peltier. Come here, Peltier."

The young man, who was moping in a corner, made his way toward them. "It 'pears tu be p'inted by fortin 'at you've got tu dance 'long wi' Mandy. Naow, you be ready tu take your place wi' her soon's we get suthin' tu eat." Then whispering into his ear like a blast of northeast wind, "Naow du try tu shake some o' the sorrow aout 'o your heart when th' dancin' begins."

"Gosh, Uncle Lisher," said Pelatiah, aghast at the plan, and casting a hopeless glance upon his big boots. "I can't dance no more'n a thirty-foot ladder."

"Wal, 'f you hain't got the tools, I do' know who hes, an' you've got tu use 'em if I hafter yard ye top o' the hot stove. Come, gals, le' 's git things sot tu rights so 't we c'n eat an' git tu the rale business o' the evenin'."

Then the guests, ranged along the walls of the kitchen and spare room, were amply served with Huldah's doughnuts, pies, and cheese, and Sam's cider received its usual compliments.

Then the young people engaged in romping games, the Needle's Eye, wherein every one who could sing and every one who could not, sang, or tried to sing, at the top of their voices:—

"The needle's eye, that doth soffy the thread that runs so treue, it has caught many a smiling lass and naow it has caught yeou!"

or with a volume and zest that would have pleased Gran'ther Hill more than the melody, "We're marching onward tow-ard Quebec." In every game the forfeits were invariably kisses, given and paid in the simplest and most direct manner, or when so decreed, in the contortions of a "double and twisted Loddy massy." The movements of another popular game were timed to the words of "Come, Philander, le' 's be a-marchin'." The elders looked on in amused toleration, while a few joined the young folks' games only to be reminded, by grudgingly paid forfeits, that the freshness of youth had departed from their wrinkled cheeks.

"Come," at last cried Uncle Lisha, who by tacit consent assumed the office of master of ceremonies, "you young folks orter be abaout cl'yed wi' bussin' an' we ol' folks has eat saour grapes long 'nough, so le' 's all turn tu an' hev a leetle sensible enj'yment a-dancin'. Where's thet aire leetle fiddler."

"He hain't come anigh," Sam answered. "He promised he'd come sartin sure, but I'm most afeerd he's run ag'in' a snag tu Hammer's 'at he won't git clear on, 'fore mornin'. It's tew tarnal bad."

"Well, that's a pretty haow de du," said the old man, "but we won't be cheated aout'n aour dancin' by one drunken fiddler. Tom Hamlin, 'd ye fetch yer jewsharp in your pocket? er can you dig one up, Samwill?" Tom "hedn't never thought on 't," nor could Sam find the only instrument upon which he ever played.

"Wal, then, I've got tu sing, which I'll make you hear me, ef I don't charm none. Chuse your pardners naow or never an' form ont' the floor. Come, Peltier, git Mandy and stan' up tu the dough dish."

Pelatiah hung back bashfully till Amanda, seeing her rival, Mary Ann, led out by Putnam, blushing with vexation, met him more than halfway, and he found his unwilling feet taking him to his place in the waiting ranks.

"All ready. Naow I'm goin' tu sing," shouted Uncle Lisha, and began to roar in stentorian tones:—

> "Lum tiddle, lum tiddle, t'l law day,
> Lum tiddle—

"Good airth an' seas! Why don't ye start yer hommels? D' ye s'pose I'm goin' tu set an' holler all night for you tu stan' an' gawp julluk tew rows o' stancheled calves?"

Thus adjured the first couple paddled and sailed down the middle, when he again took up his wordless song, and twenty-four pairs of feet, impatient for their turn, began to stamp and shuffle to its rhythm.

Antoine, sitting by Uncle Lisha, and attempting to catch the tune in snatches of undertone, played an imaginary fiddle and pranced time with both feet after the Canadian fashion, evidently considering himself the chief performer.

The dancers quickly caught the inspiration of well-meant, if unmelodious, strains, and whirled and capered in perfect abandonment to their influence. Even Pelatiah's bashfulness melted away in the excitement, and he made wild rushes at wrong moments and in wrong directions, which involved him and his partner in bewildering entanglement with other couples.

> "Turn yer pardener half way raound,
> Lum tiddle, lum tiddle, t'l law day,
> Half way raound, half way raound, do day hum, t'l law day."

Uncle Lisha sang at him vociferously, and Antoine chimed in with, "Turn yo' pahdny wrong side aout," to Pelatiah's complete bewilderment. Then young Putnam, striving to outdo his own agile steps, as he pranced down the middle with Mary Ann Jones, slipped on a fragment of apple peel and fell headlong, plowing his way along a rank of dancers and turning a furrow of them on top of himself. Uncle Lisha still sang on, his voice rising above the din of shrieks and laughter, till it dawned upon him that no one was dancing and his music was being poured forth to no purpose.

In the lull that presently succeeded the confusion the company became aware of the notes of a fiddle, whence coming no one could conjecture, faintly yet distinctly playing the familiar air of "Money Musk." While all listened, some puzzled and some breathless, and some superstitiously alarmed, Solon Briggs oracularly voiced the prevailing feeling, in a solemn, awe-stricken tone:—

"That fiddle hain't performed by no livin' han's. Watson Parmer has pairished, mis'rable, in the element of the snow, and his speerit has come to fulfill his 'pintment made to Samule. It's Watson Parmer's indivisible apperagotion."

"Beeswax," cried John Dart, listening at the open door. "Go to thunder wi' yer speerits! It's someb'dy in the woodshed. Gimme a light an' I'll see who 'tis."

Taking a candle and protecting it with his hollowed hand, he made his way to the woodshed, followed by the bolder of the company, close at his heels, the more timid crowding one another in the rear, where the light of the open door mistily illumined the falling snow. Under cover of the shed, and held high above Dart's head, the candle struggled with the gloom, till it disclosed a dismally comic little figure crouched in a limp heap, with its back against a barrel, its disproportionately long legs looped over the bar of a sawhorse on which it had attempted to seat itself. The snow-laden hat had fallen over the face, and the short body was hidden by the fiddle which the owner was playing with a skill that had survived inebriation, while in a thin and drunken voice he prompted the movements of a country dance.

"Firsh cou'le. Daow' er mi'le. Balansh. Daow a rou' shide."

"Wal, I swan," Dart ejaculated, " 'f 't ain't speerits, arter all. Hammer's, inside o' Wat Parmer. Hammer'd ortu be kicked tu death by cripples for a-lettin' on him git so. Wat," taking the hat from the fiddler's face, shaking the snow from it, and adjusting it in its proper place, "don't be a-wastin' your music on the wood pile. You can't git no dancin' aout on't. Come int' the haouse."

But the hunchback's face, vacant of everything save its habitual expression of pain, only stared blindly into space and the merry tune went on.

"You might as well talk tu a post. Take a holt o' the light, some on ye"; and giving the candle into other hands, he got behind the little man, and, placing his arms under the limp legs, lifted him as easily as one might a child, and in such a position the playing of the violin was not interrupted, and so, preceded by the candle-bearer, carried him into the house. As they entered, Palmer's drunken fancy moved him to strike up, "The Campbells are Coming."

"The camels is comin'," cried Beau Putnam. "Don't ye see the hump?"

"Shut yer head, you blasted monkey," Dart growled so savagely that the grin faded out of Putnam's face, and the laugh that his coarse jest created died out in a suppressed titter.

"Here's your music, Lovel," Dart announced, as he deposited his light burden on a chair, "the best fiddler in Charlotte county. He's a leetle mite tired jest naow, but when he gits rested he'll set all yer feet flyin' in spite of ye. Mis' Lovel, won't ye give him a cup o' tea, hot an' strong?"

When the little man had been somewhat restored to his proper self, he tuned his violin and then drew from it such blithe and melodious strains that all forgot his deformity. Even he, with loving eyes fixed upon his instrument, his worn face alight with a tender emotion that softened the lines which pain and dissipation had drawn upon it, seemed for the time also to have forgotten it.

Uncle Lisher, relieved of his musical labors, abandoned himself to the pleasures of the dance with a grace and agility that filled Aunt Jerusha's heart with pride, albeit they were such as a sportive bear exhibits. Antoine was given the floor for a while, as, to a tune of his own choosing, he danced a Canadian jig. Every one was a wideawake or active participant in the gayety except the baby and the old hound, the one sleeping, undisturbed by the noise and commotion, whereof the other was a resigned but unhappy spectator under the circumscribed shelter of the stove.

When the dance ended, and the guests, even now acknowledging no fatigue, began to depart, the morning star was shining through the breaking clouds and the day was faintly dawning upon a world whose new whiteness looked strange to eyes that last beheld it, dim and gray with the dreariness of late Autumn.

"Naow fetch on that leetle fiddler," John Dart commanded when he had tucked his Sarah Ann snugly in the buffalo-skins. "I'm a-goin' tu git him safte past Hammer's ef I hafter lock him up in his fiddle box. We wanter keep him for another apple cut. Here, Wat, cuddle in there 'twixt me an' Sary Ann, we're both on us small. Here ye be. Good-night, Lovel, ef 'tain't tew airly. I'll be on hand ef the' 's a wolf hunt. G'lang, Bob."

"It's complete trackin' snow," said Sam to a group of hunters who lingered last at his threshold, and he stooped to imprint the snowy banking with his finger. "I'll see what it's got tu tell us an' let you know. Good-mornin'."

The wagons moving over the muffled roads, and the quiet of the sleepy junketers, marked their departure with silence as noticeable as the noise of their coming.

ROSE TERRY COOKE
(1827–1892)

It is not too much to say that New England fiction as we now know it—or as we now remember it—began with the stories of Rose Terry published in the *Atlantic* under the editorship of James Russell Lowell. She had written before that, a book of poems, stories for various magazines, pot-boilers for the "firesides," but now her stories took shape around the personalities of their people. One might marvel that these stories should have been honored in their own country, seeing that there were characters in them not only life-like but often obstinate, bigoted, and so "near" that they raised parsimony to an art and a passion—unless one bears in mind the warm humor that plays about them, and the understanding that treats even twisted humanity always with a certain respect. She was tall, slight and dark, with large intense eyes. She lived in Winsted, Connecticut, after her marriage, and five years before her death, in Pittsfield, Mass. She wrote no novels, only short stories for *Harper's*, *Scribner's* and other magazines, nearly a hundred in all, thirty of them for the *Atlantic*, with this story, which appeared in June, 1891, the last of the series. It was not until 1881 that her stories began to be collected in book-form; their titles are significant: "Somebody's Neighbors" and "Huckleberries from New England Hills." In the second of these volumes this story is included.

The huckleberry-bush is as distinctive a feature of upland pasture landscape as the gray moss, leafless and springy, cushioning the rock by which it grows. Something of the spicy tang of its fruit is in this tale, though not all of it has to do with out-of-doors. Our sharpest cleavage is not between any two sections of the United States; it is between town and country, or rather, between the types of mind that cannot conceive life as really lived save in one or the other. This cleavage can show sharply in a section like this where on the one hand neighborliness is highly developed, and on the other nature is at its most compelling. It can, and in this instance does, show itself even in a family where the tie of blood is as close as in old New England it was wont to be.

A TOWN MOUSE AND A COUNTRY MOUSE

By ROSE TERRY COOKE

"WELL, Mis' Phelps, I'm reelly a-goin' to Glover to see M'lindy at last. I be, pos'tive. Don't seem as though it could be true, 't is so long sence I sot eyes on her; and I've lotted on it so much, and tried so often and failed up on't, that I can't hardly believe in't now it's comin' to pass. But I be a-goin' now, sure as you live, Providence permittin'."

The speaker was a small, thin old woman, alert and active as a chickadee, with a sharp twitter in her voice, reminding one still more of that small black and gray bird that cheers us with his gay defiance of winter, though he utter it from a fir bough bent to the ground with heavy snows. Her dark gray hair was drawn into a tight knot at the back of her head; her tear-worn eyes shone with a pathetic sort of lustre, as if joy were stranger to them than grief; her thin lips wore a doubtful smile, but still the traces of a former dimple, under that smiling influence, creased itself in one lined and sallow cheek. You saw at a glance that she had worked hard always; her small hands were knotted at the joints and callous in the palms; her shoulders were slightly bent. And you saw, too, that poverty had enforced her labor, for her dress, though scrupu-

73

lously neat, and shaped with a certain shy deference to the fashion of the day, was of poor material and scant draperies.

Amanda Hart was really a remarkable woman, but she did not know it. Her life had been one long struggle with poverty and illness in her family, to whom she was utterly devoted. She had earned her living in one way or another as long as she could remember. Her mother died when she was a mere child, and her father was always a "shift-less," miserable creature, in his later years the prey of a slow yet fatal disease, dying by inches of torture that defied doctors and wrung poor Amanda's heart with help-less sympathy.

All these years she not only nursed, but supported him; scrubbed, sewed, washed—did anything that brought in a little money—for there were doctors' bills to pay, be-sides the very necessities of life to be obtained. Her one comfort was her sister Melinda, a child ten years younger than Amanda, a rosy, sturdy, stolid creature, on whom the elder sister lavished all the deep love of a heart that was to know no other maternity. At last death mercifully re-moved old Anson Hart to some other place, but before that relief came, Melinda, by this time a young woman, had married a farmer in Glover, and Amanda had moved into Munson, and was there alone. She "kinder scratched along," as she phrased it, and earned her living, if no more, in the various ways Yankee ingenuity can discover in a large country town. She had friends who helped her to employment, and always made her welcome in their homes; for her quaint shrewdness, her very original use, or misuse, of language, her humor, and her kind heart were all pleasant to have about.

Melinda's marriage was a brief experience. She was left a widow at the end of two years, with a small house and an acre of land; and there she lived alone, on a lonely country road, three miles from the village of Glover, and with no other house in sight.

"I guess it is as good as I can do," she wrote to Amanda. "I can't sell the house, and there's quite a piece of garden to it, besides some apple-trees and quince bushes. Garden sass always was the most of my living, and there's some tailoring to be did, so as that I can get a little cash. Then folks are glad to have somebody around killing times and sech like. Mary Ann Barker used to do that, but she's been providentially removed by death, so I can step right into her shoes. I guess, any way, I'll chance it for a spell, and see how it works."

Melinda had "faculty," and her scheme did "work" so well that she lived in the tiny house for years, and in all that time Amanda had not seen her. It was a long journey, and money was hard to get. Perhaps Melinda might have gathered enough to take the journey, but she was by no means affectionate or sentimental. Life was a steady grind to her; none of its gentle amenities flourished in the red house. She had her "livin'" and was independent: that sufficed her. But Amanda was more eager every year to see her sister. She thought of her by day and dreamed of her by night; and after fifteen years her cracked teapot at last held coin enough for the expedition. Her joy was great, and the tremulous, sweet old face was pathetic in its constant smiling. She planned her journey as she sat at work, and poured her anticipations into all the neighbors' ears till their sympathy was well worn out.

But at last the day came. Amanda's two rooms were set in order, the windows closed, every fly chased out with the ferocity that inspires women against that intrusive insect, and the fire was raked down to its last spark the night before.

"I don't care for no breakfast," she said to the good woman in whose house she lived. "I should have to bile the kettle and have a cup and plate to wash up; and like enough the cloth 'd get mildewy, if I left it damp. I'll jest take a dry bite in my clean han'k'chief. I've eet up all my victuals but two cookies and a mite of cheese that I saved a puppus."

"Why, Mandy Hart! you're all of a twitter! Set right down here and hev a cup o' tea 'long o' me. You've got heaps o' time; now don't ye get into a swivet!"

"Well, Mis' Phelps, I thank you kindly; a drop of tea will taste proper good. I expect I be sort o' nervy, what with takin' a journey and the thought o' seein' Melindy. Now you tell: do I look good enough to go travelin'? I thought, first off, to wear the gown Mis' Swift give me,— that Heneryette, I b'lieve she called it; but I've sponged and pressed it till it looks as good as new, and I sort o' hate to set on 't in the dust o' them cars all day. I thought mabbe this stripid gown would do."

"You look as slick as a pin," Mrs. Phelps answered.

It was an odd pin, then! The "stripid" dress was both short and scant even for Amanda's little figure; it did not conceal an ancient pair of prunella shoes that use had well fitted to her distorted feet, and her ankle-bones, enlarged with rheumatism, showed like doorknobs under her knit cotton stockings. Over her dress she wore a brown linen duster, shiny with much washing and ironing, and her queer little face beamed from under a wide black straw hat wreathed with a shabby band of feather trimming.

But she did not look amiss or vulgar, and the joy that shone in her eyes would have transfigured sackcloth, and turned ashes into diamond dust. She was going to see Melinda! The unsatisfied mother heart in her breast beat fast at the thought. Neither absence nor silence had cooled this one love of her life.

"I expect I shall enjoy the country dretfully," she said to Mrs. Phelps. "It's quite a spell sence I've been there. Mother, she set such store by green things, trees and sech, and cinnament roses, and fennel. My land! she talked about 'em all through her last sickness, even when she was dangerous. I shall be proper glad to get out to Glover."

Poor soul! all this meant Melinda.

So she trotted off to the station, with her lunch tied up in a handkerchief in one hand and her cotton umbrella in the other, a boy following with her old cow-skin trunk on a wheelbarrow. He was a bad boy, for on the way he picked up an advertisement of a hair restorer and fastened it upon that bald trunk, chuckling fiendishly. But this was lost on Amanda; she paid him his quarter with an ambient smile, and mounted the car steps with sudden agility. The car was not full, so she sat down next a window, struggled with a pocketful of various things to find her ticket, thrust it inside her glove, to be ready, and resigned herself to the journey. Outside the window were broad fields green with new grass, budding forests, bright and tranquil rivers, distant mountains, skies of spring, blue to their depths, and flecked with white cloud-fleeces; but they were lost on Amanda. She had not inherited her mother's tastes: she saw in all this glory only Melinda, the rosy girl who had left her so long ago; to that presence she referred all nature, wondering if this quiet farmhouse were like that at Glover, if Melinda's apple-trees had bloomed like those on the hillsides she passed, or if her sister could see those far-off hills from her windows. It was a long day. The "dry bite" was a prolonged meal to our traveler. Every crumb was eaten slowly, in order to pass the weary time. Nobody spoke to her; the busy conductor had short answers for her various questions. She was tired, dusty, and half homesick when at last that official put his head in at the door and yelled: "Sha-drach! Sha-drach! Sha-drach! Change for Medway, Racketts-Town, *and* Glover!"

So Amanda grasped her handkerchief, and, helped by her sturdy umbrella, for she was stiff with long sitting, found her way to the door, and was, as she phrased it, "yanked" off the steps upon the platform by an impatient brakeman. Why should he be civil to a poor old woman? Fortunately for her, the stage for Glover stood just across the platform, and she saw the driver shoulder her bare brass-nailed trunk which was duly directed to Melinda and Glover. A long five miles lay before her. The driver was not talkative, she was the only passenger, and it seemed a journey in itself before the stage drew up at the gate in front of Mrs. Melinda Perkins's farmhouse, and she came out of the door to meet her sister. A faint color rose to Amanda's cheek, her lips trembled, her eyes glittered, but she only said, "Well, here I be."

Melinda smiled grimly. She was not used to smiling; there was no sensitive shyness about her. Tall and muscular, her heavy face, her primmed-up mouth, her hard eyes glooming under that deep fold on the lids that in moments of anger narrows the eye to a slit and gives it a snaky gleam, her flat, low forehead, from which the dull hair was strained back and tightly knotted behind,—all told of a narrow, severe nature, at once jealous and loveless, the very antithesis of Amanda's. It is true, she stooped and kissed her sister, but the kiss was as frigid as the nip of a clamshell.

"Come in," she said, in an overbearing voice. "Hiram Young, you fetch that trunk in right here into the bedroom."

"You'll hev to sleep 'long o' me, Mandy," announced Melinda, as she swung open her bedroom door, "for the' ain't no other place to sleep."

"Why, I sha'n't object, not a mite," beamed Amanda. "It'll seem like old times. But you've growed a sight, Melindy."

"I think likely, seein' it's quite a spell since you see me; but I've growed crossways, I guess," and Melinda gave a hard cackle.

"How nice you're fixed up, too!" said admiring Amanda, as she looked about her in the twilight of green paper shades and spotless cotton curtains. The room was too neat for comfort; there was a fluffy, airless scent about it; the only brightness came from the glittering brasses of the bureau, that even in that half-dark shimmered in well-scoured splendor. Outside, the sweet June day was gently fading, full of fresh odors and young breezes; but not a breath entered that apartment, for even a crack of open window might admit a fly!

Melinda introduced her guest to a tiny closet on one side of the chimney, and then went out to get tea, leaving Amanda to unpack her trunk. This was soon done, for even that small closet was more than roomy enough for her other dress, her duster, and her hat; so that she soon followed her sister, guided by savory odors of hot biscuit, "picked" codfish, and wild strawberries. This was indeed a feast to the "town mouse"; such luxuries as raised biscuit and aromatic wild fruit were not to be indulged in at her own home, and she enjoyed them even more for the faint, delicious odor of old-fashioned white roses stealing in at the open door, the scent of vernal grass in the meadows, the rustle of new leaves on the great maple that shaded the house-corner, and the sharp chirp of two saucy robins hopping briskly about the yard.

It was delightful to Amanda, but when night shut down the silence settled on her like a pall; she missed the click of feet on the pavement, the rattle of horse cars, the distant shriek of railway trains. There was literally not a sound; the light wind had died away, and it was too early in the season for crickets or katydids, too late for the evening love-songs of toads and frogs.

In vain did she try to sleep; she lay hour after hour

"listening to the silence," and trying not to stir, lest she should wake Melinda. Had a mouse, her lifelong terror, squeaked or scratched in the wall, it would have relieved her; but in this dead stillness there was that peculiar horror of a sense suddenly made useless that affects the open eye in utter darkness, or the palsied lips that can make no sound.

Night seemed endless to the poor little woman; but when at last birds began to awake and chirp to the gray dawn, she fell so soundly asleep that not even Melinda's rising, or the clatter of her preparations for breakfast in the next room, aroused her. But her sister's voice was effectual.

"Be you a-goin' to sleep all day?" said that incisive and peremptory tongue.

The question brought Amanda to her feet, quite ashamed of herself.

"You see," she explained to Melinda at breakfast, "I didn't get to sleep till nigh sun-risin', 'twas so amazin' still."

"Still! That had ought to have made ye sleep. Well, I never did! Now I can't sleep ef there's a mite o' noise. I'd hev kep' chickens but for that. Deacon Parker wanted to give me some o' his white Braymys, but I said: 'No; I've got peace and quietness, and I ain't goin' to have it broke up by roosters.'"

"I s'pose it's accordin' as we're used to 't," meekly replied Amanda, with an odd sense of being in the wrong, but she said no more; she was beginning to discover that it was not serene bliss to be with Melinda again. In their

long separation she had forgotten her sister's hard and
abrupt ways, and indeed in Melinda's solitary and very
lonely life her angles had grown sharper and sharper;
nothing had worn them off. We can enjoy idealizing a
friend, but the longer that ideal fills our hearts the harder
does reality scourge us. Amanda could not have explained
her heart-sinking to herself. She laid it to the isolation of
her sister's house, and, while Melinda made bread, went
out to walk a little way, to see if she could not enjoy the
country. All about lay green fields, wooded hills, and
blooming orchards; for spring was late here in Glover,
and only the sheltered hillsides had cast all blossoms from
the later trees. A deep sense of desolation clutched
Amanda's homesick heart; there was not a house to be
seen, not even a curl of smoke to show that one might
be hidden somewhere. Used all her days to the throng and
bustle of a large town, she found this country peace un-
endurable. She went back to the house, took up her knitting,
and tried to be conversational.

"Haven't got any neighbors at all, have ye, Melindy?"

"Nearest is Deacon Parker, 'n' he lives three mild back
behind Pond Hill."

"My sakes! what if you should be took sick?"

"But I ain't never *took* sick," snapped Melinda, looking
like a sturdy oak-tree utterly incapable of ailments.

"But you might be; nobody knows when their time is
comin'. Why, when I had the ammonia last year, I do'no
but what I should ha' died,—guess I should,—if it hadn't
been for the neighbors."

"Well, I sha'n't go over no bridges till I come to 'em,"

sharply replied Melinda, paring her potatoes with extra energy.

"Glover is quite a ways from here, ain't it?" queried Amanda.

"Three mild."

Evidently Melinda was not given to talking, but Amanda would not be discouraged.

"Don't have no county paper, do ye?"

"No, I haven't got no time to spend on them things. I can 'tend up to my own business, if other folks'll take care of theirn."

Amanda gave an inaudible sigh, and tried no more conversation. After dinner Melinda did ask a few questions, in her turn, about old acquaintances, but her sister's prattle was effectually cut short. Never in her life had Amanda found a day so dreary or a night so long, for she had it to dread beforehand. Even the sharp rattle and quick flash of a June thunder-storm was a relief to her, for it woke Melinda, and sent her about the house to shut a window here and fasten down a scuttle there, and for a brief space kept her awake; but after that little space the capable woman slept like a log,—she did not even snore,—and the night resumed its deadly silence.

Oh, how Amanda longed for the living noises that she had so often scolded about in Munson! The drunken cackle of men just out from the saloons, the rapid rush of a doctor's carriage whirling by in the small hours, a cross baby next door that would yell its loudest just when she was sleepiest,—any, all of these would have been welcome in this ghastly stillness.

The next day was Sunday, and when the rigidly recurring Sunday breakfast of baked beans and codfish balls was over Amanda inquired timidly:—

"Do you go to meetin' on the Sabbath, Melindy?"

"Well, I guess so! We ain't clear heathen."

"I didn't know but 't was too fur to walk."

" 'Tis, but Deacon Parker goes right a-past here, and stops for me. He's got a two-seater, and there'll be room for you, for he don't take nobody but me and Widder Drake."

"Where's Mis' Parker?"

"I do'no. She's dead."

Amanda's eyes opened wide at this doubtful remark about the late Mrs. Parker, but she said nothing; she satisfied herself with watching Melinda dress. Her Sunday garments were a black alpaca gown, shiny with age, what she called a "mantilly" of poor black silk edged with emaciated fringe, and the crowning horror of a Leghorn bonnet, "cut down" from its ancient dimensions into a more modern scoop, but still a scoop. It was surmounted with important bows of yellow-green satin ribbon and a fat pink rose with two stout buds. Amanda felt a chill run over her at this amazing head-gear. She did not know that the rose was Melinda's last protest against old age, her symbol of lingering youth, her "no surrender" flag.

"Why don't you wear a hat, Melindy?" she asked meekly, as she smoothed out the dejected band of her own. "Bunnets is all gone out down to Munson."

"Well, they ain't here, and I don't think it's seemly to wear them flats to meetin'; they'll do to go a-huckleberryin' or fetchin' cows home from pastur', but, to my mind, they're kinder childish for meetin'."

Amanda said nothing, and just then the deacon drove up to the gate,—a spare old man, with long scanty white hair and red-rimmed, watery eyes. Amanda was duly presented.

"Make you 'quainted with my sister, Mandy Hart, down to Munson."

"Pleased to see ye," bobbed Deacon Parker, with a toothless grin. "I'd get out to help ye in, but old Whitey don't never stand good without tyin'; and gener'lly Mis' Drake holds her, but she's gone to Shadrach this week back. She's gardeen to a child over there, and there's some court business about the prop'ty."

"Lawsy! we can get in good enough," said Melinda, alertly climbing over the hind wheel, and helping Amanda to follow.

"Spry, ain't she?" said the deacon to Amanda, with another void and formless smile. "Huddup, Whitey! We don't want to be late to the sanctooary."

The drive was beautiful, and gave poor Amanda a gentler opinion of the country. It wound by little silver brooks, under the fragrant gloom of pine woods, and the sweet breath of the fields filled her weak lungs with new life. But alas! the meeting-house was a square barn with a sharp steeple, and as she sat down on the bare seat of a corner pew, and choked with the dead odors of "meetin'-seed," the musty chill of the past week, the camphor that exhaled from Sunday clothes but recently taken from their wintry repose, and the smell of boots that had brought their scent of stable and barnyard, she longed to be back in the handsome, well-ventilated church at Munson, with the soft rustle of a well-dressed, perfumy congregation about her, and the sound of a fine organ and well-trained choir in her ears, offended now by the tuneless squalls and growls of these country singers. Poor town mouse! She was ready to exclaim with the mouse of Horace:—

"But, Lord, my friend, this savage scene!"

That very night she told Melinda that she must leave her on Tuesday, on account of promised work, and accordingly Tuesday saw her safely back again in dear Munson. Her tiny rooms seemed like a refuge to her, as she opened the blinds and let in the warm air. Her natural vivacity, subdued by Melinda and the solitude of the country, returned.

"Goodness gracious, Mis' Phelps!" Amanda exclaimed to her landlady, "I wouldn't no more live in the country than nothin'. Why 't was as still as a ear-trumpet out there. I'd ha' give all my old shoes to ha' heard a street car or a coal wagon a-rumblin' by. And lonesome! There wasn't so much as a rooster a-predicatin' by in the road. I thought I should die for want of knowin' I was alive; and the nighttime shuts down onto ye like a pot-lid. You know you can't go marvelin' round in other folks' houses. I jest had to set and knit daytimes, and sense the lonesomeness. I know I should have shockanum palsy if I had to stay there. Melindy is comin' to see me for a spell early in July, about the Fourth, when it's kinder lively, and I guess 't 'll wake her up some."

"I expect you had good country victuals and plenty o' flowers, though?" asked Mrs. Phelps, in the indirect Yankee fashion.

"Well, I did. Melindy's a most an excellent cook, and the' was a patch of wild strawberries growed to the south side of her old barn that was ripe a'ready; they have got taste into 'em, I tell ye! But, land! victuals and drink ain't the chief o' *my* diet. I'm real folksy; grasshoppers ain't no neighbors to me. I want to be amongst them that 'll talk back to me; not dumb things that won't never say nothing if you should merang 'em all day."

"Why, how you talk! How does Mis' Perkins stan' it?"

"I do'no. I expect she's hardened to it, as you may say. *I*'d jest as lives set down on a slab in the sempitery all my days as to stay out to Melindy's. I do'no but I'd ruther; for there'd be funerals, and mourners, and folks comin' to desecrate the graves with flowers, and sech, intervenin' 'most every day there. 'Twould be real lively in comparison with Melindy's house."

Now Amanda set herself to adorn her little rooms and keep them in spotless order till her sister should come; and when that happy day arrived she met her at the station, her smiling old face as pleasant as a hollyhock blossom.

"If I ain't tickled, now!" she beamed on Melinda. "I've reelly got you here."

"I said I'd come, didn't I?" answered Melinda, with a laborious smile. "I haven't fetched no great of clothes, for I can't stay long; fruit is comin' in, and I've got to make preserves for quite a few folks down to Glover."

She secretly blessed herself for making this announcement early, when she reached Amanda's little tenement: two rooms over a grocer's store, redolent with smells of kerosene, cloves, pepper, and the like, added to the fumes of bad tobacco from customers' pipes.

Not only smells, but dust and the heat of a blazing July day added to her discomfort, though she had the grace not to complain; and when Amanda had laid aside that wonderful "bunnet," and set Melinda by the north window with a fan, the country mouse felt a little more comfortable. The tea daunted her; she could not eat the sliced "Bolony," as Amanda called it; the baker's bread was dust and ashes to her taste; the orange marmalade found no favor, though it was a delicacy Armanda had kept for this special purpose, the gift of a friend. Poor Melinda gave afterward a graphic description of this dainty meal to Deacon Parker.

"I never see sech victuals in *my* life! No wonder Mandy's lean. Cake and bread jest like sawdust, and, if you'll believe it, raw sassages, actooally *raw*, sliced up on a dish! I never could eat raw meat, much less pork. And the preserves was as bitter as boneset! I went hungry to bed, you'd better believe."

Yet worse was in store for the country mouse. Amanda had given up her bed to her visitor, and lain down on the sitting-room lounge; and though it was a breathless night, at first Melinda slept, she was so tired, in spite of the noisy horse cars, rattling wagons, and click of feet.

It was the night of the third of July, and as a neighboring church clock struck twelve the first giant cracker exploded right under the bedroom window. Roused by the crash, that was followed fast by another and another, Melinda started up in all the terror of darkness and din, screaming:—

"Mandy! Mandy! where be ye? What on earth's the matter?"

Smiling superior, though but half awake, Amanda answered:—

" 'Tain't nothin'; it's the Fourth, and them boys is a-settin' off crackers. Pesky little sarpents! I s'pose there is a puppus in boys, but I've wished frequent that men growed out o' somethin' more pleasant. You turn over an' go to sleep, sister; the' won't nothin' do ye no harm."

"Oh-h!" shrieked Melinda again, as a cannon roared from the green close by, and then the whole pandemonium set in.

The cat Civilization, with the ribbon of simulated patriotism round its neck, set upon our country mouse now with feline fury. Every noise that could be made by gunpowder, horns, or bells, as well as yelling boys, crashed upon this poor woman's head till she was all but crazy. How she longed for the sweet quiet of her own home, and longed in vain, for she could not get away! Stern and silent as she seemed to be, she was but a woman, and a real feminine panic ensued.

Amanda had her hands full for the rest of the night. Her panacea of "red lavender" was useless, and this was no case for her favorite salve that cured everything. She fanned Melinda, soothed her as she best knew how, and tried with all her heart to comfort and compose the frightened woman, steadied herself by a shy sense of superiority and courage to which Melinda could not attain. But not until sunrise dispersed the crowd of celebrators, and a sort of silence replaced the clamor, could Melinda close her eyes and snatch a nap before breakfast.

Coffee, steak, and stewed potato she could eat when that breakfast came; and later on, when Amanda said timidly, "Would you like to walk out a ways? 'Tisn't quite so hot, and we can get a good place to see the percession," Melinda did not refuse. She was glad to get out-of-doors, but nothing could induce her to ride in the horse cars; so Amanda guided her about the pretty town, showed her the public buildings, the fine houses of summer residents, the various churches, and the gay shop-windows, till, worn out, they sat down on one of the hard benches set here and there on the green, to wait for the event of the day.

"Who goes into the pr'cession?" inquired Melinda.

"Oh, fire comp'nies, an' temperance s'cieties, the perlice, and th' elect men. Bands, too,—brass bands with insterments."

Melinda stared her fill at the *mélange* that soon wheeled by.

"Say, Mandy, what be them fellers with muffs on their heads, a-throwin' up sticks and ketchin' of 'em?"

"They call 'em drum majors, I b'lieve, though I don't see no drums. I do lot on seein' 'em always, they're so pompious, and yet so spry. Look! d' ye see that one catch his batten an' twirl it?"

Melinda nodded her great bonnet, which had all day

attracted nearly as much attention as she bestowed on the drum majors, but she was tired enough to go home now and enjoy a cold dinner.

Perhaps she thought the terrors of the day were over, but they were not. For years before her marriage they had all lived in the deep country, so that the most common sights of the town were unknown to her; and when Amanda insisted on her going out to see the fireworks that wound up that holiday, Melinda's nerves received another shock. The star-dropping rockets, the spitting pinwheels, the soft roar of Roman candles, the blare of "set" pieces, neither pleased nor interested her; she was in terror lest those irresponsible fire-flakes should light on her Sunday bonnet, and every fierce rush of a rocket made her jump with fresh fear.

"Don't say no more, Mandy!" she declared the next day, when her sister tried to have her stay longer. "I've *got* to go. I couldn't stan' it another minute. I'm real obleeged to ye for what ye've did to make it pleasant for me, but I can't stan' a town. I'm all broke up a'ready, and I'm as homesick as a cat to get back. I'd rather have a hovil out in the lots than a big house here. There's too many other folks here for me. I wish 't you'd come out to Glover and make it home 'long o' me."

"Land, Melindy! I couldn't live there an hour. I should die of clear lonesomeness,—I know I should. Why, when I had the neurology in my diagram, last winter, and there come a dretful snow, so as that the neighbors couldn't none of 'em happen in, I thought 't would finish me up. What should I do if was took sick to your house? No doctor, no folks around! It makes me caterpiller to think on't. But I'm jest as obleeged, and I hope you'll come to Munson some time when 't ain't the Fourth."

So Melinda went back to her solitude, and Amanda settled down again to her town life, yet with a vague sense of trouble. She could not have defined it, but it really was the consciousness that, having obtained her heart's desire, it had not satisfied her. We all come to it sooner or later. "I shall be satisfied, when I awake, with thy likeness," says David. Is not the phrase a tacit confession that nothing on earth had ever satisfied him, king and poet as he was?

A month or two after Melinda went back to Glover, Amanda received a more positive, an appreciable shock in the following letter:—

Dear Mandy,—I take my pen in hand to inform you that I am usually well and hope you enjoy the same blessing. I have been busy continual sence I come back, finding quite a little to do about the house and gardin.

I supose I had better speak wright out, though you will be some surprised I expect to hear that I am intending for to change my condishun soon. Fact is Deacon Parker and I calculate to be joined in the bans of Matrimony Monday next. 'twas quite onexpected to me when he spoke, but after a thinking of it over it looked as though the' was a Providence into it for I called to mind what you said about my being took sick here all alone, and though I am not fur along in years, nor sickly, still the' is sech a thing as accidents to be pervided against at all times. I have heered folks say that they wouldn't be no man's fourth, but law! what's the difference? The others is all dead, and buried.

We sha'n't make no weddin', but he and me will be pleased to see you when you can make it convenient to come out to Glover for a spell. Mabbe you wouldn't be so lonesome now for he keeps quite a few chickens; he's a master hand for eggs.

So no more at present from

Yourn truly   MELINDY PERKINS.

"Oh, Lordy!" shrieked Amanda, as Mrs. Phelps opened the door and she dropped her letter. "Oh! I never did! What upon airth *is* she a-thinkin' of? Heavens to Betsy! that miser'ble old stick!"

"Why, Mandy Hart, what's befell *you?*"

"Befell *me?* 'T ain't me. I ain't nobody's fool. Mis' Phelps, Melindy is a-goin' to marry a old feller out to Glover as white-headed an' red-eyed as a albinia rabbit, and as toothless as a punkin lattern. Pos'tive! I don't no more see how she can! Moreover, she sort of twits me with sayin' that I shouldn't know how to be took sick in her house, 't was so lonesome, and no doctor within five mild, and no way of gettin' to one at that. Says that put it into her head!"

"Well off, ain't he?" asked Mrs. Phelps, with the crisp acerbity of a woman who knows her world.

"She says he's got means and she'll hev a home. A home, with that little ferret a-hoverin' around the hull endurin' time! I'd ruther grind a hand-organ round Munson streets! I didn't think Melindy *could.*"

Two irrepressible tears trickled down the grieved old face from eyes that were sadder than the tears. But Amanda had made her moan. She did not answer Melinda's letter; she went on her tedious way with more patience but less cheer than ever, and the next thing she heard of her sister was the following spring when a note from Deacon Parker arrived, running thus:—

Miss Amandy Hart,—This is to inform you that your sister is real sick with a fever; the doctor thinks she's dangerous. She's kep a-askin' for you for a week back, but I didn't pay no attention to 't, thought she was kind of flighty and 'twould only be a bill of expense to send for ye. But now Doctor Fenn says she's got to hev a nuss any way, so I bethought me to send for you. I expect to pay your way so I put in a five dollar bill. If you'll come a Wednesday I shall be pleased to see ye.

Yours to command,
Ammi Parker.

Amanda was alert immediately; she had short notice to set her house in order and buy a few little delicacies for her sister. A born nurse, she knew just what to get and what to take, and was ready to set off on the early train next day. The journey seemed longer than before, the stage road was heavy, and it was much further to the deacon's house than to her sister's. She found Melinda very ill indeed.

"You poor dear soul!" Amanda said, as she bent over her sister, with her heart in her kind eyes. "I wish't you'd sent for me before. I wish I had ye down to Munson in the Home Hospittle; you'd be so much better off."

A flash of hot color surged up into the sick woman's sallow, listless face; she lifted herself, with the sudden force of will, higher on her pillow; a weak, hoarse voice issued from her blackened lips.

"I wouldn't go! Don't ye speak on 't! None o' them institootions for me. I ain't so low down as that,—not yet!"

It was the last protest of sturdy independence; she sank down again, and began muttering to herself.

Amanda looked about her to see what could be done. The room was small and dark, opening out of the kitchen. The one window faced the north; not a ray of sun ever visited it, and its outlook was on a rough lane leading to the near barnyard. On the other side of the lane was a swamp, where the first grass was just greening the tussocks, and folded cones of skunk cabbage were slowly growing up out of the black stagnant water. The window could not be opened; evidently no one had tried to open it since it was paint-stuck, years ago. She could do nothing there, so she set the door wide into the kitchen and opened the outer door. Fumes of boiling cabbage and frying pork came into the bedroom in clouds, but there was fresh air mingled with them. Melinda lay in the hollow of a feather bed, burning with typhoid fever, and Amanda could not lift her without help; the deacon was milking, and old Moll Thunder, the temporary "help," was half drunk. Amanda thought with a pang of the clean rooms and easy beds of the Cottage Hospital at Munson, the white-capped nurses, the skillful doctors, and her heart sank, though she knew, from long experiences of sickness, that no human power could save Melinda now; but it might have been otherwise, and she was her only sister, the last tie of kindred blood. She did what she could to make the poor woman comfortable, but it was too late. Melinda did not utter a rational word again: a few broken whispers,—"To home," "What a green medder!" "Tell Mandy,"—and then stupor overpowered all her faculties. There were a few hours of sonorous breathing; the stern features settled into the pinched masque of death. Melinda had gone beyond her sister's help.

"Yes," said Amanda, the week after, to Mrs. Phelps, who had come in to sympathize with her, "she was dretful sick when I got there; reelly you may say she was struck with death. And now the last one I'd got lies a-buried in the sand an' stuns in that lonesome graveyard, full o' hardhacks and mulleins. 'T wa'n't much of a funeral, but I had 'em sing Jordan, for you know it tells about 'sweet fields beyond the swellin' flood'; and she favored the country so, it seemed sort o' considerate so to do. Oh, dear! she was all the sister I'd got, Mis' Phelps, and 't is a real 'fliction. Deacon Parker was a mind to have me stay 'long o' him, for company; he was, pos'tive! But mercy! I should ha' gone crazy a-lookin' at him, if I had!"

Now Amanda was alone indeed: she had been so for years, but there had always been an aim and object to her life; Melinda was in her mind and on her heart. The pleasant expectations, the frail hopes, that had been so dear to her tried in vain to live; they had no resting-point; they recoiled on her with a dull sense of want and solitude. She grew listless, feeble and sad; yet when a friend or neighbor came in to see her she brightened up, and was so cheery that it was a surprise to them all when she took to her bed and had a doctor. He could find nothing that seemed to warrant her weakness; ordered nourishment, as doctors do, gave her some harmless pills, and went away smiling.

"He do'no nothin' what ails me," Amanda said in a half

whisper to Mrs. Phelps. "I guess I've got through. I've always looked forward to M'lindy's comin' finally to live with me; an' fust she went an' married that old Parker, an' then she up an' died. I wish't I'd ha' stayed with her longer; mabbe she wouldn't have died. She wa'n't old; not nigh so old as I be. I feel as though there wasn't nothin' to live for; but I s'pose if 't is the Lord's will I *shall* live, only I guess 't ain't. I feel a goneness that I never had ketch hold o' me before. Well, I sha'n't be lonesome, anyway; there's many mansions, and they tell about the holy city; and all my folks is there—or somewhere."

A vague look clouded her eyes for an instant, but she was too weak to speculate. Once more she spoke, very softly:—

"I hope M'lindy likes it. 'Sweet fields,'—that's what the hymn tells about."

She turned her head on the pillow, sighed—and was gone.

WILLIAM HUSSEY MACY

(1826–1891)

Whaling, once a basic industry of New England, has its prose epic in "Moby Dick" and more than one memorable record like "The Cruise of the Cachalot," but the short story has seldom used it as scene or inspiration. Fortunately for this collection it is easy to lift episodes complete in themselves from the spirited narratives of Captain Macy of Nantucket, narratives that like all the best sailors' stories are a blend of romance and reminiscence.

When William Hussey Macy died at his home on Main Street on March 14, 1891, at the age of sixty-five, the *Nantucket Inquirer and Mirror* said:

His decease removes from our midst a man of rare intellectual powers, a genial companion, and one of sterling virtues, whose name will live long in the memories of all Nantucketers as well as with a wide circle of friends scattered far beyond his place of nativity. Mr. Macy's early life, after his High School career, was spent upon the ocean, and he sailed in various whaling craft, viz.: *Potomac*, Capt. Isaac B. Hussey, 1841–1845; *Alpha*, Capt. C. B. Swain, 2d, 1850 (returning in the *Harriet Erving* in 1853); *Albion of Fairhaven*, Capt. John W. Hinds, 1854–7; brig *Homer*, Capt. George Haggerty, on a sea elephant cruise to Hurd's Island, 1858–9.

At this time he left the sea, and removed to East Boston, where he remained several years. He enlisted in the Union service in 1862, going south in November of that year as a member of Co. H. 45th Regt. M. V. M. He was wounded in the leg at the battle of Kingston, N. C., Dec. 14, 1862, and carried the bullet at the time of his death. His regiment was a part of Gen Foster's division which took part in Burnside's movement on Fredericksburg.

Soon after his return from the army, he removed to Nantucket, and in 1870 was elected Register of Deeds, since which time he has performed the duties of that office, for the past six years holding it through others, his great infirmity (blindness), which seized upon him in 1875, preventing his holding the position in his own name. Despite his loss of sight, he was thoroughly conversant with every detail of the intricacies of the common and undivided land problem of the island, and his knowledge was largely drawn upon by others. Deceased also served with great satisfaction as a member of the School Committee.

He was the author of several books, his "There She Blows!" running through a large edition. His "Here and There in Verse," was a small pamphlet containing a compilation of his poetical sketches, and is now out of print.

So, no doubt, are all his books: they rode high, spread an influence even overseas, and sank in the flood of time. But whoever finds one and reads there, finds a born writer who even on his first voyage went for to admire as well as for to see, and managed somehow to set his own wonder and delight vibrating in the reader. It was a man with a sense of the dramatic who reported the skipper's speech as he mounts higher and higher in the rigging, or set down the brief interchange of farewells as the deep-sea visiting comes to a close. It was a boy who thrilled to beauty who noted the "murmur of admiration" with which the sailors look back from the deck of the other whaler upon their own ship, hove to in the moonlight. These episodes taken from the plotless but well-woven narrative of "There She Blows!" give the same effect of standing off and looking at some familiar beauty, newly revealed by distance. In Captain Macy's book the distance was one of years: in later life he wrote it from the recollections of his first voyages, but he wrote in spirit of the boy who found them excursions into a world of wonder.

"THERE SHE BLOWS!"

By Captain William Hussey Macy

As I looked astern, when I first got my footing aloft, I caught sight of something like a small puff of steam or white smoke, rising a little and blowing off on the water. Looking intently at the same spot after a short interval, I saw another puff, rising like the former and satisfying me, from the descriptions I had heard, that some sort of whale was there. Instinctively I shouted:

"There she blows!"

"Where away?" hailed Mr. Johnson, who was just climbing the maintopmast rigging. "O yes! I see him! sperm whale, I believe—hold on a bit till he blows again— yes—thar' sh' blo-o-ows! large sperm whale! two points off the larboard! Blo-o-ows! headed to windward!"

"How far off?" shouted Mr. Grafton, from the deck.

"Three miles! 'Ere sh' blo-o-ows!"

By this time the old man was on deck, and ready for action. "Call all hands out, Mr. Grafton! Hard a star-board, there! Stand by to brace round the yards. Cook! get your breakfast down as fast as you can. Keep the run of him, there, aloft! Maintop bowline, boatsteerers! seem't's a sperm whale, eh, Mr. Johnson? Steward! give me up the glass—I must make a cleet in the gangway for that glass soon. Muster 'em all up, Mr. Grafton, and get the lines in as fast as you can (mounting the shearpole). Sing out when we head right, Mr. Johnson! Mr. Grafton, you'll have to brace sharp up, I guess (just going over the maintop). See the *Pandora*, there? O yes! I see her (halfway up the topmast rigging). Confound him! he's heading just right to see the whale, too! ('There goes flukes!' shouted the mulatto.) Yes! yes! I see him—just in time to see him (swinging his leg over the topmast crosstrees) a noble fan, too! a buster! Haul aboard that main-tack! We must have that fellow, Mr. Johnson. Steady-y! Keep her along just full and by. *We mustn't let the Pandora get him, either!*"

The *Arethusa* bent gracefully to the breeze, as, braced sharp on the port tack, she darted through the water as though instinctively snuffing her prey. The whale was one of those patriarchal old bulls, who are often found alone, and would probably stay down more than an hour before he would be seen again. Meantime, the two ships were rapidly nearing each other; and the *Pandora's* lookouts were not long in discovering that "something was up," as was evinced by her setting the main royal and foretopmast studding-sail, though they could not possibly have seen the whale yet. But the whale was apparently working slowly to windward, and the *Pandora* coming with a flowing sheet, all of which was much in her favor. The old man remained aloft, anxiously waiting the next rising, from time to time hailing the deck to know "what time it was?" and satisfying himself that the boats were in readiness, and breakfast served out to those who wanted it. As three-quarters of an hour passed, he grew more anxious and fidgety, shifting his legs about in the crosstrees, and clutching the spy-glass in his nervous grasp.

"Are you all ready, Mr. Grafton?"

"Ay, ay, sir," answered the mate from the maintop, where he had mounted to get a look at the whale when he should rise again.

"Let them hoist and swing the boats."

"Ay, ay, sir."

"I think I saw a ripple then," said the second mate, from the topsail yard directly beneath him.

"Where?" demanded the captain.

"Four points off the lee bow."

"O! no, you didn't, he won't come there. He'll rise right ahead or a little on the weather-bow. I don't think he'll go much to windward—good gracious! see that *Pandora* come down! She'll be right in the suds here, directly! I think we've run far enough, eh, Mr. Grafton? Haul the mainsail up, then! and square the main yard!"

Silence for a few minutes after this evolution was performed.

"He can't be far off when he comes up again. Look at the men old Worth has got aloft there, his crosstrees swarming, and every rattlin manned.—Look sharp! all of ye! We must see that whale when he first breaks water. That helm eased down? Haul the foresail up! and let the jib-sheets flow a little more. It can't be possible that whale has been up—no, we couldn't help seeing him, some of us —I *know* 'twas a sperm whale. I saw his fan; besides, there's Mr. Johnson—best eyes in the ship. What time is it, there? An hour and ten minutes that whale has been down—a long-winded old dog! We shall have to wear round, I'm afraid we shall forge. *Blo-o-ows!* right ahead, not one mile off! Down there and lower away! Now, Mr. Grafton, work carefully—Mr. Dunham, too; if you don't strike this rising, spread your chances well, and don't crowd each other—*but don't you let the Pandora get him!*" The captain was by this time in the stern of his own boat. "All ready, Mr. Johnson? Where's Old Jeff at my midship oar? O, here you are, eh? You ain't turned white yet— lower away! Cooper! Where's Cooper? As soon as we are all clear, wear round— *Let run that davit fall!*—Wear round and make a short board—haul up your tackle, boy. Keep to windward all you can, Cooper! Pull a little off the weatherbow, Mr. Grafton, and then set your sail! Haul in these gripes towing over the quarter— By thunder, there's Worth's boats all down! coming with fair wind, too! Out oars, lads!"

The *Pandora* had luffed to and dropped her boats a mile to windward, and they were coming down before the breeze, wing-and-wing, with their paddles flashing in the sunlight, and their immense jibs guyed out on the bow- oar as studding-sails, promising to stand about an equal chance for the whale with ourselves. The larboard boat to which I belonged proved the fastest of the three, and had a little the lead. After pulling a few quiet strokes to wind- ward, Father Grafton set his sails, and, as he gave the order to "peak the oars and take the paddles," seemed as cool and calm as when engaged in the most ordinary duty on board. There was no confusion or bustle in his boat, but with his practised eye fixed upon the huge spermaceti, he kept encouraging us in a low, dry tone, as he conned the steering oar with such skill, that he seemed to do it without effort.

"Now, lads, you face round to paddle, you can all see him. I declare, he's a noble fellow—ninety barrels under his hide, if there's a drop. Bunker, do you see that fellow? he's got a back like a ten-acre lot—paddle hard, lads—if you miss him, go right overboard yourself, and don't come up again—long and strong stroke, boys, on your paddles. See that boat coming? that's Ray, the second mate of the *Pandora*—three or four more spouts, and we'll have him— he's ours sure! they can't get here in time—scratch hard, boys! don't hit your paddles on the gunwale. Stand up, Bunker, and get your jibtack clear! Don't let them 'gally' you, if they shout in that boat."

"All right!" said his boatsteerer, with his eager hand resting on the iron pole. "Never fear, sir."

"Paddle hard, lads, a stroke or two. That's right, Bunker. Keep cool, my boy. Keep cool, and make sure of him."

A wild and prolonged shout rang on the air from six sturdy pairs of lungs in the *Pandora's* waist-boat, as Mr. Ray, seeing that he was baffled, let fly his sheets and rounded to, a ship's length to windward. It was too late, however.

"All right," said Father Grafton, in the same dry, quiet tone, as before. "Hold your hand, Bunker. Hold your hand, boy, till you're past his hump—another shoot, lads —way enough, in paddles. Now, Bunker! give it to him! Down to your oars, the rest. *Give him t'other one, boy!*

Well done! both irons to the hitches. Hold water, all! Bear a hand, now, and roll up that sail. Wet line, Tom! wet line! Where's your bucket? All ready with your sail, Bunker? Let her come then—all right. Come aft here, now, and let me get a dig at him."

The line was spinning round the loggerhead with a whizzing noise, and a smoking heat, as the huge leviathan, stung to the quick, darted down into the depths of the ocean. Bunker threw on the second round turn to check him, and jamming the bight of the line over the stern sheets, watched it carefully as it flew through his grasp; while the mate cleared his lance, and got ready to renew the attack. Every moment his anxiety increased as he kept turning his head, and looking at the tub of line, rapidly settling, as the whale ran it out. "I declare, I believe he'll take all my line. Blacksmith! pass along the drug! Check him hard, Bunker!" Then, seeing the other boats near at hand, he opened his throat, and, for the first time, we learned the power of Father Grafton's lungs.

"Spring hard, Mr. Dunham! I want your line! Cast off your craft, and stand by to throw your line to me! Spring hard! *Do!*"

The ash sticks in the waist-boat were doing their best, as the loud "Ay, ay!" was borne back o'er the water from Dunham, while the old man could be seen in the rear of the picture, wildly straining every nerve to be "in at the death," and heaving desperately at the after oar, with his hat off, his hair flying loosely in the breeze, and his whole frame writhing with eager excitement. Our line was going,

going; already there was but one flake in the tub, when the waist-boat ranged up on our quarter, and Fisher, with the coil gathered in his hand, whirled it over his head, making ready for a cast. At this instant, the strain was suddenly relieved, and the line slacked up.

"Never mind!" roared Mr. Grafton. "Hold on, Fisher! All right, he's coming! Never mind your line, Mr. Dunham, he's coming up! pull ahead and get fast! Get a lance at him if you can! Haul line, *us!* Face round here, all of ye, and haul line! Careful, Bunker, about coiling down! He'll be up now, in a minute, haul lively!"

The waist-boat had shot ahead under a fresh impulse of her oars, and the captain came drawing up abreast of the fast boat.

"Are you well fast, Mr. Grafton?"

"Ay, ay, sir; both irons chock to the socket."

"That's the talk! Got 'most all your line, hasn't he?"

"Yes, sir."

"Well, gather in as fast as you can. Spring hard, *us!* Spring! I want to grease a lance in that fish! There he is up!" he shouted as the tortured monster broke water, shoving his whole head out in his agony, and started to windward.

Fisher had bent on his craft again, and was about two ships' lengths from the whale when he rose.

"Haul quick, my lads!" said the mate, "and get this stray line in! There's Mr. Dunham going on, and the old man will be with him in a minute. There he brings to!" as the whale suddenly stopped short in his mad career, and lay swashing up and down, as if rallying his strength for a fresh effort.

"There's 'stand up' in the waist-boat! There he darts! Hurrah! two boats fast! Haul lively, *us*, and get this line in!"

The whale seemed staggered by this accumulation of cold iron in his system, and lay wallowing in the trough of the waves. It was a critical moment for him; for Mr. Dunham was getting his lance on the half-cock, ready for darting, and, as the whale suddenly "milled short round" to pass across the head of his boat, the young man saw his advantage, and cried:

"Pull ahead! Pull ahead, and we'll get a 'set' on him! Lay forward, Fisher! Lay forward hard, my lad! right on for his fin! Pull ahead! So, way enough—hold water, all"; and, driven by a strong arm, the sharp lance entered his "life," its bright shank disappearing till the pole brought it up.

"Hold her so!" said the second mate. "Way enough! just hold her so till he rises again!" as the whale hollowed his back under the sea, now crimsoned with his life-tide, and again rising, received the lance anew in his vitals; but the first "set" was enough, and the gush of clotted blood from his spiracle told how effectually it had done its work.

"There," said Father Grafton, who had just got his line gathered in and was ready to renew the assault, "there's the red flag flying at his nose! Blacksmith, we may as well put up our lance, we sha'n't want it to-day. Well done, Mr. Dunham! Thick as tar the first lance! Hold on him,

Bunker! heave on a turn!" as the whale, making a dying effort, started up to windward, passing among the *Pandora's* boats within easy hail.

"Give us your warp, Pitman, if you want a tow," said Bunker in passing to Mr. Ray's boatsteerer.

"Every dog has his day," growled Pitman, in reply.

"Yes. Come aboard to-morrow and I'll give you a 'scrap' for luck."

When in the latitude of Cape St. Augustine, being close-hauled, with light breezes at east-south-east, a ship was "raised" in the afternoon, under a cloud of light canvas, steering to the northward. As she gradually neared us, she was made out by her boats and other significant marks to be a homeward-bound whaler, and by altering her course a little, showed her intention of passing within hail and speaking us.

The meeting of two ships at sea is a beautiful and imposing affair. I was deeply interested in the sight, as the stranger drew nearer and nearer. He had hauled in his studding-sails and brailed up both courses, seeming at times to slide down to leeward on a declivity, and then to stop suddenly, as if arrested by some unseen power. The breeze was light and the sea comparatively smooth, but I was surprised to see how considerable her rolling motion was, even under these circumstances. Rough-looking men, clad in garments of more colors than the coat of Joseph ever boasted, could be seen clustered round the bows and stretching their heads over the bulwarks, and two or three had climbed into the waist-boat to get a better view. The skipper, a large, dark-looking man, sat in the head of the labored quarter-boat, from time to time turning his head to speak to his helmsman and waving his brass trumpet to enforce the order. Captain Upton, with a similar instrument, was mounted on the taffrail, his mates standing near him, a little in the background. The stillness, as the ships neared each other, was unbroken now, save by the occasional rustle of a sail aloft, or the slight rushing of the water under the bows of the stranger. The ship appeared at this moment to be heading directly into us, as though bent on striking us amidships and running us down. Some of us, clustered at the weather rail, involuntarily began to draw back, fearing a collision; but again, at a wave of the dark man's trumpet, the ship, obedient to his helm, fell slowly off, so as to pass just clear, across our stern. Silence more profound than ever.

"Who commands the *Arethusa?*" shouted a hoarse voice, through the brass tube.

"Upton!" responded the other brass tube.

"Hope you're very well, Captain Upton!" said brass tube number one, obscuring the face of the speaker like a total eclipse.

"Very well, thank you," answered tube number two in the same style. "What ship is that, pray?"

"*Mandarin,* of Nantucket."

"Hope to see you well, Captain Barney."

Much muttering now ensued among our wiseacres, each of whom had known it was the *Mandarin* all along, and had told all the rest so, half an hour ago. Anybody might have known that was the *Mandarin's* figure-head. All which somewhat interfered with the clear understanding of the rest of the dialogue, which was now carried on between the brass tubes at a furious rate. "What success?—Sixteen hundred.—What port are you from last?—Oahu.—How long are you from home?—Forty-five days.—Got any letters for us?—Yes. Come aboard.—Thank you, I will." A flourish of the trumpet, and the *Mandarin's* crew are seen running to the braces, as her helm is clapped a starboard, and she rounds to the wind at a handsome distance under our lee, with her maintopsail thrown aback for an old-fashioned "gam."

Supper is delayed for the guests to arrive; several of us dive below, embracing the opportunity to write a few lines to our friends at home; Old Jeff growls at us for being in such a hurry, and says there's plenty of time between now and midnight; for we are sure to "gam" till that time.

"Captain Barney and the old man are cronies, and they'll have to kill all the whales in the ocean across the cabin table, before they part company."

A light whale-boat is presently seen to drop from under the *Mandarin's* lee-quarter, and comes bounding to windward under the powerful impulse of her oars. A petty officer is steering, while his majesty the captain stands firmly planted in the stern sheets, with his legs spread apart in an attitude suggestive of an inverted letter Y, and benignly regards his loyal subjects at the oars, who stretch to their work in gallant style, as if conscious that they "bear Cæsar and his fortunes." The principal impelling motive, however, is their eagerness to levy contributions upon the "greenies." Already they imagine themselves returning with bundles of books and papers tied up with rope-yarns, and shirt-bosoms corpulent with new tobacco, a luxury to which their teeth have been strangers for many a day.

"Ship in, harp'neer! way enough! Look out for the warp in the waist!"

"Halloo, old man!" says Captain Barney, as he recognizes Father Grafton at the man-ropes, "you out here again?"

Then as his head rises above the rail, "How goes it, Upton? S'pose you've got a crack ship here by the look of things. Well, how did you leave old Nantucket? 'Tain't sunk yet, has it?" A common question with whalemen when they meet, and asked with as much gravity as that of the noble Thane, Macduff, "Stands Scotland where it did?" or as though islands were in the habit of submerging themselves every day in the week.

A hearty greeting and hand-shaking follows, with a few hurried questions and replies, an introduction to the other officers, and an invitation to our mate to go on board and spend the evening with Mr. Joy.

"Do you swap boats' crews, Upton?"

"Yes, I don't care; let them go."

So the boat is manned with a crew of Arethusas, myself among the number, and Mr. Grafton steers himself, not yet having arrived at the dignity of a bodyguard. It was nearly dark when we arrived alongside, and as soon as the boat was on the cranes and secured, all hands made a "grand forward movement" to supper, and I now had leisure to look about me, and to compare the vessel and her veteran looking crew with the *Arethusa* and my own shipmates.

The forecastle of the *Mandarin* was small, dingy and dark, even in the daytime, having only two small deck-lights and no sidelights, a modern luxury which had not then come into general use. She had boasted a steerage in the early part of the voyage, but this had been broken up, and all hands quartered in the forecastle—sixteen men in twelve bunks, some of them turning in and out, watch and watch. An old battered blubber-room lamp hung from a beam overhead, and gave just sufficient light to make darkness visible. Two little ones, of the kind known as "petticoat lamps," were now added, and each furnished light enough to see that the other was burning. The old adage that "a farrier's mare and a cobbler's wife are always slipshod" is fully verified in the case of a whaleman's lamp; for those who supply the world with oil burn it in its crude state.

There was room enough in the forecastle, small as it was; for not half the crew had chests, and their goods and chattels could be compressed into a very small compass. The supper was not exactly what would have tempted a gourmand; still it was all that could be expected on board a ship forty-four months from home. The cows must have gone astray, for the supply of milk had failed: *domestic* coffee, compounded of burnt peas and corn, had usurped the place of the imported article; while it was evident that the visitors, if in time for supper, had come too late for *tea*. The bread was thickly colonized, and the salt junk better adapted for the manufacture of fancy carved work and articles of *virtu* than for purposes of mastication. It was, of course, a point of honor with us green hands to overlook these little drawbacks, and even to affect an eccentric taste for the ancient viands; but our hosts were not at all backward in expressing their dissatisfaction with this state of things.

This crew were mostly "beachcombers," men who had joined the ship during the voyage, many of them in the last port, and knew little and cared less about the history of the voyage previous to the time they shipped. They were full of tales of their adventures in other vessels from which they had deserted or been discharged, and of encounters with consuls, captains of the port, *vigilantes*, and other functionaries, commonly regarded as Jack's natural enemies; while those luckless shipmasters who had availed themselves of their services must have lived in perpetual jeopardy during the time they remained on board.

I inquired of the man upon whom I was quartered at supper, "how long the ship was out."

"That's more than I can tell you," returned the cruiser. "I've been only four months in this hooker. There's Dan and 'Shorty,' they are the only two men in the fo'c'stle that came from home in her. They can tell you; all the rest of us are cruisers."

"Where did you join her?" I asked.

"In Oahu. I ran away from the *Cambridge*, of New Bedford, and stowed away here in the fore peak. The 'kikos' came aboard three times, hunting for runaway men; but I'll defy any kiko to catch *me*."

"What's a kiko?" I inquired.

"That's what they call the Kanaka policemen. They used to come down and take off the fore peak scuttle, and look down, and shove their sticks in; but you see they don't have but one pair of white trousers apiece, and don't mean to get 'em dirty. But if any kiko had crawled in where I was, he wouldn't have got out again alive."

"Why not?" I inquired, innocently.

" 'Cause I'd have let daylight through him!"

I looked at the speaker reflectively, and involuntarily hitched a little further from him on the chest, feeling somewhat doubtful of close companionship with so dangerous a character. Yet the probability is, this man was as arrant a Falstaff as could be found in a day's journey.

"What made you run away from the *Cambridge?*"

"O, me and the old man had a row. Besides, I had been eight months in her, and that's long enough to be in one craft. I'd like to see the —— hooker that would keep *me* a year."

The speaker prefixed to the word hooker a sanguinary adjective, which is not applicable to ships except after a hard-fought action.

"Do you expect to stay out the voyage in that hooker?" inquired the beachcomber.

"Yes," said I, "I think I shall. I've been well used so

far, and have nothing to complain of. I don't see any reason to leave the ship, with the chance of getting into a worse one."

"Ah, my lad, you're green yet. Wait awhile till you've seen more service, and you'll get tired of staying so long in one craft. I say, shift about and go by the cruise. Six months is plenty long enough in one hooker."

Some of the green hands were swallowing this kind of poison by wholesale; each one listening to a yarn of how the narrator had humbugged a shipping master, or bullied an American "counsle," or knocked over an officer of a ship in the discharge of his duty. The pleasures of a drunken spree and row with the police of a foreign port were duly set forth, and the peculiar delights of life in a calaboose depicted in glowing colors. But this species of conversation flagged after a time. The Mandarins boasted no musical instrument; but that curse and abomination of the forecastle, a greasy pack of cards, was produced, and furnished pastime for a small knot in one corner for a short time.

Dan and "Shorty," the two "voyagers," brought up from the depths of their chests some canes, busks, and other fancy articles or "scrimshonting," as it is termed by whalers, ingeniously fabricated from whales' teeth and jaw bones, some of which they were willing to exchange for tobacco, the principal necessary of life among seamen on long voyages, and their universal circulating medium and standard of value. An article of traffic at sea, instead of being estimated at so many dollars and cents, is rated at so many pounds of tobacco; a thing which is nearly worthless is "not worth a chaw of tobacco"; a disputed question is generally settled by betting a certain quantity of tobacco, and a notorious romancer is often interrupted in the midst of a thrilling story, with the inquiry, "How much tobacco have you got?" meaning, "How much can you give us to believe it? We'll believe anything, if you've got tobacco enough to put it through."

And yet, through all the rough entertainment there shone a vein of politeness and deference to their guests, a certain delicacy which never deserts the sailor, and which might be studied with profit by many accustomed to the most courtly circles. A man who should overstep certain bounds in his intercourse with visitors from a strange ship, or be guilty of the slightest breach of a certain etiquette, not defined by Chesterfield's laws, but natural and of spontaneous growth, as it were, would be taken to task unmercifully by his shipmates; and slights which would pass current in a fashionable evening party, with both nobs and snobs, would never be overlooked in a whaleman's "gam."

A song was called for by somebody; the motion was seconded and carried, *nem. con.*; cards were thrown aside, "scrimshonting" articles returned to their depositories; and after some little clamor, it was decided that "Old Scotty," a tall, sunburned salt, who had served, according to his own statement, in one of the maintops of his most nautical majesty William the Fourth, should open the musical programme with that delectable chorus, "The stormy winds how they blow, blow, blow," which he executed after the most approved and orthodox style, rolling up the whites of his eyes at the carlines overhead, as though he expected that the roaring chorus in which all hands joined, would lift the deck off, and afford him a view of the heavens. A burst of applause followed the last verse, which I must confess I construed to be a manifestation of joy that it was finished, and of gratitude that there was no more of it to be endured. The Arethusas were now called upon to respond, and after some comparing of notes and prompting each other, Farrell struck up the time-honored confession of the misguided Irish youth who committed matrimony at the tender age of sixteen, and "died forlorn on Steven's Green," and afterwards wrote his autobiography in common metre, his last earthly request being that his pall might be borne by six disconsolate young ladies, all dressed in white gowns and pink ribbons. This song is a stock article with Irish and seamen, for what reason it would be hard to tell. A stout, jolly-looking Mandarin next electrified the auditors with the sentimental refrain of "O no, we never mention her!" with original quavers and variations, chanted in a voice of thunder; and was followed by Old Scotty, who rolled his eyes higher than ever as he poured himself out in a heartrending ballad, describing the fate of a certain Miss Caroline of Edinboro town, who at an untimely age "shuffled off this mortal coil," and "plunged her body down," after giving precisely *three* shrieks for Henry, neither more nor less. This pathetic outbreak again brought up the Arethusas in force, and the entertainment was sustained with great vigor on both sides, the songs being of various descriptions, and some, like newspaper novelettes, broken off in the middle of a verse, "to be continued hereafter." Some of the volunteer performers would have passed for good singers where tunes were not in fashion, while others, if they had fitted all the snatches together into one, might have furnished a medley of a highly original character. The veritable history of that unfortunate mariner, William Taylor, who was sent to his last account by the contents of a brace of pistols in the hands of his slighted "ladie love," having been caught *in flagrante delicto*, basking in the smiles of another fair one, was interrupted at a most thrilling crisis by the cry of "Brace forward the mainyard!" for the *Arethusa* had forged considerably ahead, while both ships were lying aback. It took some time to do this, as by a singular fatality, nobody had a watch on deck; all the men who should by any possibility have had one had gone gamming. The *dénouement* of the fickle Taylor's story was lost, as the helm required the singer's services.

The last act of the evening partook much of the nature of the first, being filled with marvellous tales of exploits, and "moving accidents by flood," and comparison of notes touching the respective merits of ships, captains and officers. The cry of "Haul aback" cut short several half-finished stories, and brought everybody on deck to look at the *Arethusa*, now running to leeward with a light set as signal of recall for her mate and boat's crew. A murmur of admiration went round among us, at the appearance of the crack ship looming in the clear moonlight, as, having assumed the lee position, she rounded gracefully to again, when the boat was cleared away and manned, with hearty farewells on both sides.

"Good-night, Joy," said Father Grafton, as he descended the man-ropes. "Short passage home to you. Deliver my letter yourself when you get there."

"Ay, ay," returned the *Mandarin's* mate. "Greasy luck to you!"

"Thank you," said Grafton. "A large whale for you tomorrow," with the additional reservation "and two for *us*. Let go the warp! out oars—pull ahead!"

The *Mandarin* having run to leeward in her turn, the word was passed to "man the boat"; and for a wonder, they waited alongside only three-quarters of an hour. But Captain Barney was an uncommonly prompt man in his movements; the usual standard in such cases being an hour and a quarter.

In a few minutes, the rusty-looking ship was off on her northerly course for "home, sweet home," bearing messages to gladden the hearts of many interested in the fate of those on board her late consort, who was again standing by the wind to the southward.

NATHANIEL HAWTHORNE
(1804–1864)

There was a time, and a long time too, when Boston belonged to the Crown and its distinguished citizens were loyal subjects. Then came restiveness and increasing dissatisfaction and then there was Paul Revere watching for a lantern and at Concord Bridge the shot heard round the world. Before the last shot of the Revolution had been fired, pomp and circumstance had withdrawn from Boston. The last Royal Governor set sail for England and certain stiff-necked royalists followed their convictions across the sea or into Canada. Others lingered, baffled and disconsolate. They had been on the wrong side——they had sided with the past, and in a contest with the future the past, like the absent, is always wrong.

This time in our history, troubled with change and heavy with destiny as yet unrevealed, fascinated young Nathaniel Hawthorne. "Tales of the Province House" may not be the best of the "Twice Told Tales" but there can be no doubt that he wrote them because he must. The paragraph at the end of this story is the epilogue to the series; one feels in it the pull of attraction and repulsion that held him to their creation and gave him at their close the relief with which one turns from shivering darkness toward light and human company.

"Old Esther Dudley" is not only the tale of a Tory; it is a

study of a solitary. New England has never been without men and women to whom solitude is dangerously dear. There are even yet, lingering on mountain farms, old men who learned long ago how sweet a drug solitude may be. Annie Trumbull Slosson said, "They have different names for sech folks. They say they're 'cracked,' they've 'got a screw loose,' they're 'a little off,' they 'ain't all there,' and so on. But nothin' accounts for their notions so well to my mind as to say they're all jest dreamin'." Hawthorne knew the charm and the danger of such dreams; he had seen his mother give herself to solitude, as his sister was later to do. He wrote to a friend in 1838, "I want to have something to do with the material world," and in that year tried his best to break those soft chains and associated simply, happily, with village characters and even with town loafers, at North Adams. He has said that "Twice Told Tales" had "the pale tint of flowers that blossomed in too retired a shade," and he cried out to Longfellow that "there is no fate in the world so horrible as to have no share in its joys and sorrows." His happy marriage saved him from that fate, and the youth whom college-mates had called "Oberon" lived on in the person of the mature artist. But while his spirit was still in shadow he wrote this story. Old Esther, a poor creature at her best and in her old age a poor cracked creature, takes on in her despair the dignity of a symbol.

OLD ESTHER DUDLEY

By NATHANIEL HAWTHORNE

THE hour had come—the hour of defeat and humiliation
—when Sir William Howe was to pass over the threshold
of the Province House, and embark, with no such triumphal ceremonies as he once promised himself, on board the
British fleet. He bade his servants and military attendants
go before him, and lingered a moment in the loneliness
of the mansion, to quell the fierce emotions that struggled
in his bosom as with a death throb. Preferable, then, would
he have deemed his fate, had a warrior's death left him a
claim to the narrow territory of a grave within the soil
which the King had given him to defend. With an ominous
perception that, as his departing footsteps echoed adown
the staircase, the sway of Britain was passing forever from
New England, he smote his clinched hand on his brow,
and cursed the destiny that had flung the shame of a dis-
membered empire upon him.

"Would to God," cried he, hardly repressing his tears
of rage, "that the rebels were even now at the doorstep!
A blood-stain upon the floor should then bear testimony
that the last British ruler was faithful to his trust."

The tremulous voice of a woman replied to his exclamation.

"Heaven's cause and the King's are one," it said. "Go

forth, Sir William Howe, and trust in Heaven to bring back a Royal Governor in triumph."

Subduing, at once, the passion to which he had yielded only in the faith that it was unwitnessed, Sir William Howe became conscious that an aged woman, leaning on a gold-headed staff, was standing betwixt him and the door. It was old Esther Dudley, who had dwelt almost immemorial years in this mansion, until her presence seemed as inseparable from it as the recollections of its history. She was the daughter of an ancient and once eminent family, which had fallen into poverty and decay, and left its last descendant no resource save the bounty of the King, nor any shelter except within the walls of the Province House. An office in the household, with merely nominal duties, had been assigned to her as a pretext for the payment of a small pension, the greater part of which she expended in adorning herself with an antique magnificence of attire. The claims of Esther Dudley's gentle blood were acknowledged by all the successive Governors; and they treated her with the punctilious courtesy which it was her foible to demand, not always with success, from a neglectful world. The only actual share which she assumed in the business of the mansion was to glide through its passages and public chambers, late at night, to see that the servants had dropped no fire from their flaring torches, nor left embers crackling and blazing on the hearths. Perhaps it was this invariable custom of walking her rounds in the hush of midnight that caused the superstition of the times to invest the old woman with attributes of awe and mystery; fabling that she had entered the portal of the Province House, none knew whence, in the train of the first Royal Governor, and that it was her fate to dwell there till the last should have departed. But Sir William Howe, if he ever heard this legend, had forgotten it.

"Mistress Dudley, why are you loitering here?" asked he, with some severity of tone. "It is my pleasure to be the last in this mansion of the King."

"Not so, if it please your Excellency," answered the time-stricken woman. "This roof has sheltered me long. I will not pass from it until they bear me to the tomb of my forefathers. What other shelter is there for old Esther Dudley, save the Province House or the grave?"

"Now Heaven forgive me!" said Sir William Howe to himself. "I was about to leave this wretched old creature to starve or beg. Take this, good Mistress Dudley," he added, putting a purse into her hands. "King George's head on these golden guineas is sterling yet, and will continue so, I warrant you, even should the rebels crown John Hancock their king. That purse will buy a better shelter than the Province House can now afford."

"While the burden of life rests upon me, I will have no other shelter than this roof," persisted Esther Dudley, striking her staff upon the floor with a gesture that expressed immovable resolve. "And when your Excellency returns in triumph, I will totter into the porch to welcome you."

"My poor old friend!" answered the British General, —and all his manly and martial pride could no longer restrain a gush of bitter tears. "This is an evil hour for you and me. The Province which the King intrusted to my

charge is lost. I go hence in misfortune—perchance in dis-
grace—to return no more. And you, whose present being
is incorporated with the past—who have seen Governor
after Governor, in stately pageantry, ascend these steps—
whose whole life has been an observance of majestic ceremonies, and a worship of the King—how will you endure
the change? Come with us! Bid farewell to a land that
has shaken off its allegiance, and live still under a royal
government, at Halifax."

"Never, never!" said the pertinacious old dame. "Here
will I abide; and King George shall still have one true
subject in his disloyal Province."

"Beshrew the old fool!" muttered Sir William Howe,
growing impatient of her obstinacy, and shamed of the
emotion into which he had been betrayed. "She is the very
moral of old-fashioned prejudice, and could exist nowhere
but in this musty edifice. Well, then, Mistress Dudley,
since you will needs tarry, I give the Province House in
charge to you. Take this key, and keep it safe until myself, or some other Royal Governor, shall demand it of
you."

Smiling bitterly at himself and her, he took the heavy
key of the Province House, and delivering it into the old
lady's hands, drew his cloak around him for departure. As
the General glanced back at Esther Dudley's antique figure, he deemed her well fitted for such a charge, as being
so perfect a representative of the decayed past—of an
age gone by, with its manners, opinions, faith and feelings, all fallen into oblivion or scorn—of what had once
been a reality, but was now merely a vision of faded mag-

nificence. Then Sir William Howe strode forth, smiting his clinched hands together, in the fierce anguish of his spirit; and old Esther Dudley was left to keep watch in the lonely Province House, dwelling there with memory; and if Hope ever seemed to flit around her, still was it Memory in disguise.

The total change of affairs that ensued on the departure of the British troops did not drive the venerable lady from her stronghold. There was not, for many years afterwards, a Governor of Massachusetts; and the magistrates, who had charge of such matters, saw no objection to Esther Dudley's residence in the Province House, especially as they must otherwise have paid a hireling for taking care of the premises, which with her was a labor of love. And so they left her the undisturbed mistress of the old historic edifice. Many and strange were the fables which the gossips whispered about her, in all the chimney corners of the town. Among the time-worn articles of furniture that had been left in the mansion there was a tall, antique mirror, which was well worthy of a tale by itself, and perhaps may hereafter be the theme of one. The gold of its heavily-wrought frame was tarnished, and its surface so blurred, that the old woman's figure, whenever she paused before it, looked indistinct and ghost-like. But it was the general belief that Esther could cause the Governors of the overthrown dynasty, with the beautiful ladies who had once adorned their festivals, the Indian chiefs who had come up to the Province House to hold council or swear allegiance, the grim Provincial warriors, the severe clergymen—all the figures that ever swept across the broad plate of glass in former times—she could cause the whole to reappear, and people the inner world of the mirror with shadows of old life. Such legends as these, together with the singularity of her isolated existence, her age, and the infirmity that each added winter flung upon her, made Mistress Dudley the object both of fear and pity; and it was partly the result of either sentiment that, amid all the angry license of the times, neither wrong nor insult ever fell upon her unprotected head. Indeed, there was so much haughtiness in her demeanor towards intruders, among whom she reckoned all persons acting under the new authorities, that it was really an affair of no small nerve to look her in the face. And to do the people justice, stern republicans as they had now become, they were well content that the old gentlewoman, in her hoop petticoat and faded embroidery, should still haunt the palace of ruined pride and overthrown power, the symbol of a departed system, embodying a history in her person. So Esther Dudley dwelt year after year in the Province House, still reverencing all that others had flung aside, still faithful to her King, who, so long as the venerable dame yet held her post, might be said to retain one true subject in New England, and one spot of the empire that had been wrested from him.

And did she dwell there in utter loneliness? Rumor said, not so. Whenever her chill and withered heart desired warmth, she was wont to summon a black slave of Governor Shirley's from the blurred mirror, and send him in search of guests who had long ago been familiar in those deserted chambers. Forth went the sable messenger, with the starlight or the moonshine gleaming through him, and did his errand in the burial ground, knocking at the iron doors of tombs, or upon the marble slabs that covered them, and whispering to those within: "My mistress, old Esther Dudley, bids you to the Province House at midnight." And punctually as the clock of the Old South told twelve came the shadows of the Olivers, the Hutchinsons, the Dudleys, all the grandees of a by-gone generation, gliding beneath the portal into the well-known mansion, where Esther mingled with them as if she likewise were a shade. Without vouching for the truth of such traditions, it is certain that Mistress Dudley sometimes assembled a few of the stanch, though crestfallen, old tories, who had lingered in the rebel town during those days of wrath and tribulation. Out of a cobwebbed bottle, containing liquor that a royal Governor might have smacked his lips over, they quaffed healths to the King, and babbled treason to the Republic, feeling as if the protecting shadow of the throne were still flung around them. But, draining the last drops of their liquor, they stole timorously homeward, and answered not again if the rude mob reviled them in the street.

Yet Esther Dudley's most frequent and favored guests were the children of the town. Towards them she was never stern. A kindly and loving nature, hindered elsewhere from its free course by a thousand rocky prejudices, lavished itself upon these little ones. By bribes of gingerbread of her own making, stamped with a royal crown, she tempted their sunny sportiveness beneath the gloomy portal of the Province House, and would often beguile them to spend a whole play-day there, sitting in a circle round the verge of her hoop petticoat, greedily attentive to her stories of a dead world. And when these little boys and girls stole forth again from the dark, mysterious mansion, they went bewildered, full of old feelings that graver people had long ago forgotten, rubbing their eyes at the world around them as if they had gone astray into ancient times, and become children of the past. At home, when their parents asked where they had loitered such a weary while, and with whom they had been at play, the children would talk of all the departed worthies of the Province, as far back as Governor Belcher and the haughty dame of Sir William Phipps. It would seem as though they had been sitting on the knees of these famous personages, whom the grave had hidden for half a century, and had toyed with the embroidery of their rich waistcoats, or roguishly pulled the long curls of their flowing wigs. "But Governor Belcher has been dead this many a year," would the mother say to her little boy. "And did you really see him at the Province House?" "Oh yes, dear mother, yes!" the half-dreaming child would answer. "But when old Esther had done speaking about him he faded away out of his chair." Thus, without affrighting her little guests, she led them by the hand into the chambers of her own desolate heart, and made childhood's fancy discern the ghosts that haunted there.

Living so continually in her own circle of ideas, and never regulating her mind by a proper reference to present things, Esther Dudley appears to have grown partially crazed. It was found that she had no right sense of the progress and true state of the Revolutionary War, but held a constant faith that the armies of Britain were victorious on every field, and destined to be ultimately triumphant. Whenever the town rejoiced for a battle won by Washington, or Gates, or Morgan, or Greene, the news, in passing through the door of the Province House, as through the ivory gate of dreams, became metamorphosed into a strange tale of the prowess of Howe, Clinton, or Cornwallis. Sooner or later it was her invincible belief the colonies would be prostrate at the footstool of the King. Sometimes she seemed to take for granted that such was already the case. On one occasion, she startled the townspeople by a brilliant illumination of the Province House, with candles at every pane of glass, and a transparency of the King's initials and a crown of light in the great balcony window. The figure of the aged woman in the most gorgeous of her mildewed velvets and brocades was seen passing from casement to casement, until she paused before the balcony, and flourished a huge key above her head. Her wrinkled visage actually gleamed with triumph, as if the soul within her were a festal lamp.

"What means this blaze of light? What does old Esther's joy portend?" whispered a spectator. "It is frightful to see her gliding about the chambers, and rejoicing there without a soul to bear her company."

"It is as if she were making merry in a tomb," said another.

"Pshaw! It is no such mystery," observed an old man, after some brief exercise of memory. "Mistress Dudley is keeping jubilee for the King of England's birthday."

Then the people laughed aloud, and would have thrown

mud against the blazing transparency of the King's crown and initials, only that they pitied the poor old dame, who was so dismally triumphant amid the wreck and ruin of the system to which she appertained.

Oftentimes it was her custom to climb the weary staircase that wound upward to the cupola, and thence strain her dimmed eyesight seaward and countryward, watching for a British fleet, or for the march of a grand procession, with the King's banner floating over it. The passengers in the street below would discern her anxious visage, and send up a shout, "When the golden Indian on the Province House shall shoot his arrow, and when the cock on the Old South spire shall crow, then look for a Royal Governor again!"—for this had grown a byword through the town. And at last, after long, long years, old Esther Dudley knew, or perchance she only dreamed, that a Royal Governor was on the eve of returning to the Province House, to receive the heavy key which Sir William Howe had committed to her charge. Now it was the fact that intelligence bearing some faint analogy to Esther's version of it was current among the towns-people. She set the mansion in the best order that her means allowed, and, arraying herself in silks and tarnished gold, stood long before the blurred mirror to admire her own magnificence. As she gazed, the gray and withered lady moved her ashen lips, murmuring half aloud, talking to shapes that she saw within the mirror, to shadows of her own fantasies, to the household friends of memory, and bidding them rejoice with her and come forth to meet the Governor. And while absorbed in this communion, Mistress Dudley heard the tramp of many footsteps in the street, and, looking out at the window, beheld what she construed as the Royal Governor's arrival.

"O happy day! O blessed, blessed hour!" she exclaimed. "Let me but bid him welcome within the portal, and my task in the Province House, and on earth, is done!"

Then with tottering feet, which age and tremulous joy caused to tread amiss, she hurried down the grand staircase, her silks sweeping and rustling as she went, so that the sound was as if a train of spectral courtiers were thronging from the dim mirror. And Esther Dudley fancied that as soon as the wide door should be flung open, all the pomp and splendor of by-gone times would pace majestically into the Province House, and the gilded tapestry of the past would be brightened by the sunshine of the present. She turned the key—withdrew it from the lock—unclosed the door—and stepped across the threshold. Advancing up the court-yard appeared a person of most dignified mien, with tokens, as Esther interpreted them, of gentle blood, high rank, and long-accustomed authority, even in his walk and every gesture. He was richly dressed, but wore a gouty shoe, which however, did not lessen the stateliness of his gait. Around and behind him were people in plain civic dresses, and two or three war-worn veterans, evidently officers of rank, arrayed in a uniform of blue and buff. But Esther Dudley, firm in the belief that had fastened its roots about her heart, beheld only the principal personage, and never doubted that this was the long-looked-for Governor, to whom she was to surrender up her charge. As he approached, she involuntarily sank down on her knees and tremblingly held forth the heavy key.

"Receive my trust! Take it quickly!" cried she, "for methinks Death is striving to snatch away my triumph. But he comes too late. Thank Heaven for this blessed hour! God save King George!"

"That, Madam, is a strange prayer to be offered up at such a moment," replied the unknown guest of the Province House, and courteously removing his hat, he offered his arm to raise the aged woman. "Yet, in reverence for your gray hairs and long-kept faith, Heaven forbid that any here should say you nay. Over the realms which still acknowledge his sceptre, God save King George!"

Esther Dudley started to her feet, and hastily clutching back the key, gazed with fearful earnestness at the stranger; and dimly and doubtfully, as if suddenly awakened from a dream, her bewildered eyes half recognized his face. Years ago she had known him among the gentry of the province. But the ban of the King had fallen upon him! How, then, came the doomed victim here? Proscribed, excluded from mercy, the monarch's most dreaded and hated foe, this New England merchant had stood triumphantly against a kingdom's strength; and his foot now trod upon humbled Royalty as he ascended the steps of the Province House, the people's chosen Governor of Massachusetts.

"Wretch, wretch that I am!" muttered the old woman, with such a heart-broken expression that the tears gushed from the stranger's eyes. "Have I bidden a traitor welcome? Come Death! Come quickly!"

"Alas, venerable lady!" said Governor Hancock, lending her his support with all the reverence that a courtier would have shown to a queen. "Your life has been prolonged until the world has changed around you. You have treasured up all that time has rendered worthless—the principles, feelings, manners, modes of being and acting, which another generation has flung aside—and you are a symbol of the past. And I, and these around me—we represent a new race of men—living no longer in the past, scarcely in the present—but projecting our lives forward into the future. Ceasing to model ourselves on ancestral superstitions, it is our faith and principle to press onward, onward! Yet," continued he, turning to his attendants, "let us reverence, for the last time, the stately and gorgeous prejudices of the tottering Past!"

While the Republican Governor spoke, he had continued to support the helpless form of Esther Dudley; her weight grew heavier against his arm; but at last, with a sudden effort to free herself, the ancient woman sank down beside one of the pillars of the portal. The key of the Province House fell from her grasp, and clanked against the stone.

"I have been faithful unto death," murmured she. "God save the King!"

"She hath done her office!" said Hancock solemnly. "We will follow her reverently to the tomb of her ancestors; and then, my fellow-citizens, onward—onward! We are no longer children of the Past!"

As the old loyalist concluded his narrative, the enthusiasm which had been fitfully flashing within his sunken eyes, and quivering across his wrinkled visage, faded away, as if all the lingering fire of his soul were extinguished. Just then, too, a lamp upon the mantel-piece threw out a dying gleam, which vanished as speedily as it shot upward, compelling our eyes to grope for one another's features by the dim glow of the hearth. With such a lingering fire, methought, with such a dying gleam, had the glory of the ancient system vanished from the Province House, when the spirit of old Esther Dudley took its flight. And now, again, the clock of the Old South threw its voice of ages on the breeze, knolling the hourly knell of the Past, crying out far and wide through the multitudinous city, and filling our ears, as we sat in the dusky chamber, with its reverberating depth of tone. In that same mansion—in that very chamber—what a volume of history had been told off into hours, by the same voice that was now trembling in the air. Many a Governor had heard those midnight accents, and longed to exchange his stately cares for slumber. And as for mine host and Mr. Bela Tiffany and the old loyalist and me, we had babbled about dreams of the past, until we almost fancied that the clock was still striking in a bygone century. Neither of us would have wondered, had a hoop-petticoated phantom of Esther Dudley tottered into the chamber, walking her rounds in the hush of midnight, as of yore, and motioned us to quench the fading embers of the fire, and leave the historic precincts to herself and her kindred shades. But as no such vision was vouchsafed, I retired unbidden, and would advise Mr. Tiffany to lay hold of another auditor, being resolved not to show my face in the Province House for a good while hence—if ever.

THE LOWELL OFFERING
(1840–1845)

The gold rush of '49 drew young men away from farms and villages; a mild form of the same attraction had already drawn young women to the mills at Lowell, Mass. No doubt economic pressure had a good deal to do with it, ready money, never plentiful on the farm, being scarcest of all for unmarried daughters to come by. But there was a drawing-power even stronger in the thought of money all one's own, to spend, to save, or—could one come to terms with one's own conscience—to throw away, and time, however brief, in which to bring this to pass. From the first the mills founded by Francis Cabot Lowell and Nathan Appleton had their educational and social possibilities. There were plenty of night-schools, and the churches had "social circles." One might ask how a mill-girl could use these opportunities with a twelve-hour day, and when her wages were $1.75 a week clear of board, but all things are relative. Many of them came from farms where "man works from sun to sun but woman's work is never done," and the purchasing power of money was so much greater then that for the $1.25 a week allowed for mill-girls by the Corporation, women who ran the "corporation-houses" for girl boarders managed to set an excellent and plentiful table. The pianos in their parlors, as Dickens pointed out, were joint-stock affairs. The surrounding country was beautiful, and along the Merrimac

Indians often came gliding in their canoes to camp at Pawtucket Falls—not that the girls could often take the time to see all this. In all the summer there was but one full day's holiday—Fourth of July. For that they planned weeks ahead, rising at four on the great morning to ramble country roads beyond the pavement and come back to breakfast with their arms full of wild roses. But these blameless orgies were rare. When Charles Dickens, already famous and about to make them so by his praise of them in "American Notes," was proudly welcomed at Lowell, the girls could not leave their work long enough to look at the distinguished visitor, and Lucy Larcom, then at work in one of the mills, had to content herself with a pencil profile sketched by a friend as his progress passed.

Two of the social circles meeting in the vestries of local churches started little magazines for self-improvement, the *Operative's Magazine* at the First Congregational and at the Universalist the *Lowell Offering*. Within two years they merged under the latter name. The *Offering* was singularly fortunate in its editors, the most gifted being Harriet Farley, a girl of original mind and an editorial initiative ahead of her times. In those times the prevailing magazines were *Godey's* and *Graham's*, with *Godey's* more popular with women—or as they then timidly called themselves, females. With *Godey's* the *Lowell Offering* compares most favorably in everything but illustrations. These, I admit, were mainly drawings of the façades of Lowell churches, which would seem to have been dour and beetling structures, but when you take out the fashion-plates from *Godey's* —as everyone does—you have left the most unreadable letter-press through which I have ever attempted to gnaw my way. I speak with feeling, having vainly done my best to find, out of all those years of fine-print fiction, one story to put into this collection. But anyone could read the *Lowell Offering* now with a certain interest, because the stories besides being short are often refreshingly honest narratives out of the lives of girls who however inexperienced in writing for print, were neither uneducated nor on the other hand, clamped by middle-class reading-habits. These were native daughters of Massachusetts, New Hampshire, Vermont and even Maine, who had made these journeys before the railroad; these spinners often worked half the year in the mill in order to spend the other half at academies such as Bradford or Mount Holyoke. "For twenty years or so," said Lucy Larcom, "Lowell might have been looked on as a rather select industrial school for young people. . . . They had come to work with their hands, but they could not hinder the working of their minds also."

Their minds sometimes worked so much more freely than those of small-town subscribers that on one occasion at least Harriet Farley had to defend her editorial policy. The *Offering* had printed a serial story, "The Smuggler," which proved so popular that it was "printed off as fast as possible by one or two periodical establishments" giving credit neither to author nor magazine. This serial was by no means so popular with one of the subscribers, who wrote in to complain not only of the presence of smugglers in these pure pages, but of the fact that they talked in a manner unsuitable for ladies. "A female should (of all others) take a decided stand against profane swearing," said she—and this, as sometimes a letter will, got under the editorial skin. Miss Farley's spirited reply says: "To have made Edward Clapp and his followers talk like saints would have been worse than nonsense; and to have described them, without making them talk at all, would have materially detracted from the interest of the story. The language used was necessary to a truthful delineation of a smuggler's character." One seems to hear the waiting future faintly cheer. But it may have been more than coincidence that in the same number with this reply appeared a story about the doom of a girl not so careful about her language as she should have been—indeed, on one fatal occasion, while entertaining a young man believed to be on the edge of proposing, she pricked her finger on her embroidery needle and cried out "Oh the devil!" The young man immediately left for South America and has never yet returned.

At the height of its career the *Lowell Offering* had four thousand subscribers and branch offices in other cities. In England it made an impression as well as a sensation; reprinted there as "Mind Among the Spindles" it undoubtedly had its part in influencing workers' legislation, then just coming into shape. It had its part in the great philanthropic awakening of the period; this one could infer only from the tone of Dickens's report in "American Notes." Also it gave England a better notion of New England character and institutions; someone in England quoted by Miss Farley called attention to the different ways in which spinners in Lancashire and in Lowell spent their time and money; he found it a new thing under the sun for mill-girls to take to literature or learning, saying that a horse-race was far more attractive to their women operatives, and that "the mills in Manchester were stopped last month two or three days during the races, so that all might attend. Contrast this with your thronged lyceums." But this was too much praise for the honest soul of Harriet Farley to take without a wink. She wrote that "to our employers, it would be 'a new thing under the sun' to allow their work-people two or three successive days for any amusement."

I have chosen these three bits less for their literary merit than for their value as social documentation. The first, besides providing a life-like picture of a famous theocrat, may remind a modern reader from what old and distinguished families some of these operatives came, for the author is drawing on family history. The prayer story was nearly and unconsciously matched long after, when John B. Gough was in Edinburgh and attended the preaching of Dr. Finney from the seventh of Romans, "what I hate, that I do." He told Lyman Abbott that the next morning, after a night of self-question, he called upon the preacher and told him he feared that he was living in the seventh of Romans, whereupon they knelt and Dr. Finney called upon him to pray.

Mr. G.: I can't, Dr. Finney.

Dr. F.: *Pray,* Mr. Gough.

Mr. G.: I can't, Dr. Finney.

Dr. F., with renewed emphasis: *Pray,* Mr. Gough.

Mr. G.: I can't, Dr. Finney; and what is more, I won't.

Dr. F.: O Lord, have mercy on this wiry little sinner.

The second selection has given me the most accurate and precise account that I have been able to find of maple-sugaring in its social aspect. From the third, one senses the beginning of the end of old New England labor at Lowell. Long after, Lucy Larcom, who used to write for the *Offering* as "Rotha," put the problem in her poem-novel, "An Idyl of Work":

But this was waste—this woman-faculty
Tied to machinery, part of the machine
That wove cloth, when it might be clothing hearts
Or minds with queenly raiment. She foresaw
The time must come when mind itself would yield
To the machine, or leave the work to hands
That were hands only . . .
        Here was a problem, then,
For the political theorist: how to save
Mind from machinery's clutches.

None of the girls who wrote in the *Offering* and worked in the mills meant to continue permanently at that kind of work. They had learned that work could be found outside of the home, and the troubles of housekeepers with domestic service had begun. Before the Civil War that put women permanently into industry, they had taken their first steps toward the economic independence of women.

THE LOWELL OFFERING

I

FATHER MOODY

by

"ANNETTE"

"AND who," methinks I hear some one ask, "was Father Moody?" Gentle querist! he was one of the old New England clergymen, in the days o' lang syne, when they could step the earth with an air which seemed to say, "I am monarch of all I survey," and he was one of the most renowned of that noted order of men. "His fame went abroad through all the country round about," that is, the District of Maine—for that was long before it was a State —and even to the farthest corner of New England. The cause of this notoriety was probably his eccentricity, for his talents, though undisputed, raised him not so much above his fellow-men as his oddities removed him from them.

When he lived, I cannot exactly say; but as he was my great-great-great-grandfather, it must have been a great, great, great while ago. He was the minister of York, the oldest (and at that time the chief) town in Maine. The following anecdotes will illustrate his character, and none will be related but those which are well authenticated, though many others are extant.

Madam Moody was very fond of riding on horse-back,

and her husband often gratified her by a seat on the pillion, when he took an airing. But sometimes he would tell his lady to prepare for a ride, and when the horse was saddled and pillioned he would mount him and ride round the yard, while Madam was impatiently waiting upon the horse-block. After a while he would dismount, and send the horse away. "But, Mr. Moody," his spouse would exclaim, "you promised me a ride. Why do you treat me thus?"

"To teach you to bear disappointment, Mrs. Moody," would be the amiable reply. "This is to exercise your patience, and give you an opportunity for self-control."

So Mrs. Moody would exercise her locomotives by descending from the block, returning to the house, and divesting herself of her riding habiliments without uttering a reproachful word, though perhaps thinking that there is no need of *making* opportunities for the exercise of these virtues.

A young clergyman was once visiting him, and on the morning of the Sabbath he asked him if he would not preach.

"Oh no, Father Moody," was the young gentleman's reply; "I am travelling for my health, and wish to be entirely relieved from clerical duties. Besides, you, sir, are a distinguished father in Israel, and one whom I have long wished to have an opportunity of hearing, and I hope to-day for that gratification."

"Well," said the old man, as they wended their way to the meeting-house, "you will sit with me in the pulpit?"

It was perfectly immaterial, the young minister replied;

he could sit in the pulpit, or the pew, as Father Moody preferred. So when they entered the meeting-house, Father Moody stalked on, turned his companion up the pulpit stairs, and went himself into the parsonage pew.

The young man looked rather blank when he found himself alone, and waited a long while for his host to "come to the rescue." But there Father Moody sat before him, as straight and stiff as a stake or a statue, and finding there was to be no reprieve for him, he opened the Bible, and went through with the exercises. Perhaps the excitement caused by this strange treatment might have enlivened his brain; at all events, he preached remarkably well.

After the conclusion of the services, Father Moody arose in his pew, and said to the congregation, "My friends, we have had an excellent discourse this morning, from our young brother; but you are all indebted to *me* for it."

Perhaps it was the same young clergyman (and I should not wonder if it was the very night after this clerical joke) of whom the following anecdote is related. He requested his guest to lead the evening household service, but was answered by a request to be excused. "But you will pray with us," exclaimed the old man. "No, Father Moody, I wish to be excused." "But you *must* pray." "No, sir; I *must* be excused." "But you *shall* pray." "No, sir; I *shall* be excused." "I command you, in the name of Almighty God, to pray." "Mr. Moody!" replied the young man, in a determined voice, "you need not attempt to brow-beat me, for I won't pray." "Well, well," exclaimed the old gentleman, in a discomfited tone, "I believe you have more brass in your face, than grace in your heart."

A daughter of President Edwards was once at his house, upon a visit. "I shall remember you in my public prayers this morning," said he to her, one Sabbath, as they started for meeting. "No! oh, no! Father Moody, I beg of you not to do so. I entreat of you not to do it." But in his morning service, he did pray for the young lady who was then an inmate of his family, the daughter of one of the most distinguished divines, and while all eyes were probably directed to the parsonage pew, he continued, "She begged me *not* to mention her in my prayers, but I told her *I would.*"

Father Moody was very direct and fearless in his rebukes to the evil-doers; and he wished always to see them shrink and cower beneath his reproof and frown; but in one instance, at least, he was not gratified.

Col. Ingrahame, a wealthy parishioner, had retained his large stock of corn, in a time of great scarcity, in hopes of raising the price. Father Moody heard of it, and resolved upon a public attack upon the transgressor. So he arose in his pulpit, one Sabbath, and named as his text, Proverbs 11:26, "He that withholdeth corn, the people shall curse him: but blessing shall be upon the head of him that selleth it." Col. Ingrahame could not but know to whom reference was made; but he held up his head, and faced his pastor, with a look of stolid unconsciousness. Father Moody went on with some very applicable remarks, but Col. Ingrahame still pretended not to understand the allusion. Father Moody grew very warm, and became still more direct in his remarks upon matters and things. But Col. Ingrahame still held up his head, as high, perhaps a little *higher* than ever, and would not put on the coat so aptly prepared for him. Father Moody at length lost all patience. "Col. Ingrahame!" said he, "Col. Ingrahame! You *know* that I mean YOU. WHY DON'T YOU HANG DOWN YOUR HEAD?"

Mrs. Ingrahame, the Colonel's lady, was very fond of fine dress, and sometimes appeared at meeting in a style not exactly accordant with her pastor's ideas of Christian female propriety. One morning she came sweeping into church, in a new hooped dress, which was then very fashionable. "Here she comes," said Father Moody from the pulpit. "Here she comes, top and top-gallant, rigged most beautifully, and sailing most majestically; *but she has a leak that will sink her to hell.*"

The old gentleman was something of a sportsman, and occasionally, in the fall of the year, he would bring Madam Moody a fine goose, to grace her dinner table. One morning he took down his fowling-piece, and said to his wife, "If I shoot one goose, I will bring it to you, but if I bring down two, I shall devote one of them to the Lord."

"And what will you do with it?"

"I will give it to that poor widow, over the way."

He brought home two, but they were very different,— one of them a remarkably fine, large bird; the other, much inferior. Madam Moody wished him to reserve the larger one for himself. "No, no, Mrs. Moody," replied her husband. "The Lord shall have the best," and he carried it to the poor woman, in defiance of his wife's objections.

Father Moody would not receive a regular salary, and was indeed so negligent of pecuniary affairs that the parish appointed a committee to see that the parsonage house was supplied with wood, meal, meat, and other necessaries. He was very generous; and it has been said that he took his wife's shoes off her feet, to give to a bare-footed beggar. This may be true, but if so, it is probable the good lady had a better pair "up stairs."

THE LOWELL OFFERING

II

The Sugar-Making Excursion
by
"Jemima"

It was on a beautiful morning in the month of March (one of those mornings so exhilarating that they make even age and decrepitude long for a ramble) that friend H. called to invite me to visit his sugar-lot—as he called it—in company with the party which, in the preceding summer, visited Moose Mountain upon the whortleberry excursion.

A pleasant sleigh-ride of four or five miles brought us to the domicile of friend H., who had reached home an hour previously and was prepared to pilot us to his sugar camp. "Before we go," said he, "you must one and all step within doors, and warm your stomachs with some gingered cider." We complied with his request, and after a little social chat with Mrs. H. we made for the sugar camp, preceded by friend H., who walked by the side of his sleigh, which appeared to be well loaded, and which he steadied with the greatest care at every uneven place in the path.

Arrived at the camp, we found two huge iron kettles suspended on a pole, which was supported by crotched stakes driven in the ground, and each half full of boiling syrup. This was made by boiling down the sap gathered from troughs that were placed under spouts driven into rock-maple trees, an incision being first made in the tree with an auger. Friend H. told us that it had taken more than two barrels of sap to make what syrup each kettle contained. A steady fire of oak bark was burning underneath the kettles, and the boys and girls, friend H.'s sons and daughters, were busily engaged in stirring the syrup and replenishing the fire.

Abigail, the oldest daughter, went to her father's sleigh, and taking out a large rundlet, which might have contained two or three gallons, poured the contents into a couple of pails. This we perceived was milk, and as she raised one of the pails to empty the contents into the kettles, her father called out, "Ho, Abigail! has thee strained the milk?" "Yes, father," said Abigail.

"Well," said friend H., with a chuckle, "Abigail understands what she is about, as well as her mother would; and I'll warrant Hannah to make better maple sugar than any other woman in New England, or in the whole United States—and you will agree with me in that, after that sugar is turned off and cooled." Abigail turned to her work, emptied her milk into the kettles, and then stirred their contents well together, and put some bark on the fire.

"Come, Jemima," said Henry L., "let us try to assist Abigail a little, and perhaps we shall learn to make sugar ourselves; and who knows but what she will give us a 'gob' to carry home, as a specimen to show our friends; and besides, it is possible that we may have to make sugar ourselves at some time or other; and even if we do not, it will never do us any harm to know how the thing is done." Abigail furnished us each with a large brass scummer, and instructed us to take off the scum as it arose, and put it into the pails; and Henry called two others of our party to come and hold the pails.

"But tell me, Abigail," said Henry, with a roguish leer, "was that milk really intended for whitening the sugar?"

"Yes," said Abigail, with all the simplicity of a Quaker-ess, "for thee must know that the milk will all rise in a scum, and with it every particle of dirt or dust which may have found its way into the kettles."

Abigail made a second visit to her father's sleigh, ac-companied by her little brother, and brought from thence a large tin baker, and placed it before the fire. Her brother brought a peck measure two-thirds full of potatoes, which Abigail put into the baker, and leaving them to their fate, returned to the sleigh, and with her brother's assistance carried several parcels, neatly done up in white napkins, into a little log hut of some fifteen feet square, with a shed roof made of slabs. We began to fancy that we were to have an Irish lunch. Henry took a sly peep into the hut when we first arrived, and he declared that there was noth-ing inside, save some squared logs, which were placed back against the walls, and which he supposed were intended for seats. But he was mistaken in thinking that seats were every convenience which the building contained,—as will pres-ently be shown.

Abigail and her brother had been absent something like half an hour, and friend H. had in the meantime busied himself in gathering sap, and putting it in some barrels hard by. The kettles were clear from scum, and their contents were bubbling like soap. The fire was burning cheerfully, the company all chatting merrily, and a peep into the baker told that the potatoes were cooked.

Abigail and her brother came and taking up the baker carried it inside the building, but soon returned, and placed it again before the fire. Then she called to her father, who came and invited us to go and take dinner.

We obeyed the summons; but how were we surprised, when we saw how neatly arranged was everything. The walls of the building were ceiled around with boards, and side tables fastened to them, which could be raised or let down at pleasure, being but pieces of boards fastened with leather hinges and a prop underneath. The tables were covered with napkins, white as the driven snow, and loaded with cold ham, neat's tongue, pickles, bread, apple-sauce, preserves, dough-nuts, butter, cheese, and *potatoes*— without which a yankee dinner is never complete. For beverage, there was chocolate, which was made over a fire in the building—there being a rock chimney in one corner. "Now, neighbors," said friend H., "if you will but seat yourselves on these squared logs, and put up with these rude accommodations, you will do me a favor. We might have had our dinner at the house, but I thought that it would be a novelty, and afford more amusement to have it in this little hut, which I built to shelter us from what stormy weather we might have in the season of making sugar."

We arranged ourselves around the room, and right

merry were we, for friend H.'s lively chat did not suffer us to be otherwise. He recapitulated to us the manner of his life while a bachelor; the many bear-fights which he had had; told us how many bears he had killed; how a she-bear denned in his rock-dwelling the first winter after he commenced clearing his land—he having returned home to his father's to attend school; how, when he returned in the spring, he killed her two cubs, and afterwards the old bear, and made his Hannah a present of their skins to make a muff and tippet.

In the midst of dinner, Abigail came in with some hot mince pies, which had been heating in the baker before the fire out of doors. We had finished eating and were chatting merrily when one of the little boys called from without, "Father, the sugar has grained." We immediately went out and found one of the boys stirring some sugar in a bowl, to cool it. The fire was raked from beneath the kettles and Abigail and her eldest brother were stirring the contents in all haste. Friend H. put a pole within the bale of one of the kettles and raised it up, which enabled two of the company to take the other down, and having placed it in the snow, they assisted friend H. to take down the other; and while we lent a helping hand to stir and cool the sugar, friend H.'s children ate their dinners, cleared away the tables, and put what fragments were left into their father's sleigh, together with the dinner dishes, tin baker, rundlet, and the pails of scum, which were to be carried home for the swine. A firkin was also put into the sleigh; and after the sugar was sufficiently cool, it was put into the firkin, and covered up with great care.

After this we spent a short time promenading around the rock-maple grove, if leafless trees may be called a grove. A large sap-trough, which was very neatly made, struck my fancy, and friend H. said he would make me a present of it for a cradle. This afforded a subject for mirth. Friend H. said that we must not ridicule the idea of having sap-troughs for cradles; for that was touching quality, as his eldest child had been rocked many an hour in a sap-trough beneath the shade of a tree, while his wife sat beside it knitting, and he was hard by, hoeing corn.

Soon we were on our way to friend H.'s house, where we spent an agreeable evening, eating maple sugar, apples, beech-nuts, etc. We also had tea about eight o'clock, which was accompanied by every desirable luxury—after which we started for home. As we were about taking leave, Abigail made each one of us a present of a cake of sugar which was cooled in a tin heart.—"Heigh ho!" said Henry L., "how lucky! We have had an agreeable visit, a bountiful feast—have learned how to make sugar, and have all got sweet-hearts!"

THE LOWELL OFFERING

III

A SECOND PEEP AT FACTORY LIFE
(Unsigned)

THE "broad weaving-room" contains between thirty and forty looms; and broad sure enough they are. Just see how lazily the lathe drags backward and forward, and the shuttle—how spitefully it hops from one end of it to the other. But we must not stop longer, or perchance it will hop at us. You look weary; but, never mind! there was an end to Jacob's ladder, and *so* there is a termination to these stairs. Now if you please we will go up to the next room, where the spinning is done. Here we have spinning jacks or jennies that dance merrily along whizzing and singing, as they spin out their "long yarns," and it seems but pleasure to watch their movements; but it is hard work, and requires good health and much strength. Do not go too near, as we shall find that they do not understand the established rules of *etiquette*, and might unceremoniously knock us over. We must not stop here longer, for it is twelve o'clock, and we have the "carding-room" to visit before dinner. There are between twenty and thirty set of cards located closely together, and I beg of you to be careful as we go amongst them, or you will get caught in the machinery. You walk as though you were afraid of getting

154

blue. Please excuse me, if I ask you not to be afraid. 'Tis a wholesome color, and soap and water will wash it off. The girls, you see, are partially guarded against it, by over-skirts and sleeves; but as it is not *fashionable* to wear masks, they cannot keep it from their faces. You appear surprised at the hurry and bustle now going on in the room, but your attention has been so engaged that you have forgotten the hour. Just look at the clock, and you will find that it wants but five minutes to "bell time." We will go to the door, and be ready to start when the others do; and now, while we are waiting, just cast your eyes to the stair-way, and you will see another flight of stairs, leading to another spinning-room; a picker is located some-where in that region, but I cannot give you a description of it, as I have never had the courage to ascend more than five flight of stairs at a time. And—but the bell rings.

Now look out—not for the engine—but for the rush to the stair-way. O mercy! what a crowd. I do not wonder you gasp for breath; but, keep up courage; we shall soon be on terra firma again. Now, safely landed, I hope to be excused for taking you into such a crowd. Really, it would not be fair to let you see the factory girls and machinery for nothing. I shall be obliged to hurry you, as it is some way to the boarding-house, and we have but thirty minutes from the time the bell begins to ring till it is done ringing again; and then all are required to be at their work. There is a group of girls yonder, going our way; let us overtake them, and hear what they are talking about. Something unpleasant I dare say, from their earnest gestures and clouded brows.

"Well, I do think it is too bad," exclaims one.

"So do I," says another. "This cutting down wages *is* *not* what they cry it up to be. I wonder how they'd like to work as hard as we do, digging and drudging day after day, from morning till night, and then, every two or three years, have their wages reduced. I rather guess it wouldn't set very well."

"And, besides this, who ever heard, of such a thing as their being raised again," says the first speaker. "I confess that I never did, so long as I've worked in the mill, and that's been these ten years."

"Well, it is real provoking any how," returned the other, "for my part I should think they had made a clean sweep this time. I wonder what they'll do next."

"Listeners never hear any good of themselves" is a trite saying, and, for fear it may prove true in our case, we will leave this busy group, and get some dinner. There is an open door inviting us to enter. We will do so. You can hang your bonnet and shawl on one of those hooks, that extend the length of the entry for that purpose, or you can lay them on the banisters, as some do. Please to walk into the dining-room. Here are two large square tables, covered with checked cloths and loaded down with smoking viands, the odor of which is very inviting. But we will not stop here; there is the long table in the front room, at which ten or fifteen can be comfortably seated. You may place yourself at the head. Now do not be bashful or wait to be helped, but comply with the oft-made request, "help yourself" to whatever you like best; for you have but a few minutes allotted you to spend at the table. The reason why, is because you are a rational, intelligent, thinking being, and ought to know enough to swallow your food whole; whereas a horse or an ox, or any other dumb beast knows no better than to spend an hour in the *useless* process of mastication. The bell rings again, and the girls are hurrying to the mills; you, I suppose, have seen enough of them for one day, so we will walk up stairs and have a *tête-à-tête*.

You ask, if there are so many things objectionable, why we work in the mill. Well, simply for this reason,—every situation in life, has its trials which must be borne, and factory life has no more than any other. There are many things we do not like; many occurrences that send the warm blood mantling to the cheek when they must be borne in silence, and many harsh words and acts that are not called for. There are objections also to the number of hours we work, to the length of time allotted to our meals, and to the low wages allowed for labor; objections that must and will be answered; for the time has come when something, besides the clothing and feeding of the body is to be thought of; when the mind is to be clothed and fed; and this cannot be as it should be, with the present system of labor. Who, let me ask, can find that pleasure in life which they should, when it is spent in this way? Without time for the laborer's own work, and the improvement of the mind, save the few evening hours; and even then if the mind is enriched and stored with useful knowledge, it must be at the expense of health. And the feeling too, that comes over us (there is no use in denying it) when we hear the bell calling us away from repose that tired nature loudly claims—the feeling, that we are *obliged to go*. And these few hours, of which we have spoken, are far too short, three at the most at the close of day. Surely, methinks, every heart that lays claim to humanity will feel 'tis not enough. But this, we hope will, ere long, be done away with, and labor made what it should be; pleasant and inviting to every son and daughter of the human family.

There is a brighter side to this picture, over which we would not willingly pass without notice, and an answer to the question, why we work here? The time we *do* have is our own. The money we earn comes promptly; more so than in any other situation; and our work, though laborious, is the same from day to day; we know what it is, and when finished we feel perfectly free, till it is time to commence it again.

Besides this, there are many pleasant associations connected with factory life, that are not to be found elsewhere.

HENRY D. THOREAU
(1817–1862)

"If the day and the night are such that you greet them with joy, and life emits a fragrance, like flowers and sweet-scented herbs, is more elastic, starry, and immortal,—that is your success," said Thoreau, troubling the complacency of generations to come. Truths like that throw a monkey-wrench into the machinery of efficiency.

We all know about his experiment in Walden; not so many, perhaps, that he was the perfect pedestrian—one of those who can go round the world on the old Marlboro road. In 1849 he gave a completely uninterested world his "Week on the Concord and Merrimac Rivers"; in 1854 he told, in "Walden," how he "went to the woods, because I wished to live deliberately . . . and not, when I came to die, discover that I had not lived." He made his way to Maine, to Canada, up the Monadnock, and for the purposes of this collection it is fortunate that he journeyed to Cape Cod. For there he found an old man, a Wellfleet oysterman, and set him in the midst of his book.

The art with which this old man is made thus to live is subtle enough to seem a happy accident. But Thoreau did not write by rule of thumb. He was four years at Harvard, he taught, he lectured in the lyceums of the day, he knew the classics in the originals and Hindu literature in translations from London, he knew

John Herbert and John Milton. He may have been a man-of-all-work for a year or so, but it was Emerson's man-of-all-work. His style is unmistakable, but it is the hardest in our literature to imitate and it has occurred to no one to parody it. It functions as unobtrusively as a good digestion.

As for the old man of Cape Cod, it is clear that whatever his nature may be, it has been for many years getting progressively more so. All his life he has been lying in reasoned convictions and age has given him the courage of them. It was a Massachusetts woman who told me with a chuckle that it was well worth being seventy-five if but to be able to read what she wanted to, instead of what she ought to. "If my mind isn't improved by now it never will be," said she, "and I may as well enjoy it." Here is an old Massachusetts man who thoroughly enjoys his mind.

It may be also that this story will give you a new respect for a feature of New England—the clam. Calm as it looks, it has a deep-sea cousin little less than a man-eater—at least, as you will see, it has been known to get the best of a duck.

THE WELLFLEET OYSTERMAN

By Henry D. Thoreau

. . . Generally, the old-fashioned and unpainted houses on the Cape looked more comfortable, as well as picturesque, than the modern and more pretending ones, which were less in harmony with the scenery, and less firmly planted.

These houses were on the shores of a chain of ponds, seven in number, the source of a small stream called Herring River. . . . We knocked at the door of the first house, but its inhabitants were all gone away. In the meanwhile we saw the occupants of the next one looking out the window at us, and before we reached it an old woman came out and fastened the door of her bulkhead, and went in again. Nevertheless, we did not hesitate to knock at her door, when a grizzly-looking man appeared, whom we took to be sixty or seventy years old. He asked us, at first, suspiciously, where we were from, and what our business was; to which we returned plain answers.

"How far is it from Concord to Boston?" he inquired.

"Twenty miles by railroad."

"Twenty miles by railroad," he repeated.

"Didn't you ever hear of Concord of Revolutionary fame?"

"Didn't I ever hear of Concord? Why, I heard the guns

fire at the battle of Bunker Hill. [They hear the sound of heavy cannon across the Bay.] I am almost ninety; I am eighty-eight year old. I was fourteen year old at the time of Concord Fight,—and where were you then?"

We were obliged to confess that we were not in the fight.

"Well, walk in, we'll leave it to the women," said he.

So we walked in, surprised, and sat down, an old woman taking our hats and bundles, and the old man continued, drawing up to the large, old-fashioned fire-place,—

"I am a poor good-for-nothing critter, as Isaiah says: I am all broken down this year. I am under petticoat government here."

The family consisted of the old man, his wife, and his daughter, who appeared nearly as old as her mother, a fool, her son (a brutish-looking middle-aged man, with a prominent lower face, who was standing by the hearth when we entered, but immediately went out), and a little boy of ten.

While my companion talked with the women, I talked with the old man. They said that he was old and foolish, but he was evidently too knowing for them.

"These women," said he to me, "are both of them poor good-for-nothing critters. This one is my wife. I married her sixty-four years ago. She is eighty-four years old, and as deaf as an adder, and the other is not much better."

He thought well of the Bible, or at least he *spoke* well, and did not *think* ill, for that would not have been prudent for a man of his age. He said that he had read it attentively for many years, and he had much of it at his tongue's end.

He seemed deeply impressed with a sense of his own nothingness and would repeatedly exclaim,—

"I am a nothing. What I gather from my Bible is just this; that man is a poor good-for-nothing critter, and everything is just as God sees fit and disposes."

"May I ask your name?" I said.

"Yes," he answered. "I am not ashamed to tell my name. My name is ——. My great-grandfather came over from England and settled here."

He was an old Wellfleet oysterman, who had acquired a competency in that business, and had sons still engaged in it. . . .

Our host told us that the sea-clam, or hen, was not easily obtained; it was raked up, but never on the Atlantic side, only cast ashore there in small quantities in storms. The fisherman sometimes wades in water several feet deep, and thrusts a pointed stick into the sand before him. When this enters between the valves of a clam, he closes them on it, and is drawn out. It has been known to catch and hold coot and teal which were preying on it. I chanced to be on the bank of the Acushnet at New Bedford one day since this, watching some ducks, when a man informed me that, having let out his young ducks to seek their food amid the samphire (*Salicornia*) and other weeds along the riverside at low tide that morning, at length he noticed that one remained stationary, amid the weeds, something preventing it from following the others, and going to it he found its foot tightly shut in a quahog's shell. He took them up both together, carried them to his home, and his wife opened the shell with a knife, released the duck and cooked the quahog. The old man said that the great clams were good to eat, but that they always took out a certain part which was poisonous, before they cooked them. "People said it would kill a cat." I did not tell him that I had eaten a large one entire that afternoon, but began to think that I was tougher than a cat. He stated that peddlers came round there, and sometimes tried to sell the women folks a skimmer, but he told them that their women had got a better skimmer than *they* could make, in the shell of their clams; it was shaped just right for this purpose.—They call them "skim-alls" in some places. He also said that the sun-squall was poisonous to handle, and when the sailors came across it, they did not meddle with it, but heaved it out of their way. I told him that I had handled it that afternoon, and had felt no ill effects as yet. But he said it made the hands itch, especially if they had previously been scratched, or if I put it into my bosom I should find out what it was.

He informed us that no ice ever formed on the back side of the Cape, or not more than once in a century, and but little snow lay there, it being either absorbed or blown or washed away. Sometimes in winter, when the tide was down, the beach was frozen, and afforded a hard road up the back side for some thirty miles, as smooth as a floor. One winter when he was a boy, he and his father "took right out into the back side before daylight, and walked to Provincetown and back to dinner."

When I asked what they did with all that barren-looking land, where I saw so few cultivated fields,—"Nothing," he said.

"Then why fence your fields?"

"To keep the sand from blowing and covering up the whole."

"The yellow sand," said he, "has some life in it, but the white little or none."

When, in answer to his questions, I told him that I was a surveyor, he said that they who surveyed his farm were accustomed, where the ground was uneven, to loop up each chain as high as their elbows; that was the allowance they made, and he wished to know if I could tell him why they did not come out according to his deed, or twice alike. He seemed to have more respect for surveyors of the old school, which I did not wonder at. "King George the Third," said he, "laid out a road four rods wide and straight the whole length of the Cape," but where it was now he could not tell.

This story of the surveyors reminded me of a Long-Islander, who once, when I had made ready to jump from the bow of his boat to the shore, and he thought that I underrated the distance and would fall short,—though I found afterward that he judged of the elasticity of my joints by his own,—told me that when he came to a brook which he wanted to get over, he held up one leg, and then, if his foot appeared to cover any part of the opposite bank, he knew that he could jump it. "Why," I told him, "to say nothing of the Mississippi, and other small watery streams, I could blot out a star with my foot, but I would not engage to jump that distance," and asked how he knew when he had got his leg at the right elevation. But he regarded his legs as no less accurate than a pair of screw dividers or an ordinary quadrant, and appeared to have a painful recollection of every degree and minute in the arc which they described; and he would have had me believe that there was a kind of hitch in his hip-joint which answered the purpose. I suggested that he should connect his two ankles by a string of the proper length, which should be the chord of an arc, measuring his jumping ability on horizontal surfaces,—assuming one leg to be a perpendicular to the plane of the horizon, which, however, may have been too bold an assumption in this case. Nevertheless, this was a kind of geometry in the legs which it interested me to hear of.

Our host took pleasure in telling us the names of the ponds, most of which we could see from his windows, and making us repeat them after him, to see if we had got them right. They were Gull Pond, the largest and a very handsome one, clear and deep, and more than a mile in circumference, Newcomb's, Swett's, Slough, Horse-Leech, Round, and Herring Ponds, all connected at high water, if I do not mistake. The coast-surveyors had come to him for their names, and he told them of one which they had not detected. He said that they were not so high as formerly. There was an earthquake about four years before he was born, which cracked the pans of the ponds, which were of iron, and caused them to settle. I did not remember to have read of this. Innumerable gulls used to resort to them; but the large gulls were now very scarce, for, as he said, the English robbed their nests far in the north, where they breed. He remembered well when gulls were taken in the gull-house, and when small birds were killed by means of a frying-pan and fire at night. His father once lost a valuable horse from this cause. A party from Wellfleet having lighted their fire for this purpose, one dark night, on Billingsgate Island, twenty horses which were pastured there, and this colt among them, being frightened by it, and endeavoring in the dark to cross the passage which separated them from the neighboring beach, and which was then fordable at low tide, were all swept out to sea and drowned. I observed that many horses were still turned out to pasture all summer on the islands and beaches in Wellfleet, Eastham, and Orleans, as a kind of common. He also described the killing of what he called "wild hens" here, after they had gone to roost in the woods, when he was a boy. Perhaps they were "Prairie hens" (pinnated grouse) . . .

This was the merriest old man that we had ever seen, and one of the best preserved. His style of conversation was coarse and plain enough to have suited Rabelais. He would have made a good Panurge. Or rather he was a sober Silenus, and we were the boys Chromis and Mnasilus, who listened to his story.

> "Not by Haemonian hills the Thracian bard
> Nor awful Phoebus was on Pindus heard
> With deeper silence or with more regard."

There was a strange mingling of past and present in his conversation, for he had lived under King George, and might have remembered when Napoleon and the moderns generally were born. He said that one day, when the troubles between the Colonies and the mother country first broke out, as he, a boy of fifteen, was pitching hay out of a cart, one Doane, an old Tory, who was talking with his father, a good Whig, said to him, "Why, Uncle Bill, you might as well undertake to pitch that pond into the ocean with a pitchfork, as for the Colonies to undertake to gain their independence." He remembered well General Washington, and how he rode his horse along the streets of Boston, and he stood up to show us how he looked.

"He was a r—a—ther large and portly-looking man, a manly and resolute-looking officer, with a pretty good leg as he sat on his horse."—"There, I'll tell you, this was the way with Washington." Then he jumped up again, and bowed gracefully to right and left, making show as if he were waving his hat. Said he, "*That* was Washington."

He told us many anecdotes of the Revolution, and was much pleased when we told him that we had read the same in history, and that his account agreed with the written.

"O," he said, "I know, I know! I was a young fellow of sixteen, with my ears wide open; and a fellow of that age, you know, is pretty wide awake, and likes to know everything that's going on. O, I know!"

He told us the story of the wreck of the *Franklin*, which took place there the previous spring: how a boy came to his house early in the morning to know whose boat that was by the shore, for there was a vessel in distress, and he, being an old man, first ate his breakfast, and then walked over to the top of the hill by the shore, and sat down there, having found a comfortable seat, to see the ship wrecked. She was on the bar, only a quarter of a mile from him, and still nearer to the men on the beach, who had got a boat ready, but could render no assistance on account of the breakers, for there was a pretty high sea running. There were the passengers all crowded together in the forward part of the ship, and some were getting out of the cabin windows and were drawn on deck by the others.

"I saw the captain get out his boat," said he; "he had one little one; and then they jumped into it one after another, down as straight as an arrow. I counted them. There were nine. One was a woman, and she jumped as straight as any of them. Then they shoved off. The sea took them back, one wave went over them, and when they came up there were six still clinging to the boat; I counted them. The next wave turned the boat bottom upward, and emptied them all out. None of them ever came ashore alive. There were the rest of them all crowded together on the forecastle, the other parts of the ship being under water. They had seen all that happened to the boat. At length a heavy sea separated the forecastle from the rest of the wreck, and set it inside of the worst breaker, and the boat was able to reach them, and it saved all that were left, but one woman."

He also told us of the steamer *Cambria's* getting aground on his shore a few months before we were there, and of her English passengers who roamed over his grounds, and who, he said, thought the prospect from the high hill by the shore "the most delightsome they had ever seen," and also of the pranks which the ladies played with his scoop-net in the ponds. He spoke of these travellers with their purses full of guineas, just as our provincial fathers used to speak of British bloods in the time of King George the Third.

In the course of the evening I began to feel the potency of the clam which I had eaten, and I was obliged to confess to our host that I was no tougher than the cat he told of; but he answered, that he was a plain-spoken man, and he could tell me that it was all imagination. At any rate, it proved an emetic in my case, and I was made quite sick by it for a short time, while he laughed at my expense. I was pleased to read afterward, in Mourt's Relation of the landing of the Pilgrims in Provincetown Harbor, these words: "We found great muscles (the old editor says that they were undoubtedly sea-clams) and very fat and full of sea-pearl; but we could not eat them, for they made us all sick that did eat, as well sailors as passengers, . . . but they were soon well again." It brought me nearer to the Pilgrims to be thus reminded by a similar experience that I was so like them. Moreover, it was a valuable confirmation of their story, and I am prepared now to believe every word of Mourt's Relation. I was also pleased to find that man and the clam lay still at the same angle to one another. But I did not notice sea-pearl. Like Cleopatra, I must have swallowed it. I have since dug these clams on a flat in the Bay and observed them. They could squirt full ten feet before the wind, as appeared by the marks of the drops on the sand.

"Now I'm going to ask you a question," said the old man, "and I don't know as you can tell me; but you are a learned man, and I never had any learning, only what I got by natur."—It was in vain that we reminded him that he could quote Josephus to our confusion.—"I've thought, if I ever met a learned man I should like to ask him this question. Can you tell me how *Axy* is spelt, and what it means? *Axy*," says he; "there's a girl over here is named *Axy*. Now what is it? What does it mean? Is it Scripture? I've read my Bible twenty-five years over and over, and I never came across it."

"Did you read it twenty-five years for this object?" I asked.

"Well, *how* is it spelt? Wife, how is it spelt?" She said: "It is in the Bible; I've seen it."

"Well, how do you spell it?"

"I don't know. A c h, ach, s e h, seh,— Achseh."

"Does that spell Axy? Well, do *you* know what it means?" asked he, turning to me.

"No," I replied, "I never heard the sound before."

"There was a schoolmaster down here once, and they asked him what it meant, and he said it had no more meaning than a bean-pole."

I told him that I held the same opinion with the schoolmaster. I had been a schoolmaster myself, and had had strange names to deal with. I also heard of such names as Zoheth, Beriah, Amaziah, Bethuel, and Shearjashub, hereabouts.

At length the little boy, who had a seat quite in the chimney-corner, took off his stockings and shoes, warmed his feet, and having had his sore leg freshly salved, went off to bed; then the fool made bare his knotty-looking feet and legs, and followed him; and finally the old man ex-

posed his calves also to our gaze. We had never had the
good fortune to see an old man's legs before, and were
surprised to find them fair and plump as an infant's, and
we thought that he took a pride in exhibiting them. He
then proceeded to make preparations for retiring, discours-
ing meanwhile with Panurgic plainness of speech on the
ills to which old humanity is subject. We were a rare haul
for him. He could commonly get none but ministers to
talk to, though sometimes ten of them at once, and he was
glad to meet some of the laity at leisure. The evening was
not long enough for him. As I had been sick, the old lady
asked if I would not go to bed,—it was getting late for old
people; but the old man, who had not yet done his stories,
said, "You ain't particular, are you?"

"O, no," said I, "I am in no hurry. I believe I have
weathered the Clam cape."

"They are good," said he; "I wish I had some of them
now."

"They never hurt me," said the old lady.

"But then you took out the part that killed a cat," said I.

At last we cut him short in the midst of his stories, which
he promised to resume in the morning. Yet, after all, one
of the old ladies who came into our room in the night to
fasten the fire-board, which rattled, as she went out took
the precaution to fasten us in. Old women are by nature
more suspicious than old men. . . .

Before sunrise the next morning they let us out again,
and I ran over to the beach to see the sun come out of the
ocean. The old woman of eighty-four winters was already
out in the cold morning wind, bareheaded, tripping about

like a young girl, and driving up the cow to milk. She got the breakfast with despatch, and without noise or bustle; and meanwhile the old man resumed his stories, standing before us, who were sitting, with his back to the chimney, and ejecting his tobacco juice right and left into the fire behind him, without regard to the various dishes which were there preparing. At breakfast we had eels, butter-milk cake, cold bread, green beans, doughnuts, and tea. The old man talked a steady stream; and when his wife told him he had better eat his breakfast, he said: "Don't hurry me; I have lived too long to be hurried." I ate of the apple-sauce and the doughnuts, which I thought had sustained the least detriment from the old man's shots, but my companion refused the apple-sauce, and ate of the hot cake and green beans, which had appeared to him to occupy the safest part of the hearth. But on comparing notes after-ward, I told him that the buttermilk cake was particularly exposed, and I saw how it suffered repeatedly, and there-fore I avoided it; but he declared that, however that might be, he witnessed that the apple-sauce was seriously injured, and had therefore declined that. After breakfast he looked at his clock, which was out of order, and oiled it with some "hen's grease," for want of sweet oil, for he scarcely could believe that we were not tinkers or peddlers; meanwhile he told a story about visions, which had reference to a crack in the clock-case made by frost one night. He was curious to know to what religious sect we belonged. He said that he had been to hear thirteen kinds of preaching in one month, when he was young, but he did not join any of them,—he stuck to his Bible. There was nothing like any of them in

his Bible. . . . Finally, filling our pockets with doughnuts, which he was pleased to find that we called by the
same name that he did, and paying for our entertainment,
we took our departure; but he followed us out of doors,
and made us tell him the names of the vegetables which
he had raised from seeds that came out of the *Franklin*.
They were cabbage, broccoli and parsley. As I had asked
him the names of so many things, he tried me in turn with
all the plants which grew in his garden, both wild and
cultivated. It was about a quarter of an acre, which he
cultivated wholly himself. Besides the common garden
vegetables, there were Yellow Dock, Lemon Balm,
Hyssop, Gill-go-over-the-ground, Mouse-ear, Chick-
weed, Roman Wormwood, Elecampane, and other
plants. . . .

Thus, having had another crack with the old man, he
standing bare-headed under the eaves, he directed us
"athwart the fields," and we took to the beach again for
another day, it being now late in the morning.

It was but a day or two after this that the safe of the
Provincetown Bank was broken open and robbed by two
men from the interior, and we learned that our hospitable
entertainers did at least transiently harbor the suspicion
that we were the men.

LOUISA M. ALCOTT
(1833–1888)

It was in the transcendental forties that Emerson wrote to Carlyle: "We are all a little wild here with numberless projects of social reform; not a reading man but has a draft of a new community in his waistcoat pocket." In 1843 Thomas Wentworth Higginson intended to grow peaches "to secure freedom for thought by moderate labor of the hands"; in 1841 Thoreau set up his one-man commonwealth at Walden and about that time George William Curtis tried to be a farmer at Concord. And there was of course Brook Farm. "The Newness" in the air struggled to transcend the intractability of New England farming. But of all the idealistic communities founded in that decade of high dreams none was more touching in its hopes or more pathetic in its downfall than Bronson Alcott's Fruitlands.

Amos Bronson Alcott came of no famous family; he was the son of a poor farmer in Walcott, Connecticut, where he was born in 1799, went to a country school until old enough to be apprenticed to a clock-maker, and made his way as a wandering peddler of clocks and trinkets as far as North Carolina, where he was almost persuaded to become a Quaker. Always deeply and serenely concerned with philosophy, especially the philosophy of mysticism, and quietly determined in some way to relate it to the conduct of daily life, he moved thus meditatively through early manhood, gentle and firm, tending always toward the company of the high-souled, and coming at length within the circle of Reverend Samuel J. May. He married Abba May, and became in time the Father of Little Women. Honoré Willsie's biography with that title does belated honor to his gifts as a progressive educator, and shows how he anticipated some of the best of our most forward-looking educational methods. Emerson said, "He has more of the godlike than any man I have ever seen, and his presence rebukes and threatens and raises." But he must have been a trial to his family.

Sometimes I wonder if his family, with its never-failing sense of humor, may not have been something of a trial to him, once in a while. His wise and devoted wife followed wheresoever his serene philosophic spirit might lead, " 'as ballast for his balloon,' as she said in her bright way." There must have been moments when a bright way would have been a bit wearing in someone who did not believe in your balloon. But who pays the piper may call the tune, and as it was certainly his family that had constantly to do the paying, it is vastly to their credit and his that their tune was in his praise. "Duty's faithful child," his daughter Louisa, managed to admire her father for his traits almost as much as she admired her mother for hers—possibly because she tried to see him as her mother did. When this Orphic philosopher set out for the lonely farm-house near Still River, between Ayer and Lawrence, where in the summer and winter of 1843–1844 the tragic idyl of Fruitlands ran its course, his wife and his little girls were at hand and stayed by him to comfort him in his disillusion even though they had never completely shared his illusions or ecstasy.

Clara Endicott Sears, in "Bronson Alcott's Fruitlands," published by Houghton Mifflin in 1915, has gathered all the narratives and many of the opinions accessible concerning the fated experiment; its whole story, so far as can be told in words, is there. To me the most tragic feature of the book is not the hardships of the faithful or even the anguish of the founder, but the list of volumes that occupied a hundred feet of shelving in the old red farm-house, chief treasure of its simple state, that "small but valuable library recently brought by Mr. Alcott and Mr. Lane from England," and consisting, according to the *Dial*, of "one thousand volumes containing undoubtedly a richer collection of mystical writers than any other library in this country," one that was to be "the commencement of an Institution for the nurture of men in universal freedom of action, thought and being." Read these titles and you recognize that here were the garnered dreams of generations of poets and philosophers, their plans for a state of society in which men could live without cruelty or compromise. Here in Fruitlands they tried, clear down to the starvation point, to live out those beautiful dreams.

It was not till thirty years after that Bronson Alcott could bring himself to talk to outsiders about Fruitlands. Then he ended, "I have given you the facts as they were; Louisa has given the comic side in 'Transcendental Wild Oats,' but Mrs. Alcott could give you the tragic side." Even between the lines of Louisa's racy record one feels tragedy.

Between these lines of fiction, facts have had to drop through sometimes stranger than those here made into a story. There was, for instance, the true story of the man with a beard, Joseph Palmer, whose long-continued and to us amazing persecution Miss Sears records in her book. He was just out of jail in the course of this persecution when he joined Fruitlands, and when it failed he bought the place and carried on a sort of community of his own for twenty years. At eighty-four he died and was buried under a stone at North Leominster that gives his name and age, his portrait with the offending decoration, and the words, "Persecuted for Wearing the Beard." Even Emerson, it seems, was not without a slight sense of superiority to the unshaved; he classified certain reformers as "men with beards." They were not tolerated in business or the professions in the forties; curiously enough by the seventies public sentiment had swung in precisely the opposite direction.

To emphasize the documentary value of Miss Alcott's story,

here is the list given by Miss Sears of "original characters of 'Transcendental Wild Oats.'"

Timon Lion..................Charles Lane
His Son.....................William Lane
Abel Lamb...............A. Bronson Alcott
Sister Hope....................Mrs. Alcott
Her Daughters..............The Alcott girls
John Pease.................Samuel Bower
Forest Absalom..............Abram Everett
Moses White.................Joseph Palmer
Jane Gage....................Anna Page

TRANSCENDENTAL WILD OATS

By Louisa M. Alcott

On the first day of June, 184–, a large wagon, drawn by a small horse and containing a motley load, went lumbering over certain New England hills, with the pleasing accompaniments of wind, rain, and hail. A serene man with a serene child upon his knee was driving, or rather being driven, for the small horse had it all his own way. A brown boy with a William Penn style of countenance sat beside him, firmly embracing a bust of Socrates. Behind them was an energetic-looking woman, with a benevolent brow, satirical mouth, and eyes brimful of hope and courage. A baby reposed upon her lap, a mirror leaned against her knee, and a basket of provisions danced about at her feet, as she struggled with a large, unruly umbrella. Two blue-eyed little girls, with hands full of childish treasures, sat under one old shawl, chatting happily together.

In front of this lively party stalked a tall, sharp-featured man, in a long blue cloak; and a fourth small girl trudged along beside him through the mud as if she rather enjoyed it.

The wind whistled over the bleak hills; the rain fell in a despondent drizzle, and twilight began to fall. But the calm man gazed as tranquilly into the fog as if he beheld a radiant bow of promise spanning the gray sky. The

cheery woman tried to cover every one but herself with
the big umbrella. The brown boy pillowed his head on the
bald pate of Socrates and slumbered peacefully. The little
girls sang lullabies to their dolls in soft, maternal mur-
murs. The sharp-nosed pedestrian marched steadily on,
with the blue cloak streaming out behind him like a banner; and the lively infant splashed through the puddles
with a duck-like satisfaction pleasant to behold.

Thus these modern pilgrims journeyed hopefully out
of the old world, to found a new one in the wilderness.

The editors of *The Transcendental Tripod* had received
from Messrs. Lion and Lamb (two of the aforesaid pilgrims) a communication from which the following statement is an extract:—

"We have made arrangements with the proprietor of an
estate of about one hundred acres which liberates this tract
from human ownership. Here we shall prosecute our effort to initiate a Family in harmony with the primitive in-
stincts of man.

"Ordinary secular farming is not our object. Fruit,
grain, pulse, herbs, flax, and other vegetable products, re-
ceiving assiduous attention, will afford ample manual occupation, and chaste supplies for the bodily needs. It is
intended to adorn the pastures with orchards, and to super-
sede the labor of cattle by the spade and the pruning-
knife.

"Consecrated to human freedom, the land awaits the
sober culture of devoted men. Beginning with small
pecuniary means, this enterprise must be rooted in a re-
liance on the succors of an ever-bounteous Providence,

whose vital affinities being secured by this union with uncorrupted field and unworldly persons, the cares and in-
juries of a life of gain are avoided.

"The inner nature of each member of the Family is at
no time neglected. Our plan contemplates all such dis-
ciplines, cultures, and habits as evidently conduce to the
purifying of the inmates.

"Pledged to the spirit alone, the founders anticipate no
hasty or numerous addition to their numbers. The kingdom of peace is entered only through the gates of self-
denial; and felicity is the test and the reward of loyalty
to the unswerving law of Love."

This prospective Eden at present consisted of an old
red farm-house, a dilapidated barn, many acres of meadow-
land, and a grove. Ten ancient apple-trees were all the
"chaste supply" which the place afforded as yet; but, in
the firm belief that plenteous orchards were soon to be
evoked from their inner consciousness, these sanguine
founders had christened their domain Fruitlands.

Here Timon Lion intended to found a colony of Latter
Day Saints, who, under his patriarchal sway, should regenerate the world and glorify his name forever. Here
Abel Lamb, with the devoutest faith in the high ideal
which was to him a living truth, desired to plant a Paradise, where Beauty, Virtue, Justice, and Love might live
happily together, without the possibility of a serpent entering in. And here his wife, unconverted but faithful to
the end, hoped, after many wanderings over the face of
the earth, to find rest for herself and a home for her
children.

"There is our new abode," announced the enthusiast, smiling with a satisfaction quite undamped by the drops dripping from his hat-brim, as they turned at length into a cart-path that wound along a steep hillside into a barren-looking valley.

"A little difficult of access," observed his practical wife, as she endeavored to keep her various household goods from going overboard with every lurch of the laden ark.

"Like all good things. But those who earnestly desire and patiently seek will soon find us," placidly responded the philosopher from the mud, through which he was now endeavoring to pilot the much-enduring horse.

"Truth lies at the bottom of a well, Sister Hope," said Brother Timon, pausing to detach his small comrade from a gate, whereon she was perched for a clearer gaze into futurity.

"That's the reason we so seldom get at it, I suppose," replied Mrs. Hope, making a vain clutch at the mirror, which a sudden jolt sent flying out of her hands.

"We want no false reflections here," said Timon, with a grim smile, as he crunched the fragments under foot in his onward march.

Sister Hope held her peace, and looked wistfully through the mist at her promised home. The old red house with a hospitable glimmer at its windows cheered her eyes; and, considering the weather, was a fitter refuge than the sylvan bowers some of the more ardent souls might have preferred.

The new-comers were welcomed by one of the elect precious,—a regenerate farmer, whose idea of reform consisted mainly in wearing white cotton raiment and shoes of untanned leather. This costume, with a snowy beard, gave him a venerable, and at the same time a somewhat bridal appearance.

The goods and chattels of the Society not having arrived, the weary family reposed before the fire on blocks of wood, while Brother Moses White regaled them with roasted potatoes, brown bread and water, in two plates, a tin pan, and one mug; his table service being limited. But, having cast the forms and vanities of a depraved world behind them, the elders welcomed hardship with the enthusiasm of new pioneers, and the children heartily enjoyed this foretaste of what they believed was to be a sort of perpetual picnic.

During the progress of this frugal meal, two more brothers appeared. One a dark, melancholy man, clad in homespun, whose peculiar mission was to turn his name hind part before and use as few words as possible. The other was a bland, bearded Englishman, who expected to be saved by eating uncooked food and going without clothes. He had not yet adopted the primitive costume, however; but contented himself with meditatively chewing dry beans out of a basket.

"Every meal should be a sacrament, and the vessels used should be beautiful and symbolical," observed Brother Lamb mildly, righting the tin pan slipping about on his knees. "I priced a silver service when in town, but it was too costly; so I got some graceful cups and vases of Britannia ware."

"Hardest things in the world to keep bright. Will

whiting be allowed in the community?" inquired Sister Hope, with a housewife's interest in labor-saving institutions.

"Such trivial questions will be discussed at a more fitting time," answered Brother Timon, sharply, as he burnt his fingers with a very hot potato. "Neither sugar, molasses, milk, butter, cheese nor flesh are to be used among us, for nothing is to be admitted which has caused wrong or death to man or beast."

"Our garments are to be linen till we learn to raise our own cotton or some substitute for woolen fabrics," added Brother Abel, blissfully basking in an imaginary future as warm and brilliant as the generous fire before him.

"Haou abaout shoes?" asked Brother Moses, surveying his own with interest.

"We must yield that point till we can manufacture an innocent substitute for leather. Bark, wood, or some durable fabric will be invented in time. Meanwhile, those who desire to carry out our idea to the fullest extent can go barefooted," said Lion, who liked extreme measures.

"I never will, nor let my girls," murmured rebellious Sister Hope, under her breath.

"Haou do you cattle'ate to treat the ten-acre lot? Ef things ain't 'tended to right smart, we shan't hev no crops," observed the practical patriarch in cotton.

"We shall spade it," replied Abel, in such perfect good faith that Moses said no more, though he indulged in a shake of the head as he glanced at hands that had held nothing heavier than a pen for years. He was a paternal old soul and regarded the younger men as promising boys on a new sort of lark.

"What shall we do for lamps, if we cannot use any animal substance? I do hope light of some sort is to be thrown upon the enterprise," said Mrs. Lamb, with anxiety, for in those days kerosene and camphene were not, and gas unknown in the wilderness.

"We shall go without till we have discovered some vegetable oil or wax to serve us," replied Brother Timon, in a decided tone, which caused Sister Hope to resolve that her private lamp should be always trimmed, if not burning.

"Each member is to perform the work for which experience, strength, and taste best fit him," continued Director Lion. "Thus drudgery and disorder will be avoided and harmony prevail. We shall rise at dawn, begin the day by bathing, followed by music, and then a chaste repast of fruit and bread. Each one finds congenial employment till the meridian meal; when some deep-searching conversation gives rest to the body and development to the mind. Healthful labor again engages us till the last meal, when we assemble in social communion, prolonged till sunset, when we retire to sweet repose, ready for the next day's activity."

"What part of the work do you incline to yourself?" asked Sister Hope, with a humorous glimmer in her keen eyes.

"I shall wait till it is made clear to me. Being in preference to doing is the great aim, and this comes to us rather by a resigned willingness than a wilful activity, which is a check to all divine growth," responded Brother Timon.

"I thought so." And Mrs. Lamb sighed audibly, for during the year he had spent in her family Brother Timon had so faithfully carried out his idea of "being, not doing," that she had found his "divine growth" both an expensive and unsatisfactory process.

Here her husband struck into the conversation, his face shining with the light and joy of the splendid dreams and high ideals hovering before him.

"In these steps of reform, we do not rely so much on scientific reasoning or physiological skill as on the spirit's dictates. The greater part of man's duty consists in leaving alone much that he now does. Shall I stimulate with tea, coffee, or wine? No. Shall I consume flesh? Not if I value health. Shall I subjugate cattle? Shall I claim property in any created thing? Shall I trade? Shall I adopt a form of religion? Shall I interest myself in politics? To how many of these questions—could we ask them deeply enough and could they be heard as having relation to our eternal welfare—would the response be 'Abstain'?"

A mild snore seemed to echo the last word of Abel's rhapsody, for Brother Moses had succumbed to mundane slumber and sat nodding like a massive ghost. Forest Absalom, the silent man, and John Pease, the English member, now departed to the barn; and Mrs. Lamb led her flock to a temporary fold, leaving the founders of the "Consociate Family" to build castles in the air till the fire went out and the symposium ended in smoke.

The furniture arrived next day, and was soon bestowed;

for the principal property of the community consisted in books. To this rare library was devoted the best room in the house, and the few busts and pictures that still survived many flittings were added to beautify the sanctuary, for here the family was to meet for amusement, instruction, and worship.

Any housewife can imagine the emotions of Sister Hope, when she took possession of a large, dilapidated kitchen, containing an old stove and the peculiar stores out of which food was to evolve for her little family of eleven. Cakes of maple sugar, dried peas and beans, barley and hominy, meal of all sorts, potatoes, and dried fruit. No milk, butter, cheese, tea, or meat appeared. Even salt was considered a useless luxury and spice entirely forbidden by these lovers of Spartan simplicity. A ten years' experience of vegetarian vagaries had been good training for this new freak, and her sense of the ludicrous supported her through many trying scenes.

Unleavened bread, porridge, and water for breakfast; bread, vegetables, and water for dinner; bread, fruit, and water for supper was the bill of fare ordained by the elders. No teapot profaned that sacred stove, no gory steak cried aloud for vengeance from her chaste gridiron; and only a brave woman's taste, time, and temper were sacrificed on that domestic altar.

The vexed question of light was settled by buying a quantity of bayberry wax for candles; and, on discovering that no one knew how to make them, pine knots were introduced, to be used when absolutely necessary. Being summer the evenings were not long, and the weary fraternity found it no great hardship to retire with the birds. The inner light was sufficient for most of them. But Mrs. Lamb rebelled. Evening was the only time she had to herself, and while the tired feet rested the skilful hands mended torn frocks and little stockings, or anxious heart forgot its burden in a book.

So "mother's lamp" burned steadily, while the philosophers built a new heaven and earth by moonlight; and through all the metaphysical mists and philanthropic pyrotechnics of that period Sister Hope played her own little game of "throwing light," and none but the moths were the worse for it.

Such farming probably was never seen before since Adam delved. The band of brothers began by spading garden and field; but a few days of it lessened their ardor amazingly. Blistered hands and aching backs suggested the expediency of permitting the use of cattle till the workers were better fitted for noble toil by a summer of the new life.

Brother Moses brought a yoke of oxen from his farm,— at least, the philosophers thought so till it was discovered that one of the animals was a cow; and Moses confessed that he "must be let down easy, for he couldn't live on garden sarse entirely."

Great was Dictator Lion's indignation at this lapse from virtue. But time pressed, the work must be done; so the meek cow was permitted to wear the yoke and the recreant brother continued to enjoy forbidden draughts in the barn, which dark proceeding caused the children to regard him as one set apart for destruction.

The sowing was equally peculiar, for, owing to some mistake, the three brethren, who devoted themselves to this graceful task, found when about half through the job that each had been sowing a different sort of grain in the same field; a mistake which caused much perplexity, as it could not be remedied; but, after a long consultation and a good deal of laughter, it was decided to say nothing and see what would come of it.

The garden was planted with a generous supply of useful roots and herbs; but, as manure was not allowed to profane the virgin soil, few of these vegetable treasures ever came up. Purslane reigned supreme, and the disappointed planters ate it philosophically, deciding that Nature knew what was best for them, and would generously supply their needs, if they could only learn to digest her "sallets" and wild roots.

The orchard was laid out, a little grafting done, new trees and vines set, regardless of the unfit season and entire ignorance of the husbandmen, who honestly believed that in the autumn they would reap a bounteous harvest.

Slowly things got into order, and rapidly rumors of the new experiment went abroad, causing many strange spirits to flock thither, for in those days communities were the fashion and transcendentalism raged wildly. Some came to look on and laugh, some to be supported in poetic idleness, a few to believe sincerely and work heartily. Each member was allowed to mount his favorite hobby and ride it to his heart's content. Very queer were some of the riders, and very rampant some of the hobbies.

One youth, believing that language was of little consequence if the spirit was only right, startled new-comers by blandly greeting them with "Good-morning, damn you," and other remarks of an equally mixed order. A second irrepressible being held that all the emotions of the soul should be freely expressed, and illustrated his theory by antics that would have sent him to a lunatic asylum, if, as an unregenerate wag said, he had not already been in one. When his spirit soared, he climbed trees and shouted; when doubt assailed him, he lay upon the floor and groaned lamentably. At joyful periods he raced, leaped, and sang; when sad, he wept aloud; and when a great thought burst upon him in the watches of the night, he crowed like a jocund cockerel, to the great delight of the children and the great annoyance of their elders. One musical brother fiddled whenever so moved, sang sentimentally to the four little girls, and put a music-box on the wall when he hoed corn.

Brother Pease ground away at his uncooked food, or browsed over the farm on sorrel, mint, green fruit, and new vegetables. Occasionally he took his walks abroad, airily attired in an unbleached cotton *poncho*, which was the nearest approach to the primeval costume he was allowed to indulge in. At midsummer he retired to the wilderness, to try his plan where the woodchucks were without prejudices and huckleberry-bushes were hospitably full. A sun-stroke unfortunately spoiled his plan, and he returned to semi-civilization a sadder and wiser man.

Forest Absalom preserved his Pythagorean silence, cultivated his fine dark locks, and worked like a beaver, setting an excellent example of brotherly love, justice, and fidelity by his upright life. He it was who helped over-worked Sister Hope with her heavy washes, kneaded the endless succession of batches of bread, watched over the children, and did the many tasks left undone by the brethren, who were so busy discussing and defining great duties that they forgot to perform the small ones.

Moses White placidly plodded about, "chorin' raound," as he called it, looking like an old-time patriarch, with his silver hair and flowing beard, and saving the community from many a mishap by his thrift and Yankee shrewdness.

Brother Lion domineered over the whole concern; for, having put the most money into the speculation, he was resolved to make it pay,—as if anything founded on an ideal basis could be expected to do so by any but enthusi-asts.

Abel Lamb simply revelled in the Newness, firmly be-lieving that his dream was to be beautifully realized and in time not only little Fruitlands, but the whole earth, be turned into a Happy Valley. He worked with every muscle of his body, for *he* was in deadly earnest. He taught with his whole head and heart; planned and sacrificed, preached and prophesied, with a soul full of the purest aspirations, most unselfish purposes, and desires for a life devoted to God and man, too high and tender to bear the rough usage of this world.

It was a little remarkable that only one woman ever joined this community. Mrs. Lamb merely followed wheresoever her husband led,—"as ballast for his bal-loon," as she said, in her bright way.

Miss Jane Gage was a stout lady of mature years, sentimental, amiable, and lazy. She wrote verses copiously, and had vague yearnings and graspings after the unknown, which led her to believe herself fitted for a higher sphere than any she had yet adorned.

Having been a teacher, she was set to instructing the children in the common branches. Each adult member took a turn at the infants; and, as each taught in his own way, the result was a chronic state of chaos in the minds of these much-afflicted innocents.

Sleep, food, and poetic musings were the desires of dear Jane's life, and she shirked all duties as clogs upon her spirit's wings. Any thought of lending a hand with the domestic drudgery never occurred to her; and when to the question, "Are there any beasts of burden on the place?" Mrs. Lamb answered, with a face that told its own tale, "Only one woman!" the buxom Jane took no shame to herself, but laughed at the joke, and let the stout-hearted sister tug on alone.

Unfortunately, the poor lady hankered after the flesh-pots, and endeavored to stay herself with private sips of milk, crackers, and cheese, and on one dire occasion she partook of fish at a neighbor's table.

One of the children reported this sad lapse from virtue, and poor Jane was publicly reprimanded by Timon.

"I only took a little bit of the tail!" sobbed the penitent poetess.

"Yes, but the whole fish had to be tortured and slain that you might tempt your carnal appetite with that one taste of the tail. Know ye not, consumers of flesh meat, that ye are nourishing the wolf and the tiger in your bosoms?"

At this awful question and the peal of laughter which arose from some of the younger brethren, tickled by the ludicrous contrast between the stout sinner, the stern judge, and the naughty satisfaction of the young detective, poor Jane fled from the room to pack her trunk and return to a world where fishes' tails were not forbidden fruit.

Transcendental wild oats were sown broadcast that year, and the fame thereof has not yet ceased in the land; for, futile as this crop seemed to outsiders, it bore an invisible harvest, worth much to those who planted in earnest. As none of the members of this particular community have ever recounted their experiences before, a few of them may not be amiss, since the interest in these attempts has never died out and Fruitlands was the most ideal of all these castles in Spain.

A new dress was invented, since cotton, silk, and wool were forbidden as the product of slave-labor, worm-slaughter, and sheep-robbery. Tunics and trowsers of brown linen were the only wear. The women's skirts were longer, and their straw hat-brims wider than the men's, and this was the only difference. Some persecution lent a charm to the costume, and the long-haired, linen-clad reformers quite enjoyed the mild martyrdom they endured when they left home.

Money was abjured, as the root of all evil. The produce of the land was to supply most of their wants, or be exchanged for the few things they could not grow. This idea had its inconveniences; but self-denial was the fashion, and it was surprising how many things one can do without. When they desired to travel, they walked, if possible, begged the loan of a vehicle or boldly entered car or coach, and, stating their principles to the officials, took the consequences. Usually their dress, their earnest frankness, and gentle resolution won them a passage; but now and then they met with hard usage and had the satisfaction of suffering for their principles.

On one of these penniless pilgrimages they took passage on a boat, and, when fare was demanded, artlessly offered to talk, instead of pay. As the boat was well under way and they actually had not a cent, there was no help for it. So Brothers Lion and Lamb held forth to the assembled passengers in their most eloquent style. There must have been something effective in this conversation, for the listeners were moved to take up a contribution for these inspired lunatics, who preached peace on earth and goodwill to man so earnestly, with empty pockets. A goodly sum was collected; but when the captain presented it the reformers proved that they were consistent even in their madness, for not a penny would they accept, saying, with a look at the group about them, whose indifference or contempt had changed to interest and respect, "You see how well we get on without money"; and so went serenely on their way, with their linen blouses flapping airily in the cold October wind.

They preached vegetarianism everywhere and resisted all temptations of the flesh, contentedly eating apples and bread at well-spread tables, and much afflicting hospitable hostesses by denouncing their food and taking away their appetites, discussing the "horrors of shambles," the "incorporation of the brute in man," and "on elegant abstinence the sign of a pure soul." But, when the perplexed or offended ladies asked what they should eat, they got in reply a bill of fare consisting of "bowls of sunrise for breakfast," "solar seeds of the sphere," "dishes from Plutarch's chaste table," and other viands equally hard to find in any modern market.

Reform conventions of all sorts were haunted by these brethren, who said many wise things and did many foolish ones. Unfortunately, these wanderings interfered with their harvest at home; but the rule was to do what the spirit moved, so they left their crops to Providence and went a-reaping in wider and, let us hope, more fruitful fields than their own.

Luckily, the earthly providence who watched over Abel Lamb was at hand to glean the scanty crop yielded by the "uncorrupted land," which, "consecrated to human freedom," had received "the sober culture of devout men."

About the time the grain was ready to house, some call of the Oversoul wafted all the men away. An easterly storm was coming up and the yellow stacks were sure to be ruined. Then Sister Hope gathered her forces. Three little girls, one boy (Timon's son), and herself, harnessed to clothes-baskets and Russia-linen sheets, were the only teams she could command; but with these poor appliances the indomitable woman got in the grain and saved food for her young, with the instinct and energy of a mother-bird with a brood of hungry nestlings to feed.

This attempt at regeneration had its tragic as well as comic side, though the world only saw the former.

With the first frosts, the butterflies, who had sunned themselves in the new light through the summer, took flight, leaving the few bees to see what honey they had stored for winter use. Precious little appeared beyond the satisfaction of a few months of holy living.

At first it seemed as if a chance to try holy dying also was to be offered them. Timon, much disgusted with the failure of the scheme, decided to retire to the Shakers, who seemed to be the only successful community going.

"What is to become of us?" asked Mrs. Hope, for Abel was heart-broken at the bursting of his lovely bubble.

"You can stay here, if you like, till a tenant is found. No more wood must be cut, however, and no more corn ground. All I have must be sold to pay the debts of the concern, as the responsibility rests with me," was the cheering reply.

"Who is to pay us for what we have lost? I gave all I had,—furniture, time, strength, six months of my children's lives,—and all are wasted. Abel gave himself body and soul, and is almost wrecked by hard work and disappointment. Are we to have no return for this, but leave to starve and freeze in an old house, with winter at hand, no money, and hardly a friend left; for this wild scheme has alienated nearly all we had. You talk much about justice. Let us have a little, since there is nothing else left."

But the woman's appeal met with no reply but the old one: "It was an experiment. We all risked something, and must bear our losses as we can."

With this cold comfort, Timon departed with his son, and was absorbed into the Shaker brotherhood, where he soon found that the order of things was reversed, and it was all work and no play.

Then the tragedy began for the forsaken little family. Desolation and despair fell upon Abel. As his wife said, his new beliefs had alienated many friends. Some thought him mad, some unprincipled. Even the most kindly thought him a visionary, whom it was useless to help till he took more practical views of life. All stood aloof, saying: "Let him work out his own ideas, and see what they are worth."

He had tried, but it was a failure. The world was not ready for Utopia yet, and those who attempted to found it only got laughed at for their pains. In other days, men could sell all and give to the poor, lead lives devoted to holiness and high thought, and, after the persecution was over, find themselves honored as saints or martyrs. But in modern times these things are out of fashion. To live for one's principles, at all costs, is a dangerous speculation; and the failure of an ideal, no matter how humane and noble, is harder for the world to forgive and forget than bank robbery or the grand swindles of corrupt politicians.

Deep waters now for Abel, and for a time there seemed no passage through. Strength and spirits were exhausted by hard work and too much thought. Courage failed when, looking about for help, he saw no sympathizing face, no hand outstretched to help him, no voice to say cheerily, "We all make mistakes, and it takes many experiences to shape a life. Try again, and let us help you."

Every door was closed, every eye averted, every heart cold, and no way open whereby he might earn bread for his children. His principles would not permit him to do many things that others did; and in the few fields where conscience would allow him to work, who would employ a man who had flown in the face of society, as he had done?

Then this dreamer, whose dream was the life of his life, resolved to carry out his idea to the bitter end. There seemed no place for him here,—no work, no friend. To go begging conditions was as ignoble as to go begging money. Better perish of want than sell one's soul for the sustenance of the body. Silently he lay down upon his bed, turned his face to the wall, and waited with pathetic patience for death to cut the knot which he could not untie. Days and nights went by, and neither food nor water passed his lips. Soul and body were dumbly struggling together, and no word of complaint betrayed what either suffered.

His wife, when tears and prayers were unavailing, sat down to wait the end with a mysterious awe and submission; for in this entire resignation of all things there was an eloquent significance to her who knew him as no other human being did.

"Leave all to God," was his belief; and in this crisis the loving soul clung to this faith, sure that the Allwise Father would not desert this child who tried to live so near to Him. Gathering her children about her, she waited the issue of the tragedy that was being enacted in that solitary room, while the first snow fell outside, untrodden by the footprints of a single friend.

But the strong angels who sustain and teach perplexed and troubled souls came and went, leaving no trace without, but working miracles within. For, when all other sentiments had faded into dimness, all other hopes died utterly; when the bitterness of death was nearly over, when body was past any pang of hunger or thirst, and soul stood ready to depart, the love that outlives all else refused to die. Head had bowed to defeat, hand had grown weary with too heavy tasks, but heart could not grow cold to those who lived in its tender depths, even when death touched it.

"My faithful wife, my little girls,—they have not forsaken me, they are mine by ties that none can break. What right have I to leave them alone? What right to escape from the burden and the sorrow I have helped to bring? This duty remains to me, and I must do it manfully. For their sakes, the world will forgive me in time; for their sakes, God will sustain me now."

Too feeble to rise, Abel groped for the food that always lay within his reach, and in the darkness and solitude of that memorable night ate and drank what was to him the bread and wine of a new communion, a new dedication of heart and life to the duties that were left him when the dreams fled.

In the early dawn, when that sad wife crept fearfully to

see what change had come to the patient face on the pillow, she found it smiling at her, saw a wasted hand outstretched to her, and heard a feeble voice cry bravely, "Hope!"

What passed in that little room is not to be recorded except in the hearts of those who suffered and endured much for love's sake. Enough for us to know that soon the wan shadow of a man came forth, leaning on the arm that never failed him, to be welcomed and cherished by the children, who never forgot the experiences of that time.

"Hope" was the watchword now; and, while the last logs blazed on the hearth, the last bread and apples covered the table, the new commander, with renewed courage, said to her husband,—

"Leave all to God—and me. He has done his part, now I will do mine."

"But we have no money, dear."

"Yes, we have, I sold all we could spare, and have enough to take us away from this snow-bank."

"Where can we go?"

"I have engaged four rooms at our good neighbor, Lovejoy's. There we can live cheaply till spring. Then for new plans and a home of our own, please God."

"But, Hope, your little store won't last long, and we have no friends."

"I can sew and you can chop wood. Lovejoy offers you the same pay as he gives his other men; my old friend, Mrs. Truman, will send me all the work I want; and my blessed brother stands by us to the end. Cheer up, dear heart, for while there is work and love in the world we shall not suffer."

"And while I have my good angel Hope, I shall not despair, even if I wait another thirty years before I step beyond the circle of the sacred little world in which I still have a place to fill."

So one bleak December day, with their few possessions piled on an oxsled, the rosy children perched atop, the parents trudging arm in arm behind, the exiles left their Eden and faced the world again.

"Ah me! my happy dream. How much I leave behind that can never be mine again," said Abel, looking back at the lost Paradise, lying white and chill in its shroud of snow.

"Yes, dear; but how much we bring away," answered brave-hearted Hope, glancing from husband to children.

"Poor Fruitlands! The name was as great a failure as the rest!" continued Abel, with a sigh, as a frostbitten apple fell from a leafless bough at his feet.

But the sigh changed to a smile as his wife added, in a half-tender, half-satirical tone,—

"Don't you think Apple Slump would be a better name for it, dear?"

(Note by Clara Endicott Sears in her book, *Bronson Alcott's Fruitlands*, Houghton Mifflin Co., 1915:—After so many years Louisa Alcott very naturally forgot a few unimportant details when she wrote "Transcendental Wild Oats," yet they are important enough to set straight. Papers lately found show the exit from Fruitlands to have taken place in January. She also speaks of stoves in the old house. This is a mistake. The old chimney was taken down by Joseph Palmer's grandson, Mr. Alvin Holman, many years after the Community was broken up.)

OLIVER WENDELL HOLMES
(1809–1894)

"Elsie Venner" had scarcely appeared—at first under the title of "The Professor's Story" in 1859—before a lady of his acquaintance called it his "medicated novel," and the epithet has clung even to this day. It was to be sure the work of a doctor not only practising but teaching his profession, and it did involve a medical theory that even Dr. Holmes considered debatable— though after the book appeared he was glad to get reported instances that seemed to support it. But though the novel was, on his own statement, "the outcome of a theory," it was not this medical theory, long since discredited, that it was written to demonstrate. It was meant "to stir the mighty question of automatic agency in its relation to self-determination"—in words less theological, it was to be one more document in the long Puritan discussion of the tragic dilemma of free will and moral responsibility.

But with the snake charm and terror of the doomed Elsie this collection has nothing to do: it draws upon the book as a rich mine of information on those social distinctions so sharply made and so vigorously maintained in earlier days of our national life. They were nowhere more clearly defined than in republican Massachusetts, and no one was on better terms with them than Oliver Wendell Holmes. He was on such good terms that he

could laugh, not so much at, as about them. In this very book
he makes the famous definition and description of the "Brahmin
caste" of New England, and does it so well that it has gone
by that name ever since. No one has more precisely indicated the
three social divisions of a prosperous inland town of the period
as indicated by their dwellings: mansion-house families, two-
story people with front yards, and farmhouse folks. Each rep-
resents a way of life, a complete social environment. For the first
he has an evident preference based on admiration and respect; for
the last, an affection that makes the paragraph beginning "There
were a good many comfortable farmhouses scattered about Rockland" rise before its close to a true lyric cry. But in the third, the
intermediary state, he found his greatest literary opportunity.
For it was pretentious, "genteel," with "neither the luxury of the
mansion-house nor the comfort of the farmhouse,"—and Dr.
Holmes was not only a humorist, he was a satirist to the bone.

This may well be why the chapter we have chosen—so nearly
complete in itself that by leaving out only the paragraph or two
in which Elsie appears it amounts to a short story—has every
chance of being remembered whatever else in the novel may be
forgotten. Colonel Sprowle's party was almost too much for Dr.
Holmes's dignity and all the better for his success; he fairly let
himself go, not even pausing at actual slap-stick comedy in the
episode of Deacon Soper and the ice-cream. But from the time the
first guests begin to inspect the furnishings of the ladies' dressing-
room—indeed from the first words on which the invitations go
out, it is a real party in days when parties were never impromptu.
This is not the only formal entertainment in the novel; there
is the tea-party given by the Widow Rowens for a more select
assembly, but this one has a grand general sweep.

The Rockland of "Elsie Venner" seems to have been in the
Connecticut Valley, in the region of Northampton; a fellow-
resident wrote that Dr. Holmes "made some pretty close studies
for his novels of scenes and events in Pittsfield," but "as he used
them to purify a moral atmosphere, it would be better not to

try to identify them too closely." I am not so sure he meant Colonel Sprowle's party to exert an influence, purifying or otherwise, on the moral atmosphere: I think he wrote it to enjoy himself, out of pure exuberance. Certainly it has raised my spirits ever since I was a little girl, to read it. It may be worth setting down that he said "In 'Elsie Venner' I made the word *chrysocracy*, thinking it would take its place; but it didn't; *plutocracy*, meaning the same thing, was adopted instead." He was more successful with *anaesthesia*, a word with which he did enrich the dictionary.

Dr. Crothers said that Dr. Holmes's wit was like a safety match that struck on the prepared surface of the box in which it came, and Boston was the box. Certainly he never felt that it confined him; "better a hash at home than a roast with strangers," he wrote back once from a journey—though his long life in and around Boston was never on a hash basis. Born at Cambridge thirty-four years after Concord Fight, he graduated from Harvard, studied medicine there and in France, practised in Boston, and was Parkman Professor at Harvard Medical School. In his old age he lived on Beacon Street: "Through this window," he said, "I can see Cambridge where I was born, Harvard where I was educated, and Mount Auburn where I shall rest. There are few men who can see so much of their lives at a single glance." In 1894, at a great age, in his home beside the Charles River, he ceased breathing.

THE EVENT OF THE SEASON

By OLIVER WENDELL HOLMES

"Mr. and Mrs. Colonel Sprowle's compliments to Mr. Langdon, and request the pleasure of his company at a social entertainment on Wednesday evening next.

"Elm St.   Monday."

On paper of a pinkish color and musky smell, with a large S at the top, and an embossed border. Envelope adherent, not sealed. Addressed,

—— Langdon, Esq.
                              Present.

Brought by H. Frederic Sprowle, youngest son of the Colonel,—the H., of course, standing for the paternal Hezekiah, put in to please the father, and reduced to its initial to please the mother, she having a marked preference for Frederic. Boy directed to wait for an answer.

"Mr. Langdon has the pleasure of accepting Mr. and Mrs. Colonel Sprowle's polite invitation for Wednesday evening."

On plain paper, sealed with an initial.

In walking along the main street, Mr. Bernard had noticed a large house of some pretensions to architectural display, namely, unnecessarily projecting eaves, giving it a mushroomy aspect, wooden mouldings at various available points, and a grandiose arched portico. It looked a little swaggering by the side of one or two of the mansion-houses that were not far from it, was painted too bright

for Mr. Bernard's taste, had rather too fanciful a fence
before it, and had some fruit-trees planted in the front
yard, which to this fastidious young gentleman implied a
defective sense of the fitness of things, not promising in
people who lived in so large a house, with a mushroom
roof and a triumphal arch for its entrance.

This place was known as "Colonel Sprowle's villa,"
(genteel friends,)—as "the elegant residence of our distinguished fellow-citizen, Colonel Sprowle," (Rockland
Weekly Universe,)—as "the neew Haouse," (old settlers,)—as "Spraowle's Folly," (disaffected and possibly
envious neighbors,)—and in common discourse, as "the
Colonel's."

Hezekiah Sprowle, Esquire, Colonel Sprowle of the
Commonwealth's Militia, was a retired "merchant." An
India merchant he might, perhaps, have been properly
called; for he used to deal in West India goods, such as
coffee, sugar, and molasses, not to speak of rum,—also in
tea, salt fish, butter and cheese, oil and candles, dried fruit,
agricultural "p'dóose" generally, industrial products, such
as boots and shoes, and various kinds of iron and wooden
ware, and at one end of the establishment in calicoes and
other stuffs,—to say nothing of miscellaneous objects of
the most varied nature, from sticks of candy, which tempted
in the smaller youth with coppers in their fists, up to orna-
mental articles of apparel, pocket-books, breast-pins, gilt-
edged Bibles, stationery,—in short, everything which was
likely to prove seductive to the rural population. The
Colonel had made money in trade, and also by matrimony.
He had married Sarah, daughter and heiress of the late

Tekel Jordan, Esq., an old miser, who gave the town-clock, which carries his name to posterity in large gilt letters as a generous benefactor of his native place. In due time the Colonel reaped the reward of well-placed affections. When his wife's inheritance fell in, he thought he had money enough to give up trade, and therefore sold out his "store," called in some dialects of the English language *shop*, and his business.

Life became pretty hard work to him, of course, as soon as he had nothing particular to do. Country people with money enough not to have to work are in much more danger than city people in the same condition. They get a specific look and character, which are the same in all the villages where one studies them. They very commonly fall into a routine, the basis of which is going to some lounging-place or other, a bar-room, a reading-room, or something of the kind. They grow slovenly in dress, and wear the same hat forever. They have a feeble curiosity for news perhaps, which they take daily as a man takes his bitters, and then fall silent and think they are thinking. But the mind goes out under this regimen, like a fire without a draught; and it is not very strange, if the instinct of mental self-preservation drives them to brandy-and-water, which makes the hoarse whisper of memory musical for a few brief moments, and puts a weak leer of promise on the features of the hollow-eye future. The Colonel was kept pretty well in hand as yet by his wife, and though it had happened to him once or twice to come home rather late at night with a curious tendency to say the same thing twice and even three times over, it had always been in very cold weather,—and everybody knows that no one is safe to drink a couple of glasses of wine in a warm room and go suddenly out into the cold air.

Miss Matilda Sprowle, sole daughter of the house, had reached the age at which young ladies are supposed in technical language to have *come out*, and thereafter are considered to be *in company*.

"There's one piece o' goods," said the Colonel to his wife, "that we ha'n't disposed of, nor got a customer for yet. That's Matildy. I don't mean to set *her* up at vaandoo. I guess she can have her pick of a dozen."

"She's never seen anybody yet," said Mrs. Sprowle, who had had a certain project for some time, but had kept quiet about it. "Let's have a party, and give her a chance to show herself and see some of the young folks."

The Colonel was not very clear-headed, and he thought, naturally enough, that the party was his own suggestion, because his remark led to the first starting of the idea. He entered into the plan, therefore, with a feeling of pride as well as pleasure, and the great project was resolved upon in a family council without a dissentient voice. This was the party, then, to which Mr. Bernard was going. The town had been full of it for a week. "Everybody was asked." So everybody said that was invited. But how in respect of those who were not asked? If it had been one of the old mansion-houses that was giving a party, the boundary between the favored and the slighted families would have been known pretty will beforehand, and there would have been no great amount of grumbling. But the Colonel, for all his title, had a forest of poor relations and a brushwood swamp of shabby friends, for he had scrambled up to fortune, and now the time was come when he must define his new social position.

This is always an awkward business in town or country. An exclusive alliance between two powers is often the same thing as a declaration of war against a third. Rockland was soon split into a triumphant minority, invited to Mrs. Sprowle's party, and a great majority, uninvited, of which the fraction just on the border line between recognized "gentility" and the level of the ungloved masses was in an active state of excitement and indignation.

"Who is she, I should like to know?" said Mrs. Saymore, the tailor's wife. "There was plenty of folks in Rockland as good as ever Sally Jordan was, if she *had* managed to pick up a merchant. Other folks could have married merchants, if their families wasn't as wealthy as them old skinflints that willed her their money," etc., etc. Mrs. Saymore expressed the feeling of many beside herself. She had, however, a special right to be proud of the name she bore. Her husband was own cousin to the Saymores of Freestone Avenue (who write the name *Seymour*, and claim to be of the Duke of Somerset's family, showing a clear descent from the Protector to Edward Seymour, (1630,)—then a jump that would break a herald's neck to one Seth Saymore, (1783,)—from whom to the head of the present family the line is clear again). Mrs. Saymore, the tailor's wife, was not invited, because her husband *mended* clothes. If he had confined himself strictly to *making* them, it would have put a different face upon the matter.

The landlord of the Mountain House and his lady were invited to Mrs. Sprowle's party. Not so the landlord of Pollard's Tahvern and his lady. Whereupon the latter vowed that they would have a party at their house too, and made arrangements for a dance of twenty or thirty couples, to be followed by an entertainment. Tickets to this "Social Ball" were soon circulated, and, being accessible to all at a moderate price, admission to the "Elegant Supper" included, this second festival promised to be as merry, if not as select, as the great party.

Wednesday came. Such doings had never been heard of in Rockland as went on that day at the "villa." The carpet had been taken up in the long room, so that the young folks might have a dance. Miss Matilda's piano had been moved in, and two fiddlers and a clarionet-player engaged to make music. All kinds of lamps had been put in requisition, and even colored wax-candles figured on the mantel-pieces. The costumes of the family had been tried on the day before: the Colonel's black suit fitted exceedingly well; his lady's velvet dress displayed her contours to advantage; Miss Matilda's flowered silk was considered superb; the eldest son of the family, Mr. T. Jordan Sprowle, called affectionately and elegantly "Geordie," voted himself "stunnin' "; and even the small youth who had borne Mr. Bernard's invitation was effective in a new jacket and trousers, buttony in front, and baggy in the reverse aspect, as is wont to be the case with the home-made garments of inland youngsters.

Great preparations had been made for the refection which was to be part of the entertainment. There was much

clinking of borrowed spoons, which were to be carefully
counted, and much clicking of borrowed china, which was
to be tenderly handled,—for nobody in the country keeps
those vast closets full of such things which one may see in
rich city-houses. Not a great deal could be done in the
way of flowers, for there were no greenhouses, and few
plants were out as yet; but there were paper ornaments
for the candle-sticks, and colored mats for the lamps, and
all the tassels of the curtain and bells were taken out of
those brown linen bags, in which, for reasons hitherto
undiscovered, they are habitually concealed in some house-
holds. In the remoter apartments every imaginable operation was going on at once,—roasting, boiling, baking, beating, rolling, pounding in mortars, frying, freezing; for
there was to be ice-cream to-night of domestic manufacture;—and in the midst of all these labors, Mrs. Sprowle
and Miss Matilda were moving about, directing and helping as they best might, all day long. When the evening
came, it might be feared they would not be in just the
state of mind and body to entertain company. . . . The
Colonel himself had been pressed into the service. He had
pounded something in the great mortar. He had agitated a
quantity of sweetened and thickened milk in what was
called a cream-freezer. At eleven o'clock A. M., he retired
for a space. On returning, his color was noted to be somewhat heightened, and he showed a disposition to be jocular
with the female help,—which tendency, displaying itself
in livelier demonstrations than were approved at head-
quarters, led to his being detailed to out-of-door duties,
such as raking gravel, arranging places for horses to be

hitched to, and assisting in the construction of an arch of wintergreen at the porch of the mansion. . . .

Evening came at last, and the ladies were forced to leave the scene of their labors to array themselves for the coming festivities. The tables had been set in a back room, the meats were ready, the pickles were displayed, the cake was baked, the blanc-mange had stiffened, and the ice-cream had frozen.

At half past seven o'clock, the Colonel, in costume, came into the front parlor, and proceeded to light the lamps. Some were good-humored enough and took the hint of a lighted match at once. Others were as vicious as they could be,—would not light on any terms, any more than if they were filled with water, or lighted and smoked one side of the chimney, or sputtered a few sparks and sulked themselves out, or kept up a faint show of burning, so that their ground glasses looked as feebly phosphorescent as so many invalid fireflies. With much coaxing and screwing and pricking, a tolerable illumination was at last achieved. At eight there was a grand rustling of silks, and Mrs. and Miss Sprowle descended from their respective bowers or boudoirs. Of course they were pretty well tired by this time, and very glad to sit down,—having the prospect before them of being obliged to stand for hours. The Colonel walked about the parlor, inspecting his regiment of lamps. By and by Mr. Geordie entered.

"Mph! mph!" he sniffed, as he came in. "You smell of lamp-smoke here."

That always galls people,—to have a new-comer accuse them of smoke or close air, which they have got used to and do not perceive. The Colonel raged at the thought of his lamps' smoking, and tongued a few anathemas inside of his shut teeth, but turned down two or three wicks that burned higher than the rest.

Master H. Frederic next made his appearance, with questionable marks upon his fingers and countenance. Had been tampering with something brown and sticky. His elder brother grew playful, and caught him by the baggy reverse of his more essential garment.

"Hush!" said Mrs. Sprowle,—"there's the bell!"

Everybody took position at once, and began to look very smiling and altogether at ease.—False alarm. Only a parcel of spoons,—"loaned," as the inland folks say when they mean lent, by a neighbor.

"Better late than never!" said the Colonel, "let me heft them spoons."

Mrs. Sprowle came down into her chair again as if all her bones had been bewitched out of her.

"I'm pretty nigh beat out a'ready," said she, "before any of the folks has come."

They sat silent awhile, waiting for the first arrival. How nervous they got! and how their senses were sharpened!

"Hark!" said Miss Matilda,—"what's that rumblin'?"

It was a cart going over a bridge more than a mile off, which at any other time they would not have heard. After this there was a lull, and poor Mrs. Sprowle's head nodded once or twice. Presently a crackling and grinding of gravel; —how much that means, when we are waiting for those whom we long or dread to see! Then a change in the tone of the gravel-crackling.

"Yes, they have turned in at our gate. They're comin'! Mother! mother!"

Everybody in position, smiling and at ease. Bell rings. Enter the first set of visitors. The Event of the Season has begun.

"Law! it's nothin' but the Cranes' folks! I do believe Mahala's come in that old green de-laine she wore at the Surprise Party!"

Miss Matilda had peeped through a crack of the door and made this observation and the remark founded thereon. Continuing her attitude of attention, she overheard Mrs. Crane and her two daughters conversing in the attiring-room, up one flight.

"How fine everything is in the great house!" said Mrs. Crane,—"jest look at the picters!"

"Matildy Sprowle's drawin's," said Ada Azuba, the eldest daughter.

"I should think so," said Mahala Crane, her younger sister,—a wide-awake girl, who hadn't been to school for nothing, and performed a little on the lead pencil herself. "I should like to know whether that's a hay-cock or a mountain!"

Miss Matilda winced; for this must refer to her favorite monochrome, executed by laying on heavy shadows and stumping them down into mellow harmony,—the style of drawing which is taught in six lessons, and the kind of specimen which is executed in something less than one hour. Parents and other very near relatives are sometimes gratified with these productions, and cause them to be framed and hung up, as in the present instance.

"I guess we won't go down jest yet," said Mrs. Crane, "as folks don't seem to have come."

So she began a systematic inspection of the dressing-room and its conveniences.

"Mahogany four-poster,—come from the Jordans', I cal'late. Marseilles quilt. Ruffles all round the piller. Chintz curtings,—jest put up,—o' purpose for the party, I'll lay ye a dollar.—What a nice washbowl!" (Taps it with a white knuckle belonging to a red finger.) "Stone chaney.—Here's a bran'-new brush and comb,—and here's a scent-bottle. Come here, girls, and fix yourselves in the glass, and scent your pocket-handkerchers."

And Mrs. Crane bedewed her own kerchief with some of the *eau de Cologne* of native manufacture,—said on its label to be much superior to the German article.

It was a relief to Mrs. and the Miss Cranes when the bell rang and the next guests were admitted. Deacon and Mrs. Soper,—Deacon Soper of the Rev. Mr. Fairweather's church, and his lady. Mrs. Deacon Soper was directed, of course, to the ladies' dressing-room, and her husband to the other apartment, where gentlemen were to leave their outside coats and hats. Then came Mr. and Mrs. Briggs, and then the three Miss Spinneys, then Silas Peckham, Head of the Apollinean Institute, and Mrs. Peckham, and more after them, until at last the ladies' dressing-room got so full that one might have thought it was a trap none of them could get out of. In truth, they all felt a little awkwardly. Nobody wanted to be first to venture down-stairs. At last Mr. Silas Peckham thought it was time to make a move for the parlor, and for this purpose presented himself at the door of the ladies' dressing-room.

"Lorindy, my dear!" he exclaimed to Mrs. Peckham,—
"I think there can be no impropriety in our joining the family down-stairs."

Mrs. Peckham laid her large, flaccid arm in the sharp angle made by the black sleeve which held the bony limb her husband offered, and the two took the stair and struck out for the parlor. The ice was broken, and the dressing-room began to empty itself into the spacious, lighted apartments below.

Mr. Silas Peckham slid into the room with Mrs. Peckham alongside, like a shad convoying a jelly-fish.

"Good-evenin', Mrs. Sprowle! I hope I see you well this evenin'. How's your haälth, Colonel Sprowle?"

"Very well, much obleeged to you. Hope you and your good lady are well. Much pleased to see you. Hope you'll enjoy yourselves. We've laid out to have everything in good shape,—spared no trouble nor ex—"

—"pense,"—said Silas Peckham.

Mrs. Colonel Sprowle, who, you remember, was a Jordan, had nipped the Colonel's statement in the middle of the word Mr. Peckham finished, with a look that jerked him like one of those sharp twitches women keep giving a horse when they get a chance to drive one.

Mr. and Mrs. Crane, Miss Ada Azuba, and Miss Mahala Crane made their entrance. There had been a discussion about the necessity and propriety of inviting this family, the head of which kept a small shop for hats and boots and shoes. The Colonel's casting vote had carried it in the affirmative.—How terribly the poor old green de-laine did cut up in the blaze of so many lamps and candles.

Stop at the threshold! This is a hall of judgment you are entering; the court is in session; and if you move five steps forward, you will be at its bar. . . .

Miss Mahala Crane did not have these reflections; and no young girl ever did, or ever will, thank Heaven! Her keen eyes sparkled under her plainly parted hair and the green de-laine moulded itself in those unmistakable lines of natural symmetry in which Nature indulges a small shop-keeper's daughter occasionally as well as a wholesale deal-er's young ladies. She would have liked a new dress as much as any other girl, but she meant to go and have a good time at any rate.

The guests were now arriving in the drawing-room pretty fast, and the Colonel's hand began to burn a good deal with the sharp squeezes which many of the visitors gave it. Conversation, which had begun like a summer-shower in scattering drops, was fast becoming continuous, and occasionally rising into gusty swells, with now and then a broad-chested laugh from some Captain or Major or other military personage,—for it may be noted that all large and loud men in the unpaved districts bear military titles.

Deacon Soper came up presently and entered into con-versation with Colonel Sprowle.

"I hope to see our pastor present this evenin'," said the Deacon.

"I don't feel quite sure," the Colonel answered. "His

dyspepsy has been bad on him lately. He wrote to say, that Providence permittin', it would be agreeable to him to take a part in the exercises of the evenin', but I mistrusted he didn't mean to come. To tell the truth, Deacon Soper, I rather guess he don't like the idee of dancin', and some of the other little arrangements."

"Well," said the Deacon, "I know there's some condemns dancin'. I've heerd a good deal of talk about it among the folks round. Some have it that it never brings a blessin' on a house to have dancin' in it. Judge Tileston died, you remember, within a month after he had his great ball, twelve year ago, and some thought it was in the natur' of a judgment. I don't believe in any of them notions. If a man happened to be struck dead the night after he'd been givin' a ball," (the Colonel loosened his black stock a little, and winked and swallowed two or three times,) "I shouldn't call it a judgment,—I should call it a coincidence. But I'm a little afraid our pastor won't come. Somethin' or other's the matter with Mr. Fairweather. I should sooner expect to see the old Doctor come over out of the Orthodox parsonage-house."

"I've asked him," said the Colonel.

"Well?" said Deacon Soper.

"He said he should like to come, but he didn't know what his people would say. For his part, he loved to see young people havin' their sports together, and very often felt as if he should like to be one of 'em himself. 'But,' says I, 'Doctor, I don't say there won't be a little dancin'.' 'Don't!' says he, 'for I want Letty to go,' (She's his granddaughter that's been stayin' with him,) 'and Letty's mighty fond of dancin'. You know,' says the Doctor, 'it isn't my business to settle whether other people's children should dance or not.' And the Doctor looked as if he should like to rigadoon and sashy across as well as the young one he was talkin' about. He's got blood in him, the old Doctor has. . . ."

Mr. Silas Peckham and his lady joined the group.

"Is this to be a Temperance Celebration, Mrs. Sprowle?" asked Mr. Silas Peckham.

Mrs. Sprowle replied, "that there would be lemonade and srub for those that preferred such drinks, but that the Colonel had given folks to understand that he didn't mean to set in judgment on the marriage in Canaan, and that those that didn't like srub and such things would find somethin' that would suit them better."

Deacon Soper's countenance assumed a certain air of restrained cheerfulness. . . .

The dancing went on briskly. Some of the old folks looked on, others conversed in groups and pairs, and so the evening wore along, until a little after ten o'clock. About this time there was noticed an increased bustle in the passages, with a considerable opening and shutting of doors. Presently it began to be whispered about that they were going to have supper. Many, who had never been to any large party before, held their breath for a moment at this announcement. It was rather with a tremulous interest than with open hilarity that the rumor was generally received.

One point the Colonel had entirely forgotten to settle. It was a point involving not merely propriety, but perhaps

principle also, or at least the good report of the house,—
and he had never thought to arrange it. He took Judge
Thornton aside and whispered the important question to
him,—in his distress of mind, mistaking pockets and taking
out his bandanna instead of his white handkerchief to wipe
his forehead.

"Judge," he said, "do you think, that, before we commence refreshing ourselves at the tables, it would be the
proper thing to—crave a—to request Deacon Soper or
some other elderly person—to ask a blessing?"

The Judge looked as grave as if he were about giving
the opinion of the Court in the great India-rubber case.

"On the whole," he answered, after a pause, "I should
think it might, perhaps, be dispensed with on this occasion.
Young folks are noisy, and it is awkward to have talking
and laughing going on while a blessing is being asked.
Unless a clergyman is present and makes a point of it, I
think it will hardly be expected."

The Colonel was infinitely relieved. "Judge, will you
take Mrs. Sprowle in to supper?" And the Colonel returned the compliment by offering his arm to Mrs. Judge
Thornton.

The door of the supper-room was now open, and the
company, following the lead of the host and hostess, began
to stream into it, until it was pretty well filled.

There was an awful kind of pause. Many were beginning to drop their heads and shut their eyes, in anticipation
of the usual petition before a meal; some expected the
music to strike up,—others, that an oration would now be
delivered by the Colonel.

"Make yourselves at home, ladies and gentlemen," said the Colonel; "good things were made to eat, and you're welcome to all you see before you."

So saying he attacked a huge turkey which stood at the head of the table; and his example being followed first by the bold, then by the doubtful, and lastly by the timid, the clatter soon made the circuit of the tables. Some were shocked, however, as the Colonel had feared they would be, at the want of the customary invocation. Widow Leech, a kind of relation, who had to be invited, and who came with her old, back-country-looking string of gold beads round her neck, seemed to feel very serious about it.

"If she'd ha' known that folks would begrutch cravin' a blessin' over sech a heap o' provisions, she'd rather ha' staid t' home. It was a bad sign, when folks wasn't grateful for the baounties of Providence."

The elder Miss Spinney, to whom she made this remark, assented to it, at the same time ogling a piece of frosted cake, which she presently appropriated with great refinement of manner,—taking it between her thumb and forefinger, keeping the others well spread and the little finger in extreme divergence, with a graceful undulation of the neck, and a queer little sound in her throat, as of an *m* that wanted to get out and perished in the attempt.

The tables now presented an animated spectacle. Young fellows of the more dashing sort, with high stand-up collars and voluminous bows to their neckerchiefs, distinguished themselves by cutting up fowls and offering portions thereof to the buxom girls these knowing ones had commonly selected.

"A bit of the wing, Roxy, or of the—under limb?"

The first laugh broke out at this, but it was premature, a *sporadic* laugh, as Dr. Kittredge would have said, which did not become epidemic. People were very solemn as yet, many of them being new to such splendid scenes, and crushed, as it were, in the presence of so much crockery and so many silver spoons, and such a variety of unusual viands and beverages. When the laugh rose around Roxy and her saucy beau, several looked in that direction with an anxious expression, as if something had happened,— a lady fainted, for instance, or a couple of lively fellows come to high words.

"Young folks will be young folks," said Deacon Soper. "No harm done. Least said soonest mended."

"Have some of these shell-oysters?" said the Colonel to Mrs. Trecothick.

A delicate emphasis on the word *shell* implied that the Colonel knew what was what. To the New England inland native, beyond the reach of the east winds, the oyster un- conditioned, the oyster absolute, without a qualifying ad- jective, is the *pickled* oyster. Mrs. Trecothick, who knew very well that an oyster long out of his shell (as is apt to be the case with the rural bivalve) gets homesick and loses his sprightliness, replied, with the pleasantest smile in the world, that the chicken she had been helped to was too delicate to be given up even for the greater rarity. But the word "shell-oyster" had been overheard; and there was a perceptible crowding movement towards their newly dis- covered habitat, a large soup-tureen.

Silas Peckham had meantime fallen upon another locality of these recent mollusks. He said nothing, but helped himself freely, and made a sign to Mrs. Peckham.

"Lorindy," he whispered, "shell-oysters!"

And ladled them out to her largely, without betraying any emotion, just as if they had been the natural inland or pickled article.

After the more solid portion of the banquet had been duly honored, the cakes and sweet preparations of various kinds began to get their share of attention. There were great cakes and little cakes, cakes with raisins in them, cakes with currants, and cakes without either; there were brown cakes and yellow cakes, frosted cakes, glazed cakes, hearts and rounds, and *jumbles*, which playful youth slip over the forefinger before spoiling their annular outline. There were mounds of *blo'monje*, of the arrowroot variety,— that being undistinguishable from such as is made with Russia isinglass. There were jellies, which had been shaking, all the time the young folks were dancing in the next room, as if they were balancing to partners. There were built-up fabrics, called *Charlottes*, caky externally, pulpy within; there were also *marangs*, and likewise custards,— some of the indolent-fluid sort, others firm, in which every stroke of the teaspoon left a smooth, conchoidal surface like the fracture of chalcedony, with here and there a little eye like what one sees in cheeses. Nor was that most wonderful object of domestic art called *trifle* wanting, with its charming confusion of cream and cake and almonds and jam and jelly and wine and cinnamon and froth; nor yet the marvellous *floating-island*,—name suggestive of all that is romantic in the imaginations of youthful palates.

"It must have cost you a sight of work, to say nothin' of money, to get all this beautiful confectionary made for the party," said Mrs. Crane to Mrs. Sprowle.

"Well, it cost some consid'able labor, no doubt," said Mrs. Sprowle. "Matilda and our girls and I made 'most all the cake with our own hands, and we all feel some tired; but if folks get what suits 'em, we don't begrudge the time nor the work. But I do feel thirsty," said the poor lady, "and I think a glass of srub would do my throat good; it's dreadful dry. Mr. Peckham, would you be so polite as to pass me a glass of srub?"

Silas Peckham bowed with great alacrity, and took from the table a small glass cup, containing a fluid reddish in hue and subacid in taste. This was *srub*, a beverage in local repute, of questionable nature, but suspected of owing its tints and sharpness to some kind of syrup derived from the maroon-colored fruit of the sumac. There were similar small cups on the table filled with lemonade, and here and there a decanter of Madeira wine, of the Marsala kind, which some prefer to, and many more cannot distinguish from, that which comes from the Atlantic island.

"Take a glass of wine, Judge," said the Colonel; "here is an article that I rather think'll suit you."

The Judge knew something of wines, and could tell all the famous old Madeiras from each other,—"Eclipse," "Juno," the almost fabulously scarce and precious "White-top," and the rest. He struck the nativity of the Mediterranean Madeira before it had fairly moistened his lip.

"A sound wine, Colonel, and I should think of a genuine vintage. Your very good health."

"Deacon Soper," said the Colonel, "here is some Madary Judge Thornton recommends. Let me fill you a glass of it."

The Deacon's eyes glistened. He was one of those consistent Christians who stick firmly by the first miracle and Paul's advice to Timothy.

"A little good wine won't hurt anybody," said the Deacon. "Plenty,—plenty,—plenty. There!" He had not withdrawn his glass, while the Colonel was pouring, for fear it should spill, and now it was running over.

—It is very odd how all a man's philosophy and theology are at the mercy of a few drops of a fluid which the chemists say consists of nothing but C_4, O_2, H_6. The Deacon's theology fell off several points towards latitudinárianism in the course of the next ten minutes. He had a deep inward sense that everything was as it should be, human nature included. The little accidents of humanity, known collectively to moralists as sin, looked very venial to his growing sense of universal brotherhood and benevolence.

"It will all come right," the Deacon said to himself,— "I feel a joyful conviction that everything is for the best. I am favored with a blessed peace of mind, and a very precious season of good feelin' toward my fellow-creturs."

A lusty young fellow happened to make a quick step backward just at that instant, and put his heel, with his weight on top of it, upon the Deacon's toes.

"Aigh! What the d' d' didos are y' abaout with them great huffs o' yourn?" said the Deacon, with an expression upon his features not exactly that of peace and good-will to men. The lusty young fellow apologized; but the Deacon's face did not come right, and his theology backed round several points in the direction of total depravity.

Some of the dashing young men in stand-up collars and extensive neckties, encouraged by Mr. Geordie, made quite free with the "Madary," and even induced some of the more stylish girls—not of the mansion-house set, but of the tip-top two-story families—to taste a little. Most of these young ladies made faces at it, and declared it was "perfectly horrid," with that aspect of veracity peculiar to their age and sex.

About this time a movement was made on the part of some of the mansion-house people to leave the supper-table. Miss Jane Trecothick had quietly hinted to her mother that she had had enough of it. Miss Arabella Thornton had whispered to her father that he had better adjourn this court to the next room. There were signs of migration,—a loosening of people in their places,—a looking about for arms to hitch on to.

"Stop!" said the Colonel. "There's something coming yet.—Ice-cream!"

The great folks saw that the play was not over yet, and that it was only polite to stay and see it out. The word "ice-cream" was no sooner whispered than it passed from one to another all down the tables. The effect was what might have been anticipated. Many of the guests had never seen this celebrated product of human skill, and to all the two-story population of Rockland it was the last expression of the art of pleasing and astonishing the human palate. Its appearance had been deferred for several reasons: first, because everybody would have attacked it, if it had come in with the other luxuries; secondly, because undue apprehensions were entertained (owing to want of experience) of its tendency to deliquesce and resolve itself with alarming rapidity into puddles of creamy fluid; and, thirdly, because the surprise would make a grand climax to finish off the banquet.

There is something so audacious in the conception of ice-cream, that it is not strange that a population undebauched by the luxury of great cities looks upon it with a kind of awe and speaks of it with a certain emotion. This defiance of the seasons, forcing Nature to do her work of congelation in the face of her sultriest noon, might well inspire a timid mind with fear lest human art were revolting against the Higher Powers, and raise the same scruples which resisted the use of ether and chloroform in certain contingencies. Whatever may be the cause, it is well known that the announcement at any private rural entertainment that there is to be ice-cream produces an immediate and profound impression. It may be remarked, as aiding this impression, that exaggerated ideas are entertained as to the dangerous effects this congealed food may produce on persons not in the most robust health.

There was silence as the pyramids of ice were placed on the table, everybody looking on in admiration. The Colonel took a knife and assailed the one at the head of the table. When he tried to cut off a slice, it didn't seem to understand it, however, and only tipped, as if it wanted to upset. The Colonel attacked it on the other side, and it tipped just as badly the other way. It was awkward for the Colonel. "Permit me," said the Judge,—and he took the knife and struck a sharp slanting stroke which sliced off a piece just of the right size, and offered it to Mrs. Sprowle. This act of dexterity was much admired by the company.

The tables were all alive again.

"Lorindy, here's a plate of ice-cream," said Silas Peckham.

"Come, Mahaly," said a fresh-looking young fellow with a saucerful in each hand, "here's your ice-cream;—let's go in the corner and have a celebration, us two." And the old green de-laine, with the young curves under it to make it sit well, moved off as pleased apparently as if it had been silk velvet with thousand-dollar laces over it.

"Oh, now, Miss Green! do you think it's safe to put that cold stuff into your stomick?" said the Widow Leech to a young married lady, who, finding the air rather warm, thought a little ice would cool her down very nicely. "It's jest like eatin' snowballs. You don't look very rugged; and I should be dreadful afeard, if I was you—"

"Carrie," said old Dr. Kittredge, who had overheard this,—"how well you're looking this evening! But you must be tired and heated;—sit down here, and let me give you a good slice of ice-cream. How you young folks do grow up, to be sure! I don't feel quite certain whether it's you or your older sister, but I know it's somebody I call Carrie, and that I've known ever since—"

A sound something between a howl and an oath startled the company and broke off the Doctor's sentence. Everybody's eyes turned in the direction from which it came.

A group instantly gathered round the person who had uttered it, who was no other than Deacon Soper.

"He's chokin'! he's chokin'!" was the first exclamation, —"slap him on the back!"

Several heavy fists beat such a tattoo on his spine that the Deacon felt as if at least one of his vertebræ would come up.

"He's black in the face," said Widow Leech,—"he's swallered somethin' the wrong way. Where's the Doctor? —let the Doctor get to him, can't ye?"

"If you will move, my good lady, perhaps I can," said Doctor Kittredge, in a calm tone of voice.—"He's not choking, my friends," the Doctor added immediately, when he got sight of him.

"It's apoplexy,—I told you so,—don't you see how red he is in the face?" said old Mrs. Peake, a famous woman for "nussin'" sick folks,—determined to be a little ahead of the Doctor.

"It's not apoplexy," said Dr. Kittredge.

"What is it, Doctor, what is it? Will he die? Is he dead? —Here's his poor wife, the Widow Soper that is to be, if she a'n't a'ready—"

"Do be quiet, my good woman," said Dr. Kittredge,— "Nothing serious, I think, Mrs. Soper.—Deacon!"

The sudden attack of Deacon Soper had begun with the extraordinary sound mentioned above. His features had immediately assumed an expression of intense pain, his eyes staring wildly, and, clapping his hands to his face, he had rocked his head backward and forward in speechless agony.

At the Doctor's sharp appeal the Deacon lifted his head.

"It's all right," said the Doctor, as soon as he saw his face. "The Deacon had a smart attack of neuralgic pain. That's all. Very severe, but not at all dangerous."

The Doctor kept his countenance, but his diaphragm was shaking the change in his waistcoat-pockets with subterranean laughter. He had looked through his spectacles and seen at once what had happened. The Deacon, not being in the habit of taking his nourishment in the congealed state, had treated the ice-cream as a pudding of a rare species, and, to make sure of doing himself justice in its distribution, had taken a large mouthful of it without the least precaution. The consequence was a sensation as if a dentist were killing the nerves of twenty-five teeth at once with hot irons, or cold ones, which would hurt rather worse.

The Deacon swallowed something with a spasmodic effort, and recovered pretty soon and received the congratulations of his friends. There were different versions of the expressions he had used at the onset of his complaint,—some of the reported exclamations involving a breach of propriety, to say the least,—but it was agreed that a man in an attack of neuralgy wasn't to be judged of by the rules that applied to other folks.

The company soon after this retired from the supper-room. The mansion-house gentry took their leave, and the two-story people soon followed. Mr. Bernard had stayed an hour or two, and left soon after he found that Elsie Venner and her father had disappeared. . . . The planet Mars was burning like a red coal; the northern constellation was slanting downward about its central point of flame; and while he looked, a falling star slid from the zenith and was lost.

He reached his chamber and was soon dreaming over the Event of the Season.

HARRIET BEECHER STOWE
(1811–1896)

Mrs. Stowe was well aware that though she would live in history through "Uncle Tom's Cabin," it would take another novel to give her a chance to live in literature. It was through "Oldtown Folks" that she hoped to hold that place. "It is more to me than a story," she said; "it is my résumé of the whole spirit and body of New England." She put her whole soul into it and took her own time—so much of it that the presses had often to be stopped while everyone waited for the return of proofs, from the far south sometimes, for though she wrote most of the novel in "Glenwood," the house she had built in 1892 on the bank of Park River at Hartford, Connecticut, she made meanwhile long visits to Florida. The book has a definite plot-structure and a romantic interest, but it is quite possible to forget the solution of the mystery of the old Dench House and yet remember scenes as vividly as if one had lived through them. Mrs. Stowe herself did not live through them; the time of the story is before her time—not long after the Revolutionary War, while yet a certain aristocratic glamour clung about old Tory families like that of Miss Deborah Kittery, and here and there a title, like that of Lady Lothrop, lived on by courtesy even on the lips of staunch republicans. The parson is one of the best instances in our fiction of a clergyman of the old régime still maintaining by sheer personal prestige the power of a lost social authority.

It was not a time rich in festivals. "Poganuc People" uses Mrs. Stowe's own childhood memories of Litchfield, when Christmas was as yet a holiday proscribed for Puritans; in "Oldtown Folks" the boy telling the story had not the faintest idea what Easter Sunday was until Lady Lothrop offered to take him to Boston in her carriage next day, but he "felt it to be something vague, strange, and remotely suggestive of the supernatural." Sam Lawson encompassed the observance with his large, lazy tolerance when Polly said it was all pagan flummery about Easter. "Lordy massy, we mustn't be hard on nobody," said he, "can't 'spect everybody to be right all round; it's what I tell Polly when she sniffs at Lady Lothrop keepin' Christmas and Easter and sich. 'Lordy massy, Polly,' says I, 'if she reads her Bible, and 's good to the poor, and don't speak evil o' nobody, why, let her have her Easter; what's the harm on't?' But, lordy massy bless your soul and body! there's no kind o' use talkin' to Polly." Even the warm-hearted, large-souled grandmother, who agreed that "there's good folks among 'em all," hoped that when the boy spent Easter in Boston he would go out on Copp's Hill and see the graves of the Saints, whose legends in Cotton Mather's "Magnalia" they were never tired of hearing. The place of all these high days and holidays was taken by the great festival of Thanksgiving. Herein a story within a story, taken from "Oldtown Folks," is the real New England feast, crown and glory of the year, set down at the height of its grandeur in spirit and detail, culinary and social. And here, seen through the steam and smoke of preparation, is the lank and languid form of the incomparable Sam Lawson.

Sam had appeared in "Oldtown Fireside Stories," which began in the *Atlantic* in 1870, and destroyed their chance of being real stories by his very perfection. For he is a rural philosopher who cannot be hurried or diverted; who must meander at his own rate and after his own notion; he needed more space and time, as Mrs. J. T. Field has pointed out, than he could ever hope to get in a short story. So he wanders and slouches at his own pace, or enjoys "the excitement of an occasional odd bit of work with which he had clearly no concern, and which had no sort of tendency toward his own support or that of his family," through this novel, "entered according to Act of Congress in the year 1869" and reaching, as my copy shows, its twenty-seventh edition in 1884. Wherever he appears, the novel tightens and brightens.

Mrs. Stowe lived to be eighty-five. Her husband had been professor of divinity at Bowdoin, where she wrote "Uncle Tom's Cabin," which in America alone sold thirty thousand copies in a year. By the next year the Staffordshire potteries in England, always quick to meet a popular demand, were turning out statuettes of Eva and Uncle Tom reading the Scriptures under a transatlantic arbor. They were once to be found the length and breadth of Britain, in cottage parlors; I came upon one the last time I prowled about the second-hand shops near the Elephant-and-Castle, and brought it back with me to the land of its inspiration.

HOW WE KEPT THANKSGIVING AT OLDTOWN

By Harriet Beecher Stowe

Are there any of my readers who do not know what Thanksgiving day is to a child? Then let them go back with me, and recall the image of it as we kept it in Oldtown.

People have often supposed, because the Puritans founded a society where there were no professed public amusements, that therefore there was no fun going on in the ancient land of Israel, and that there were no cakes and ale, because they were virtuous. They were never more mistaken in their lives. There was an abundance of sober, well-considered merriment; and the hinges of life were well oiled with that sort of secret humor which to this day gives the raciness to real Yankee wit. Besides this, we must remember that life itself is the greatest possible amusement to people who really believe they can do much with it,—who have that intense sense of what can be brought to pass by human effort, that was characteristic of the New England colonies. To such it is not exactly proper to say that life is an amusement, but it certainly is an engrossing interest that takes the place of all amusements.

Looking over the world on a broad scale, do we not find that public entertainments have very generally been the sops thrown out by engrossing upper classes to keep lower classes from inquiring too particularly into their rights, and to make them satisfied with a stone, when it was not quite convenient to give them bread? Wherever there is a class that is to be made content to be plundered of its rights, there is an abundance of fiddling and dancing, and amusements, public and private, are in great requisition. It may also be set down, I think, as a general axiom, that people feel the need of amusements less and less, precisely in proportion as they have solid reasons for being happy.

Our good Puritan fathers intended to form a state of society of such quality of conditions, and to make the means of securing the goods of life so free to all, that everybody should find abundant employment for his facilities in a prosperous seeking of his fortunes. Hence, while they forbade theatres, operas, and dances, they made a state of unparalleled peace and prosperity, where one could go to sleep at all hours of day or night with house door wide open, without bolt or bar, yet without apprehension of any to molest or make afraid.

There were, however, some few national fêtes:—Election day, when the Governor took his seat with pomp and rejoicing, and all the housewives outdid themselves in election cake, and one or two training days, when all the children were refreshed, and our military ardor quickened, by the roll of drums, and the flash of steel bayonets, and marchings and evolutions—sometimes ending in that sublimest of military operations, a sham fight, in which nobody was killed. The Fourth of July took high rank, after the Declaration of Independence; but the king and high priest of all festivals was the autumn Thanksgiving.

When the apples were all gathered and the cider was all made, and the yellow pumpkins were rolled in from many a hill in billows of gold, and the corn was husked, and the labors of the season were done, and the warm, late days of Indian Summer came in, dreamy and calm and still, with just frost enough to crisp the ground of a morning, but with warm trances of benignant, sunny hours at noon, there came over the community a sort of genial repose of spirit,—a sense of something accomplished, and of a new golden mark made in advance on the calendar of life,— and the deacon began to say to the minister, of a Sunday, "I suppose it's about time for the Thanksgiving proclamation."

Rural dress-makers about this time were extremely busy in making up festival garments, for everybody's new dress, if she was to have one at all, must appear on Thanksgiving day.

Aunt Keziah and Aunt Lois and my mother talked over their bonnets, and turned them round and round on their hands, and discoursed sagely of ribbons and linings, and of all the kindred bonnets that there were in the parish, and how they would probably appear after Thanksgiving. My grandmother, whose mind had long ceased to wander on such worldly vanities, was at this time officiously reminded by her daughters that her bonnet wasn't respectable, or it was announced to her that she *must* have a new gown. Such were the distant horizon gleams of the Thanksgiving festival.

We also felt its approach in all departments of the

household,—the conversation at this time beginning to turn on high and solemn culinary mysteries and receipts of wondrous power and virtue. New modes of elaborating squash pies and quince tarts were now ofttimes carefully discussed at the evening fireside by Aunt Lois and Aunt Keziah, and notes seriously compared with the experiences of certain other Aunties of high repute in such matters. I noticed that on these occasions their voices often fell into mysterious whispers, and that receipts of especial power and sanctity were communicated in tones so low as entirely to escape the vulgar ear. I still remember the solemn shake of the head with which my Aunt Lois conveyed to Miss Mehitable Rossiter the critical properties of *mace*, in relation to its powers of producing in corn fritters a suggestive resemblance to oysters. As ours was an oyster-getting district, and as that charming bivalve was perfectly easy to come at, the interest of such an imitation can be accounted for only by the fondness of the human mind for works of art.

For as much as a week beforehand, "we children" were employed in chopping mince for pies to a most wearisome fineness, and in pounding cinnamon, allspice, and cloves in a great lignumvitae mortar; and the sound of this pounding and chopping reëchoed through all the rafters of the old house with a hearty and vigorous cheer, most refreshing to our spirits.

In those days there were none of the thousand ameliorations of the labors of housekeeping which have since arisen, —no ground and prepared spices and sweet herbs; everything came into our hands in the rough, and in bulk, and the reducing of it into a state for use was deemed one of the most appropriate labors of childhood. Even the very salt that we used in cooking was rock-salt, which we were required to wash and dry and pound and sift, before it became fit for use.

At other times of the year we sometimes murmured at these labors, but those that were supposed to usher in the great Thanksgiving festival were always entered into with enthusiasm. There were signs of richness all around us,—stoning of raisins, cutting of citron, slicing of candied orange-peel. Yet all these were only dawnings and intimations of what was coming during the week of real preparation, after the Governor's proclamation had been read.

The glories of that proclamation! We knew beforehand the Sunday it was to be read, and walked to church with alacrity, filled with gorgeous and vague expectations.

The cheering anticipation sustained us through what seemed to us the long waste of the sermon and prayers; and when at last the auspicious moment approached,—when the last quaver of the last hymn had died out,—the whole house rippled with a general movement of complacency, and a satisfied smile of pleased expectation might be seen gleaming on the faces of all the young people, like a ray of sunshine through a garden of flowers.

Thanksgiving now was dawning! We children poked one another, and fairly giggled with unreproved delight as we listened to the crackle of the slowly unfolding document. That great sheet of paper impressed us as something supernatural, by reason of its mighty size, and by the broad seal of the State affixed thereto; and when the minister read therefrom, "By his Excellency, the Governor of the Commonwealth of Massachusetts, a Proclamation," our mirth was with difficulty repressed by admonitory glances from our sympathetic elders. Then, after a solemn enumeration of the benefits which the Commonwealth had that year received at the hands of Divine Providence, came at last the naming of the eventful day, and, at the end of all, the imposing heraldic words, "God save the Commonwealth of Massachusetts." And then, as the congregation broke up and dispersed, all went their several ways with schemes of mirth and feasting in their heads.

And now came on the week in earnest. In the very watches of the night preceding Monday morning, a preternatural stir below stairs, and the thunder of the pounding-barrel, announcing that the washing was to be got out of the way before daylight, so as to give "ample scope and room enough" for the more pleasing duties of the season.

The making of *pies* at this period assumed vast proportions that verged upon the sublime. Pies were made by forties and fifties and hundreds, and made of everything on the earth and under the earth.

The pie is an English institution, which, planted on American soil, forthwith ran rampant and burst forth into an untold variety of genera and species. Not merely the old traditional mince pie, but a thousand strictly American seedlings from the main stock, evinced the power of American housewives to adapt old institutions to new uses. Pumpkin pies, cranberry pies, huckleberry pies, cherry pies, green-currant pies, peach, pear and plum pies, custard pies, apple pies, Marlborough-pudding pies,—pies with top crusts, and pies without,—pies adorned with all sorts of fanciful flutings and architectural strips laid across and around, and otherwise varied, attested the boundless fertility of the feminine mind, when once let loose in a given direction.

Fancy the heat and vigor of the great pan-formation, when Aunt Lois and Aunt Keziah, and my mother and grandmother, all in ecstasies of creative inspiration, ran, bustled, and hurried,—mixing, rolling, tasting, consulting, —alternately setting us children to work when anything could be made of us, and then chasing us all out of the kitchen when our misinformed childhood ventured to take too many liberties with sacred mysteries. Then out we would all fly at the kitchen door, like sparks from a blacksmith's window.

In the corner of the great kitchen, during all these days, the jolly old oven roared and crackled in great volcanic billows of flame, snapping and gurgling as if the old fellow entered with joyful sympathy into the frolic of the hour; and then, his great heart being once warmed up, he brooded over successive generations of pies and cakes, which went in raw and came out cooked, till butteries and dressers and shelves and pantries were literally crowded with a jostling abundance.

A great cold northern chamber, where the sun never shone, and where in winter the snow sifted in at the window-cracks, and ice and frost reigned with undisputed sway, was fitted up to be the storehouse of these surplus treasures. There, frozen solid, and thus well preserved in their icy fetters, they formed a great repository for all the winter months; and the pies baked at Thanksgiving often came out fresh and good with the violets of April.

During this eventful preparation week, all the female part of my grandmother's household, as I have before remarked, were at a height above any ordinary state of mind, —they moved about the house rapt in a species of prophetic frenzy. It seemed to be considered a necessary feature of such festivals, that everybody should be in a hurry, and everything in the house should be turned bottom upwards with enthusiasm,—so at least we children understood it, and we certainly did our part to keep the ball rolling.

Moreover, my grandmother's kitchen at this time began to be haunted by those occasional hangers-on and retainers, of uncertain fortunes, whom a full experience of her bountiful habits led to expect something at her hand at this time of the year. All the poor, loafing tribes, Indian and half-Indian, who at other times wandered, selling baskets and other light wares, were sure to come back to Oldtown a little before Thanksgiving time, and report themselves in my grandmother's kitchen.

The great hogshead of cider in the cellar, which my grandfather called the Indian Hogshead, was on tap at all hours of the day; and many a mugful did I draw and dispense to the tribes that basked in the sunshine of our door.

Aunt Lois never had a hearty conviction of the propriety of these arrangements; but my grandmother, who had a prodigious verbal memory, bore down upon her with such strings of quotations from the Old Testament that she was utterly routed.

"Now," says my Aunt Lois, "I s'pose we've got to have Betty Poganut and Sally Wonsamug, and old Obscue and his wife, and the whole tribe down, roosting around our doors, till we give 'em something. That's just mother's way; she always keeps a whole generation at her heels."

"How many times must I tell you, Lois, to read your Bible?" was my grandmother's rejoinder; and loud over the sound of pounding and chopping in the kitchen could be heard the voice of her quotations: "If there be among you a poor man in any of the gates of the land which the Lord thy God giveth thee, thou shalt not harden thy heart, nor shut thy hand, from thy poor brother. Thou shalt surely give him; and thy heart shall not be grieved when thou givest to him, because that for this thing the Lord thy God shall bless thee in all thy works; for the poor shall never cease from out of the land."

These words seemed to resound like a sort of heraldic proclamation to call around us all that softly shiftless class, who, for some reason or other, are never to be found with anything in hand at the moment that it is wanted.

"There, to be sure," said Aunt Lois, one day when our preparations were in full blast—"there comes Sam Lawson down the hill, limpsy as ever; now he'll have his doleful story to tell, and mother'll give him one of the turkeys."

And so, of course, it fell out.

Sam came in with his usual air of plaintive assurance, and seated himself a contemplative spectator in the

chimney-corner, regardless of the looks and signs of un-
welcome on the part of Aunt Lois.

"Lordy massy, how prosperous everything does seem
here!" he said, in musing tones, over his inevitable mug of
cider; "so different from what 't is t' our house. There's
Hepsy, she's all in a stew, an' I've just been an' got her
thirty-seven cents' wuth o' nutmegs, yet she says she's
sure she don't see how she's to keep Thanksgiving, an' she's
down on me about it, just as ef 't was my fault. Yeh see,
last winter our old gobbler got froze. You know, Mis'
Badger, that 'ere cold night we hed last winter. Wal, I was
off with Jake Marshall that night; ye see, Jake, he hed
to take old General Dearborn's corpse into Boston to the
family vault, and Jake, he kind o' hated to go alone, 't
was a drefful cold time, and he ses to me, 'Sam, you jes
go 'long with me'; so I was sort o' sorry for him, and I
kind o' thought I'd go 'long. Wal, come 'long to Josh
Bissel's tahvern, there at the Half-way House, you know,
't was so swinging cold we stopped to take a little suthin'
warmin', and we sort o' sot an' sot over the fire, till, fust
we knew, we kind o' got asleep; an' when we woke up we
found we'd left the old General hitched up t' th' post
pretty much all night. Wal, didn't hurt him none, poor
man; 't was allers a favorite spot o' his'n. But, takin' one
thing with another, I didn't get home till about noon next
day, an', I tell you, Hepsy she was right down on me. She
said the baby was sick, and there hadn't been no wood
split, nor the barn fastened up, nor nothin'. Lordy massy,
I didn't mean no harm; I thought there was wood enough,

and I thought likely Hepsy'd git out an' fasten up the barn. But Hepsy, she was in one o' her contrary streaks, an' she wouldn't do a thing; an', when I went out to look, why, sure 'nuff, there was our old tom-turkey froze as stiff as a stake,—his claws jist a stickin' right straight up like this." Here Sam struck an expressive attitude, and looked so much like a frozen turkey as to give a pathetic reality to the picture.

"Well now, Sam, why need you be off on things that's none of your business?" said my grandmother. "I've talked to you plainly about that a great many times, Sam," she continued, in tones of severe admonition. "Hepsy is a hard-working woman, but she can't be expected to see to everything, and you oughter 'ave been at home that night to fasten up your own barn and look after your own creeturs."

Sam took the rebuke all the more meekly as he perceived the stiff black legs of a turkey poking out from under my grandmother's apron while she was delivering it. To be exhorted and told of his shortcomings, and then furnished with a turkey at Thanksgiving, was a yearly part of his family programme. In time he departed, not only with a turkey, but with us boys in procession after him, bearing a mince and a pumpkin pie for Hepsy's children.

"Poor things!" my grandmother remarked; "they ought to have something good to eat Thanksgiving day; 'tain't their fault that they've got a shiftless father."

Sam, in his turn, moralized to us children, as we walked beside him: "A body'd think that Hepsy'd learn to trust in Providence," he said, "but she don't. She allers has a

Thanksgiving dinner pervided; but that 'ere woman ain't grateful for it, by no manner o' means. Now she'll be just as cross as she can be, 'cause this 'ere ain't *our* turkey, and these 'ere ain't our pies. Folks doos lose so much, that hes sech dispositions."

A multitude of similar dispensations during the course of the week materially reduced the great pile of chickens and turkeys which black Caesar's efforts in slaughtering, picking, and dressing kept daily supplied.

Besides these offerings to the poor, the handsomest turkey of the flock was sent, dressed in first-rate style, with Deacon Badger's dutiful compliments, to the minister; and we children, who were happy to accompany black Caesar on this errand, generally received a seed-cake and a word of acknowledgment from the minister's lady.

Well, at last, when all the chopping and pounding and baking and brewing, preparatory to the festival, were gone through with, the eventful day dawned. All the tribes of the Badger family were to come back home to the old house, with all the relations of every degree, to eat the Thanksgiving dinner. And it was understood that in the evening the minister and his lady would look in upon us, together with some of the select aristocracy of Oldtown.

Great as the preparations were for the dinner, everything was so contrived that not a soul in the house should be kept from the morning service of Thanksgiving in the church, and from listening to the Thanksgiving sermon, in which the minister was expected to express his views freely concerning the politics of the country, and the state of things in society generally, in a somewhat more secular vein of thought than was deemed exactly appropriate to the Lord's day. But it is to be confessed, that, when the good man got carried away by the enthusiasm of his subject to extend these exercises beyond a certain length, anxious glances, exchanged between good wives, sometimes indicated a weakness of the flesh, having a tender reference to the turkeys and chickens and chicken pies, which might possibly be overdoing in the ovens at home. But your old brick oven was a true Puritan institution, and backed up the devotional habits of good housewives by the capital care which he took of whatever was committed to his capacious bosom. A truly well-bred oven would have been ashamed of himself all his days, and blushed redder than his own fires, if a God-fearing house-matron, away at the temple of the Lord, should come home and find her pie-crust either burned or underdone by his over or under zeal; so the old fellow generally managed to bring things out exactly right.

When sermons and prayers were all over, we children rushed home to see the great feast of the year spread.

What chitterings and chatterings there were all over the house, as all the aunties and uncles and cousins came pouring in, taking off their things, looking at one another's bonnets and dresses, and mingling their comments on the morning sermon with various opinions on the new millinery outfits, and with bits of home news, and kindly neighborhood gossip.

The best room on this occasion was thrown wide open, and its habitual coldness had been warmed by the burning down of a great stack of hickory logs, which had been heaped up unsparingly since morning. It takes some hours to get a room warm where a family never sits, and which therefore has not in its walls one particle of the genial vitality which comes from the in-dwelling of human beings. But on Thanksgiving day, at least, every year, this marvel was effected in our best room.

Although all servile labor and vain recreation on this day were by law forbidden, according to the terms of the proclamation, it was not held to be a violation of the precept, that all the nice old aunties should bring their knitting-work and sit gently trotting their needles around the fire; nor that Uncle Bill should start a full-fledged romp among the girls and children, while the dinner was being set on the long table in the neighboring kitchen. Certain of the good elderly female relatives, of serious and discreet demeanor, assisted at this operation.

But who shall do justice to the dinner, and describe the turkey, and chickens, and chicken pies, with all that endless variety of vegetables which the American soil and climate have contributed to the table, and which, without regard to the French doctrine of courses, were all piled together in jovial abundance upon the smoking board? There was much carving and laughing and talking and eating, and all showed that cheerful ability to despatch the provisions which was the ruling spirit of the hour. After the meat came the plum-puddings, and then the endless array of pies, till human nature was actually bewildered and overpowered by the tempting variety; and even we children turned from the profusion offered to us, and wondered what was the matter that we could eat no more.

When all was over, my grandfather rose at the head of the table, and a fine venerable picture he made as he stood there, his silver hair flowing in curls down each side of his clear, calm face, while, in conformity to the old Puritan custom, he called their attention to a recital of the mercies of God in His dealings with their family.

It was a sort of family history, going over and touching upon the various events which had happened. He spoke of my father's death, and gave a tribute to his memory; and closed all with the application of a time-honored text, expressing the hope that as years passed by we might "so number our days as to apply our hearts unto wisdom"; and then he gave out that psalm which in those days might be called the national hymn of the Puritans.

This we all united in singing to the venerable tune of St. Martin's, an air which, the reader will perceive, by its multiplicity of quavers and inflections gave the greatest possible scope to the cracked and trembling voices of the ancients, who united in it with even more zeal than the younger part of the community.

And now, the dinner being cleared away, we youngsters, already excited to a tumult of laughter, tumbled into the best room, under the supervision of Uncle Bill, to relieve ourselves with a game of "blind-man's-buff," while the elderly women washed up the dishes and got the house in order, and the men folks went out to the barn to look at the cattle, and walked over the farm and talked of the crops.

In the evening the house was all open and lighted with the best of tallow candles, which Aunt Lois herself had made with especial care for this illumination. It was understood that we were to have a dance, and black Caesar, full of turkey and pumpkin pie, and giggling in the very jollity of his heart, had that afternoon rosined his bow, and tuned his fiddle, and practised jigs and Virginia reels, in a way that made us children think him a perfect Orpheus.

As soon as the candles were lighted came in Miss Mehitable with her brother Jonathan, and Tina, like a gay little tassel, hanging on her withered arm.

After them soon arrived the minister and his lady,—she in a grand brocade satin dress, open in front to display a petticoat brocaded with silver flowers. With her well-formed hands shining out of a shimmer of costly lace, and her feet propped on high-heeled shoes, Lady Lothrop justified the prestige of good society which always hung about her. Her lord and master, in the spotless whiteness of his ruffles on wrist and bosom, and in the immaculate keeping and neatness of all his clerical black, and the perfect *pose* of his grand full-bottomed clerical wig, did honor to her conjugal cares. They moved through the room like a royal prince and princess, with an appropriate, gracious, well-considered word for each and every one. They even returned, with punctilious civility, the awe-struck obeisance of black Caesar, who giggled over straightway with joy and exultation at the honor.

But conceive of my Aunt Lois's pride of heart, when, following in the train of these august persons, actually came Ellery Davenport, bringing upon his arm Miss Deborah Kittery. Here was a situation! Had the whole island of Great Britain waded across the Atlantic Ocean to call on Bunker Hill, the circumstance would scarcely have seemed to her more critical.

"Mercy on us!" she thought to herself, "all these Episcopalians coming! I do hope mother'll be careful; I hope she won't feel it necessary to give them a piece of her mind, as she's always doing."

Miss Deborah Kittery, however, knew her soundings, and was too genuine an Englishwoman not to know that "every man's house is his castle," and that one must respect one's neighbor's opinions on his own ground.

As to my grandmother, her broad and buxom heart on this evening was so full of motherliness, that she could have patted the very King of England on the head, if he had been there, and comforted his soul with the assurance that she supposed he meant well, though he didn't exactly know how to manage; so, although she had a full consciousness that Miss Deborah Kittery had turned all America over to unconvented mercies, she nevertheless shook her warmly by the hand, and told her she hoped she'd make herself at home.

Whenever or wherever it was that the idea of the sinfulness of dancing arose in New England, I know not; it is a certain fact that at Oldtown, at this time, the presence of the minister and his lady was held not to be in the slightest degree incompatible with this amusement. I appeal to many of my readers, if they or their parents could not recall a time in New England when in all the large towns dancing assemblies used to be statedly held, at which the minister and his lady, though never uniting in the dance, always gave an approving attendance, and where all the decorous, respectable old church-members brought their children, and stayed to watch an amusement in which they no longer actively partook. No one looked on with a more placid and patronizing smile than Dr. Lothrop and his lady, as one after another began joining the exercise, which, commencing first with the children and young people, crept gradually upwards among the elders.

Uncle Bill would insist on leading out Aunt Lois, and the bright color rising to her thin cheeks brought back a fluttering image of what might have been beauty in some fresh, early day. Ellery Davenport insisted upon leading forth Miss Deborah Kittery, notwithstanding her oft-repeated refusals and earnest protestations to the contrary. As to Uncle Fliakim he jumped and frisked and gyrated among the single sisters and maiden aunts, whirling them into the dance as if he had been the little black gentleman himself. With that true spirit of Christian charity which marked all his actions, he invariably chose out the homeliest and most neglected, and thus worthy Aunt Keziah, dear old soul, was for a time made quite prominent by his attentions.

Of course the dances in those days were of a strictly moral nature. The very thought of one of the round dances of modern times would have sent Lady Lothrop behind her big fan in helpless confusion, and exploded my grandmother like a full-charged arsenal of indignation. As it was, she stood, her broad pleased face radiant with satisfaction, as the wave of joyousness crept up higher and higher round her, till the elders, who stood keeping time with their hands and feet, began to tell one another how they had danced with their sweethearts in good old days gone by, and the elder women began to blush and bridle, and boast of steps that they could take in their youth, till the music finally subdued them, and into the dance they went.

"Well, well!" quoth my grandmother; "they're all at it so heartily, I don't see why I shouldn't try it myself." And into the Virginia reel she went, amid screams of laughter from all the younger members of the company.

But I assure you my grandmother was not a woman to be laughed at; for whatever she once set on foot, she "put through" with a sturdy energy befitting a daughter of the Puritans.

"Why shouldn't I dance?" she said, when she arrived red and resplendent at the bottom of the set. "Didn't Mr. Despondency and Miss Muchafraid and Mr. Readytohalt all dance together in the Pilgrim's Progress?"—and the minister in his ample flowing wig, and my lady in her stiff brocade, gave to my grandmother a solemn twinkle of approbation.

As nine o'clock struck, the whole scene dissolved and melted; for what well-regulated village would think of carrying festivities beyond that hour?

And so ended our Thanksgiving at Oldtown.

EDWARD EVERETT HALE
(1822–1909)

Tradition at Harvard has it that when Edward Everett Hale was an undergraduate he used to sleep until the last stroke of the bell, spring out of bed, throw his clothes over the stairway, and jump into them on the way down. All traditions, however flamboyant, have at least a psychological basis of fact, and no doubt in his Harvard days the boy was already jumping into life and work and fun with the same *élan* the man was to keep up for well on to a century. "Live with all your might," was one of his mottoes, "and you will have more life with which to live."

He was great-nephew of Nathan Hale and nephew of Edward Everett, and was born in Boston. Henry Ward Beecher once asked an old friend of mine where she was born. "In Boston," she replied, proudly. "That's nice," said he, "you won't have to be born again." This precaution as to birthplace has been taken by a number of American writers who reinforced it further by staying as near to the city as well they might for a good part of their days. Edward Everett Hale was one of these. He spent most of his long life as pastor and at last as pastor emeritus in Boston. He was a strong and valued supporter of every movement for the betterment of man, from freeing the slave and helping the freedman, to prison improvement and civil service reform, but above all he was a good neighbor, extending the definition of neighborliness ever more widely without losing its warm personal interest. From his stories arose those practical examples of this principle, King's Daughters and Lend-a-Hand Clubs with the societies arising indirectly from them; he himself considered his "In His Name" his best story, and "Ten Times One is Ten" has his famous motto: "Look up and not down; look forward and not back; look out and not in; and lend a hand." At length this neighborliness—whose vital impulse was a primitive Christianity—expressed itself in a plan for a permanent world court of justice, whose creation he foretold in a sermon preached in 1899 at Washington, D. C., and which he had outlined at the Lake Mohunk Conference four years earlier. He began to write in 1848, not so much for purely literary purposes as in line with his social and philanthropic activities, and the collected edition of his works numbered 120 titles in ten volumes.

The story by which he is here represented was written in 1867, for the Christmas number of the *Boston Daily Advertiser,* of which his father was owner and editor, and was included in his first volume of short stories, published under the descriptive title of "If, Yes, and Perhaps: Four Possibilities and Six Exaggerations, with some bits of fact." This volume also included "The Man Without a Country" and "My Double and How he Undid Me." Like these far more famous fables, this story is evidently made on the plan he used for all in this collection: "Set up some imaginative fancy and show how it would have been had it been a fact." This fancy is made fact in Boston, just as in his charming apologue of a modern psyche he re-tells an ancient myth in terms of literary society, names and all, in Boston's golden age. There is a significant poem of Vachel Lindsay's, "So Much the Worse for Boston," in which a rocky mountain cat, explaining to a man from the East what sort of place he believes Boston to be, meets the protests of the man that Boston is by no means so noble and idealistic a place, with "So much the worse for Boston." The neighborliness of this tale, the village-spirit of mutual lend-a-hand, is one of the special possibilities of a city whose special glamour, for all its size and dignity, is that it yet retains something of the best village, or even rural spirit. If they never really did anything like this on a Boston Christmas in the sixties, one must agree that it was so much the worse for Boston.

CHRISTMAS WAITS IN BOSTON

By EDWARD EVERETT HALE

I

I ALWAYS give myself a Christmas present. And on this particular year the present was a Carol party,—which is about as good fun, all things consenting kindly, as a man can have.

Many things must consent, as will appear. First of all there must be good sleighing,—and second, a fine night for Chrismas Eve. Ours are not the carollings of your poor shivering little East Angles or South Mercians, where they have to plod around afoot in countries where they do not know what a sleigh-ride is.

I had asked Harry to have sixteen of the best voices in the chapel school to be trained to eight or ten good carols without knowing why. We did not care to disappoint them if a February thaw setting in on the twenty-fourth of December should break up the spree before it began. Then I had told Howland that he must reserve for me a span of good horses and a sleigh that I could pack sixteen small children into, tight-stowed. Howland is always good about such things, knew what the sleigh was for, having done the same in other years, and doubled the span of horses of his own accord, because the children would like it better, and "it would be no difference to him." Sunday night, as the weather nymphs ordered, the wind hauled round to the northwest and everything froze hard. Monday night things moderated, and the snow began to fall steadily,—so steadily;—and so Tuesday night the Metropolitan people gave up their unequal contest, all good men and angels rejoicing at their discomfiture, and only a few of the people in the very lowest *Bolgie* being ill-natured enough to grieve. And thus it was, that by Thursday evening there was one hard compact roadway from Copp's Hill to the Bone-burner's Gehenna, fit for good men and angels to ride over, without jar, without noise, and without fatigue to horse or man. So it was that when I came down with Lycidas to the chapel at seven o'clock, I found Harry had gathered there his eight pretty girls and his eight jolly boys, and had them practising for the last time:

> "Carol, carol Christians,
> Carol joyfully;
> Carol for the coming
> Of Christ's nativity."

I think the children had got inkling of what was coming, or perhaps Harry had hinted it to their mothers. Certainly they were warmly dressed, and when, fifteen minutes afterwards, Howland came round himself with the sleigh, he had put in as many rugs and bear-skins as if he thought the children were to be taken new-born from their respective cradles. Great was the rejoicing as the bells of the horses rang beneath the chapel windows, and Harry did not get his last *da capo* for his last carol, not much matter indeed, for they were perfect enough in it before midnight.

Lycidas and I tumbled in on the back seat, each with a child on his lap to keep us warm; I was flanked by Sam Perry, and he by John Rich, both of the mercurial age, and therefore good to do errands. Harry was in front somewhere, flanked in likewise, and the twelve other children lay in miscellaneously between, like sardines when you have first opened the box. I had invited Lycidas, because, besides being my best friend, he is the best fellow in the world, and so deserves the best Christmas Eve can give him. Under the full moon, on the snow still white, with sixteen children at the happiest, and with the blessed memories of the best the world has ever had, there can be nothing better than two or three such hours.

"First, driver, out on Commonwealth Avenue. That will tone down the horses. Stop on the left after you have passed Fairfield Street." So we dashed up to the front of Haliburton's palace, where he was keeping his first Christmastide. And the children, whom Harry had hushed down for a square or two, broke forth with good full voice under his strong lead in

"Shepherd of tender sheep,"

singing with all that unconscious pathos with which children do sing, and starting the tears in your eyes in the midst of your gladness. The instant the horses' bells stopped, their voices began. In an instant more we saw Haliburton and Anna run to the window and pull up the shades, and, in a minute more, faces at all the windows. And so the children sung through Clement's old hymn.

Little did Clement think of bells and snow, as he taught it in his Sunday school there in Alexandria. But perhaps to-day, as they pin up the laurels and the palm in the chapel at Alexandria, they are humming the words, not thinking of Clement more than he thought of us. As the children closed with

> "Swell the triumphant song
> To Christ, our King,"

Haliburton came running out, and begged me to bring them in. But I told him, "No," as soon as I could hush their shouts of "Merry Christmas;" that we had a long journey before us, and must not alight by the way. And the children broke out with

> "Hail to the night,
> Hail to the day,"

rather a favorite,—quicker and more to the childish taste, perhaps, than the other,—and with another "Merry Christmas" we were off again.

Off, the length of Commonwealth Avenue, to where it crosses the Brookline branch of the Mill-Dam,—dashing along with the gayest of sleighing-parties as we came back into town, up Chestnut Street, through Louisburg Square, —we ran the sleigh into a bank on the slope of Pinckney Street in front of Walter's house,—and before they suspected there that any one had come, the children were singing

> "Carol, carol Christians,
> Carol joyfully."

Kisses flung from the window; kisses flung back from the street. "Merry Christmas" again and a good-will, and then one of the girls began

> "When Anna took the baby,
> And pressed his lips to hers"—

and all of them fell in so cheerily. O dear me! it is a scrap of old Ephrem the Syrian, if they did but know it! And when, after this, Harry would fain have driven on, how the little witches begged that they might sing just one song more there, because Mrs. Alexander had been so kind to them, when she showed them about the German stitches. And then up the hill and over to the North End, and as far as we could get the horses up into Moon Court, that they might sing to the Italian image-man who gave Lucy the boy and dog in plaster, when she was sick in the spring. For the children had, you know, the choice of where they would go; and they select their best friends, and will be more apt to remember the Italian image-man than Chrysostom himself, though Chrysostom should have "made a few remarks" to them seventeen times in the chapel. Then the Italian image-man heard for the first time in his life:

> "Now is the time of Christmas come,"

and

> "Jesus in his babes abiding."

And then we came up Hanover Street and stopped under Mr. Gerry's chapel, where they were dressing the walls with their evergreens, and gave them

"Hail to the night,
Hail to the day:"

And so down State Street and stopped at the *Advertiser* office, because when the boys gave their Literary Entertainment, Mr. Hale put in their advertisement for nothing, and up in the old attic there the compositors were relieved to hear

"No war nor battle sound,"

and

"The waiting world was still."

Even the leading editor relaxed from his gravity and the "In General" man from his more serious views, and the *Daily* the next morning wished everybody a "Merry Christmas" with even more unction, and resolved that in coming years it would have a supplement, large enough to contain all the good wishes. So away again to the houses of confectioners who had given the children candy,—to Miss Simonds' house, because she had been so good to them in school,—to the palaces of millionaires who had prayed for these children with tears if the children only knew it,—to Dr. Frothingham in Summer Street, I remember, where we stopped because the Boston Association of Ministers met there,—and out on Dover Street Bridge, that the poor chair mender might hear our carols sung once more before he heard them better sung in another world where nothing needs mending. . . . O, we went to twenty places that night, I suppose; we went to the grandest places in Boston, and we went to the meanest. At nine we brought up at my house, D Street, three doors from the corner, and the children picked out their very best for Polly and my six little girls to hear, and then for the first time we let them jump out and run in. Polly had some hot oysters for them, so that the frolic was crowned with a treat. There was a Christmas cake cut into sixteen pieces, which they took home to dream upon; and then hoods and mufflers on again, and by ten o'clock or a little after, we had all the girls and all the little ones at their homes . . .

II

Lycidas and I both thought that the welcome of these homes was perhaps the best part of it all, as we went into these modest houses, to leave the children, to say they had been good, and to wish a "Merry Christmas" ourselves to fathers, mothers, and to guardian aunts. . . . Here was brave Mrs. Masury. I had not seen her since her mother died. "Indeed, Mr. Ingham, I got so used to watching then, that I cannot sleep well yet o'nights; I wish you knew some poor creature that wanted me to-night, if it were only in memory of Bethlehem" . . . "What can I send to your children," said Dalton, who was finishing sword-blades. (Ill wind was Fort Sumter, but it blew good to poor Dalton, whom it set up in the world with his sword-factory.) "Here's an old-fashioned tape-measure for the girl, and a Sheffield wimble for the boy. What, there is no boy? Let one of the girls have it, then; it will count one more present for her." And so he pressed his brown-paper parcel into my hand. From every house, though it were the humblest, a word of love, as sweet, in truth, as if we could have heard the voice of angels singing in the sky.

I bade Harry good-night; took Lycidas to his house, and gave his wife my Christmas wishes and good-night; and, coming down to the sleigh again, gave way to the feeling which I think you will all understand, that this was not the time to stop, but just the time to begin. For the streets were stiller now, and the moon brighter than ever, and the blessings of these simple people and of the proud people, and of the very angels in heaven, who are not bound to the misery of using words when they have anything worth saying,—all these wishes and blessings were round me, all the purity of the still winter night, and I didn't want to lose it all by going to bed to sleep. So I put the boys all together, where they could chatter, and then, passing through Charles Street . . . I noticed the lights in Woodhull's house, and, seeing they were up, thought I would make Fanny a midnight call. She came to the door herself. I asked if she were waiting for Santa Claus, but I saw in a moment that I must not joke with her. She said she had hoped I was her husband. In a minute was one of those contrasts which make life, life . . . Poor Fanny's mother had been blocked up in the Springfield train as she was coming on for Christmas. The old lady had been chilled through, and was here in bed now with pneumonia. Both Fanny's children had been ailing when she came, and this morning the doctor had pronounced it scarlet fever. Fanny had not undressed herself since Monday, nor slept, I thought, in the same time. So while we had been singing carols and wishing Merry Christmas, the poor child had been waiting, hoping that her husband or Edward, both of whom were on the tramp, would find for her and bring to her the model nurse, who had not yet arrived, nor had either of the men returned. Professional paragons, dear reader, are shy of scarlet fever. I told the poor child that it was better as it was. I wrote a line for Sam Perry to take to his aunt, Mrs. Masury, in which I simply said: "Dear mamma, I have found the poor creature who wants you to-night. Come back in this carriage." I bade him take a hack at Barnard's, where they were all up waiting for the assembly to be done at Papanti's. I sent him over to Albany Street; and really as I sat there trying to soothe Fanny, it seemed to me less time than it has taken me to dictate this little story about her, before Mrs. Masury rang gently, and I left them, having made Fanny promise that she would consecrate the day, which at that moment was born, by trusting God, by going to bed and going to sleep, knowing that her children were in much better hands than hers . . .

And so I walked home. Better so, perhaps, after all, than in the lively sleigh with the tinkling bells. What an eternity it seemed since I started with those children singing carols!

"Within that province far away
    Went plodding home a weary boor;
A streak of light before him lay,
    Fallen through a half-shut stable door
Across his path. He passed, for naught

Told what was going on within:
How keen the stars, his only thought,
The air how calm and cold and thin,
In the solemn midnight,
Centuries ago!"

"Streak of light"—Is there a light in Lycidas's room?
They not in bed? That is making a night of it! Well, there
are few hours of the day or night when I have not been in
Lycidas's room, so I let myself in by the night-key he
gave me, and ran up the stairs,—it is a horrid seven-storied
first-class, apartment-house. For my part, I had as lief live
in a steeple. Two flights I ran up, two steps at a time,—
I was younger then than I am now,—pushed open the
door which was ajar, and saw such a scene of confusion as
I never saw in Mary's over-nice parlor before. Queer!
I remember the first thing that I saw was wrong was a
great ball of white German worsted on the floor. Her
basket was upset. A great Christmas tree lay across the
rug, quite too high for the room; a large, sharp-pointed
Spanish clasp-knife was by it, with which they had been
lopping it; there were two immense baskets of white
papered presents, both upset; but what frightened me most
was the centre-table. Three or four handkerchiefs on it,—
towels, napkins, I know not what,—all brown and red and
almost black with blood! I turned, heart-sick, to look into
the bedroom,—and I really had a sense of relief when I
saw somebody . . . Lycidas, but just now so strong and
well, lay pale and exhausted . . . while over him bent
Mary and Morton. I learned afterwards that poor Lycidas,
while trimming the Christmas tree and talking merrily

with Mary and Morton,—who, by good luck, had brought round his presents late, and was staying to tie on glass balls and apples,—had given himself a deep and dangerous wound with the point of the unlucky knife, and had lost a great deal of blood before the hemorrhage could be controlled. Just before I entered, the stick tourniquet which Morton had temporised had slipped in poor Mary's unpractised hand, at the moment he was about to secure the artery . . .

"O Fred," said Morton, without looking up, "I am glad you are here."

"And what can I do for you?"

"Some whiskey,—first of all."

"There are two bottles," said Mary, "in the cupboard behind his dressing-glass."

I took Bridget with me, struck a light in the dressing-room (how she blundered about the match) and found the cupboard door locked! Key doubtless in Mary's pocket, —probably in pocket of "another dress." I did not ask. Took my own bunch, willed tremendously that my account-book drawer key should govern the lock, and it did. If it had not, I should have put my fist through the panels. Bottle marked "bay rum;" another bottle with no mark; two bottles of Saratoga water. "Set them all on the floor, Bridget." A tall bottle of cologne. Bottle marked in manuscript. What in the world is it? "Bring that candle, Bridget." "Eau distillée, Marron, Montreal." What in the world did Lycidas bring distilled water from Montreal for? And then Morton's clear voice from the other room, "As quick as you can, Fred." "Yes! in one moment. Put all these on the floor, Bridget." Here they are at last. "Corkscrew, Bridget."

"Indade, sir, and where is it?" "Where? I don't know. Run as quick as you can, and bring it. His wife cannot leave him." So Bridget ran, and I meanwhile am driving a silver pronged fork into the Bourbon corks, and the blade of my own penknife for the other side.

"Now, Fred," from Morton, within. "Yes, in one moment," I replied. Penknife blade breaks off, fork pulls right out, two crumbs of cork with it. Will that girl never come?

I turned round; I found a goblet on the wash-stand; I took Lycidas's heavy clothes-brush and knocked off the neck of the bottle . . . It smashed like a Prince Rupert's drop in my hand, crumbled into seventy pieces,—a nasty smell of whiskey on the floor,—and I, holding just the hard bottom of the thing with two large spikes running worthless up into the air. But I seized the goblet, poured into it what was left in the bottom, and carried it into Morton as quietly as I could. He bade me give Lycidas as much as he could swallow; then showed me how to compress the great artery. When he was satisfied that he could trust me, he began his work again, silently. . . . When all was secure, he glanced at the ghastly white face, with beads of perspiration on the forehead and upper lip, laid his finger on the pulse and said, "We will have a little more whiskey. No, Mary, you are overdone already; let Fred bring it." The truth was that poor Mary was almost as white as Lycidas. She would not faint,—that was the only reason she did not,—and at the moment I wondered that she did not fall. Bridget, you see, was still nowhere.

So I retired again, to attack that other bottle. Would that Kelt ever come? I passed the bell-rope as I went into the dressing-room, and rang as hard as I could ring. I took the other bottle and bit steadily with my teeth at the cork, only, of course, to wrench the end of it off. Morton called me, and I stepped back. "No," said he, "bring your whiskey."

Mary had just rolled gently back on the floor. I went again in despair. But I heard Bridget's step this time. She ran in, in triumph, with a *screw-driver!*

"No!" I whispered,—"no. The crooked thing you draw corks with," and I showed her the bottle again. "Find one somewhere and don't come back without it."

"Frederic!" said Morton. I think he never called me so before . . . "Frederic!" "Yes," I said. But why did I say "Yes"? "Father of Mercy, tell me what to do."

And my mazed eyes, dim with tears,—did you ever shed tears from excitement?—fell on an old razor-strop of those days of shaving, made by *C. Whittaker,* SHEFFIELD. The Sheffield stood in black letters out from the rest like a vision. They make corkscrews in Sheffield too. If this Whittaker had only made a corkscrew! And what is a "Sheffield wimble?"

Hand in my pocket—brown paper parcel.

"Where are you, Frederic?" "Yes," said I for the last time. Twine off! brown paper off! And I learned that the "Sheffield wimble" was one of those things whose name you never heard before, which people sell you in Thames Tunnel, where a hoof-cleaner, a gimlet, a screw-driver and a *corkscrew* fold into one handle. "Yes," said I again. "Pop," said the cork. "Bubble, bubble, bubble," said the whiskey. Bottle in one hand, full tumbler in the other, I walked in. Morton poured half a tumblerful down Lycidas's throat that time . . . I found that there was need of it, from what he said of the pulse when it was all over . . .

This was the turning-point. He was exceedingly weak, and we sat by him through the night, . . . but there was no real danger after that.

As we turned away from the house on Christmas morning,—I to preach and he to visit his patients,—he said to me, "Did you *make* that whiskey?"

"No," said I, "but poor Dod Dalton had to furnish the corkscrew."

And I went down to the chapel to preach. The sermon had been lying ready at home on my desk, and Polly had brought it round to me, for there had been no time for me to go from Lycidas's home to D Street and to return. There was the text, all as it was the day before:

They helped every one his neighbor, and every one said to his brother, Be of good courage. So the carpenter encouraged the goldsmith, and he that smootheth with the hammer him that smote the anvil.

And there were the pat illustrations, as I had finished them yesterday . . . And I said to them all, "O, if I could tell you, my friends, what every twelve hours of my life tells me,—of the way in which woman helps woman, and man helps man, when only the ice is broken,—how we are all rich as soon as we find out that we are all brothers, and how we are all in want, unless we can call at any moment for a brother's hand,—then I could make you understand something, in the lives you lead every day, of what the New Covenant, the New Commonwealth, the New Kingdom, is to be . . ."

But when we had our tree in the evening at home, I did tell all this story to Polly and the bairns, and I gave Alice her measuring-tape,—precious with a spot of Lycidas's blood,—and Bertha her Sheffield wimble. "Papa," said old Clara, who is the next child, "all the people gave presents, did not they, as they did in the picture in your study?"

"Yes," said I, "though they did not all know they were giving them."

"Why do they not give such presents every day?" said Clara.

"O child," I said, "it is only for thirty-six hours of the three hundred and sixty-five days that all people remember that they are all brothers and sisters, and those are the hours that we call, therefore, Christmas Eve and Christmas Day."

HENRY A. SHUTE

Those who go back summer by summer to the same farm-house in the hills make a practice of what might be called visits of reassurance, to places like the brook, the haymow or the attic, to convince themselves that like Kate Nickleby's miniature, they are still "unmoved, unchanged." In the farm-house I know best one of these places is the what-not in the best parlor, because it holds certain books it is part of vacation routine annually to re-read. The collection goes back as far as "Queechy" and "Meadow Brook," and sometime just before the Great War someone en-riched it with Judge Shute's "Plupy." Anyone taking this book may be located for some time after, anywhere on the place, by outbursts of laughter; other addicts know thereby that he has reached the rescue of the chicken (when Plupy's father found he was trying to lift the whole barn), or the debate, or the break-up of the minstrel show. I have even heard, far in the silent night, a sharp yelp from the barn-chamber, forced from a fifteen-year old visitor enjoying his annual re-reading by an untimely candle.

Judge Shute is a distinguished townsman of Exeter, New Hampshire, a town whose history is distinguished; he has an im-pressive paragraph in *Who's Who*, but he lives in our literature because when he was in school he kept a singularly uninhibited journal. This he re-discovered, published serially in the local paper in later life, and in 1902 gave to the world in book-form as "The Real Diary of a Real Boy." Not for Judge Shute the title-page prudence of "All characters in this book are entirely fictitious"; he included a key giving full names and in some cases subsequent careers of his people—Keene and Cele, Beany, Pewt and all the rest. He himself was Plupy, and in later volumes of which "Plupy" reached the highest point, he set forth the career of this youth in a dignified but still naïve New England town not long after the Civil War. He is a bad boy only by the Thomas Bailey Aldrich definition; there is no resemblance save perhaps ingenuity between Plupy and Peck's Bad Boy. He is not even disobedient in general, his difficulties with authority arising mainly from his ingenuity in breaking rules that have not yet been made, because authority could not work fast enough to forecast what that boy could think up. Generally he does not even think it up, the charm of this record being the joyous irresponsibility with which he flings himself headlong into the occasion.

It is with something of a shock that one finds ten- and fifteen-cent script in circulation in New Hampshire when Plupy had to pay for the broken window out of his cornet money. It is almost the only feature of the tale that ties it firmly to the past. Boys in New Hampshire still spear green apples on withes and "let ding" at dogs and sometimes at men; in large and cheerful families brothers and sisters yet wrangle over the respective pressure of their domestic duties; above all, boys are still misunderstood. Penrod and Plupy could confide in each other regarding parental misunderstanding—and each would resent the other's condolence as swiftly and in the same way that Plupy resented his friend's agreement that his father was mean. Families may not be so large, time, even in vacation, not so spacious, and even in small towns, opportunities for initiative not so open. But owing to the proverbial preference of boys to be boys this story probably dates less than any other in the collection.

"LIFE IS ONE DARN THING AFTER ANOTHER"

By Henry A. Shute

PLUPY was grumpy. There was no doubt of it. Anyone who saw him as he sat on the fence in front of his house, dangling his long legs in the air, or idly drumming his heels on the boards, scowling fiercely at the world, would have known that deep in his heart dwelt a mighty indignation.

The day had begun inauspiciously for him. He had forgotten to split his kindlings the night before and had incurred condign punishment that seemed to him unjust and wholly out of proportion to the offense.

If his father had whipped him he would have gotten over it long before this. But he had ordered him to stay in the yard all day. And he had promised to go fishing with Pewt and Potter, and Pewt knew where there were some bully perch, old lunkers. He almost wished his father was dead. Anyway his father would be sorry when he was dead. That was just the way, nothing ever went right. What did he have to split up kindlings for anyway? Why didn't they come all split?

If people only knew enough to cut down little trees instead of big ones, they would be little enough for kindlings anyway, and it was easier to cut up little ones than big ones. When he was a man he would never make his boy split kindlings, but would buy them all split.

He bet his father would feel bad if he drowned himself. He guessed he would miss him when he was gone. And his mother too, she might have said something when his father told him to stay in.

He pictured himself lying dead in the river with the boats full of people with boat-hooks and eel spears, and the banks lined with other pale-faced scared people, and he pictured himself brought home limp and dripping, and brought into the house amid the cries and groans of his father, the father who had driven him to this dreadful death.

And he drew so affecting a picture of their unavailing grief that the tears filled his eyes and a lump arose in his throat as big as the yarn-covered, rubber-cored ball in his pocket.

As his swimming eyes roamed wistfully around in search of something to lighten the dreary monotony of staying in the yard all day, they fell on the huge old apple-tree whose deep-green leaves stirred slightly in the light breeze, and were dappled all over by flecks of golden sunshine.

Suddenly a thought struck him, the green apples were just large enough to throw with an elastic switch. "Bully," he would be the first to do it this season. He sprang from the fence and started for the tree. Then a most unusual spasm of obedience struck him. "Mother," he called, "Mother-er-er," he shrieked, as she did not immediately answer.

"What is it?" a voice replied from the house.

"Kin I plug some green apples with a stick?"

"Why, y-e-e-s, I think so," his mother replied, somewhat doubtfully, "only," she continued, "don't throw them at people and don't break any windows."

"All right, mother," he replied, swarming up the tree for a limber switch. The tree, a high old Baldwin, was too large for his arms and legs to go around, although they were of abnormal length and thinness for a boy of his age, but as it bent slightly to the east and as there was a cavity about eight feet from the ground, it was climbed in this ingenious manner.

Plupy stepped upon the wooden railing around the currant bushes which was nailed to the tree, from there sprang straddlewise up the trunk until his fingers reached the cavity, where he squirmed and inched and twisted himself along until he reached the bend in the tree whence he could pull himself up by the branches.

When he had selected a suitable withe he found he had left his knife in the house, whereupon he began to yell for someone to bring it out. "Keene, Cele, Georgie," he shouted, until one of the young ladies mentioned, a black-eyed, saucy-looking, round-faced girl, appeared in a blue checked apron with a dish-cloth and a plate in her hands.

"Whatcher howlin' like that for, Harry?" she asked in a tone of indignant remonstrance. "Whatcher want?"

"Wantcher to gwup in my room 'n git my jack knife. S'in my linen britches."

"Guess if you want it, you can go'n get it yerself. I'm washin' dishes."

"Oh, gollong 'n git it, woncher? don't be so mean," urged Plupy.

"Go yourself, I won't," said Keene decidedly, turning her back on the suppliant, "I won't."

"Mother-er!" shouted Plupy, "can't Keene just gwup and get my knife for me?"

"Why," said the much-wanted woman, "I should think she might."

"Ma, he can go jesswell as I, he hasn't anything to do and I'm jest as busy as I can be," said Keene, attacking a platter with a great splash of water.

"Make her, mother, she jes does it to be mean. I don't believe I can get up here again in a week," said Plupy.

"Come, Keene," said her mother good-naturedly, "run up and get his knife." Whereupon that young lady with a frown and a defiant swing of her square shoulders, walked upstairs with some rather unnecessary noise, but soon returned saying she couldn't find his old knife.

" 'Twas right in the pocket of my linen britches," said Plupy, "betcher didn't look."

"Did too," asserted the young lady.

"Cornelia," said her mother with a warning light in her eyes, "go straight upstairs and bring down Harry's knife."

There was but one reply to this argument, and in a trice "Cornelia" mounted the stairs and returned with the knife, which she tossed indignantly to her grinning brother, who caught it deftly, and jeeringly said "Ya-ah-ya-ah, had to, didn't yer?"

"Smarty, you wait and see," replied black-eyes, tossing her head and returning to her dishes.

Left alone, Plupy cut a stout but limber switch and carefully trimmed off the twigs and leaves, whistling shrilly a popular band tune. Then he whittled the end to a sharp point on which to impale his projectiles. If he could only harden the end in fire it wouldn't split and would last longer.

There was Sam Dyer's blacksmith shop just across the garden, but then he couldn't go out of the yard. Perhaps, however, Sam would harden it for him. So he dropped his switch to the ground where he speedily followed it, letting himself down from a bending branch.

Arrived at the boundary fence he climbed to the top rail and accosted the blacksmith who was sousing a hot iron in the water trough.

"Mr. Dyer," he said with more deference than he generally used in accosting that gentleman, "wilyer please hold the end of this stick in your fire a minute, just to harden it."

Mr. Dyer looked up with a momentary frown. His experience with Plupy had been somewhat extensive and of such a nature as to put him in the condition of being constantly on guard. But he was an extremely good-natured and simple-hearted man and his frown was speedily chased away by a cheerful grin.

"Why, in course, in course, sonny, come right over," he said hospitably.

"No, you do it, I can't come over, gotter stay in the yard all day," said Plupy, shamefacedly.

"Watcher bin doin' naou?" queried Sam.

"Didn't split no kindlin's las' night."

"H'm, that all?" said the blacksmith, leaning on his smutty arms on the fence, "didn't know but yer'd bin breakin' winders or ringin' door-bells er suthin' like that."

"No, honest, now, twant nothin' but jest that," affirmed Plupy, "hope to die and cross my throat," he added, drawing his fingers crosswise over his skinny neck, which with the boys was then and may possibly be now the most solemn oath possible.

"Well," said Sam, "gimme yer stick an' I'll singe it for ye," and he obligingly did so, returning it with the point in quite a delightfully adamantine condition.

Plupy, in great elation, thanked him and ran back to the apple-tree where he filled his pockets with hard green apples of about the size of bantam's eggs. Then choosing one he tentatively bit it, made a wry face and spat. Then, impaling it on the point of his withe, he lightly swung the switch into the air to try its temper, then gave it a throwing motion with all the strength of his arm.

"Whoof," sang the withe as it cut through the air. Away went the apple with an audible hum, leaving the point at just the right moment. Away, away it soared, ascending for an incredible distance, where it passed out of sight among the trees.

Another was tried with equal success. The third left the point too soon and ascended perpendicularly until it was lost to sight, then fell in the next yard. Plupy forgot all his troubles, he was happy. But whenever a boy has anything to throw projectiles with, be it a bean blower, pop-gun, bow'narrer, arrow-rifle or slingshot, some sort of a target is necessary for perfect enjoyment.

And so after trying long-distance shots for a while, Plupy began to look about for something to hit. He soon found it. Across two gardens, nearly one hundred yards away, sat two men on a fence. They had been hired to work in a neighbor's garden, and in the absence of that neighbor, were improving their time by political discussion. The fact that they were doing wrong in neglecting their employer's work was no reason why Plupy should seek to even up matters by using them as a target.

But so he did, and with poor success for a while. The shots went like lightning, but wide of the mark. At last Plupy began to get the range, and finally, to his intense delight, a hard round apple took one of the disputants a prodigious thump on the back of the head.

In an instant he sprang from the fence with a whoop, and came charging toward the place from which the missile had come, pouring out blasphemies and threats. Plupy dodged behind the fence and dived into the barn to a hiding place near a small window, through which he could see the performances of old Seth Tanner, which was that frantic gentleman's name. Across the street came Skinny Brice and Tady Finton, whistling and wholly unconscious of approaching doom.

Seeing the enraged Tanner charging them with horrid curses, they stopped not to argue the matter or to inquire his intentions. His warlike demonstrations were enough. They fled, he followed. They crawled under the fence, he jumped over. They dived under a big beach wagon standing in front of the blacksmith's shop, he was compelled to go around, and fell over the pole, which, while it added fresh fuel to his wrath and great fluency to his vocal attainments, gave them a few rods' start, and though he rose and followed, he never had a ghost of a show of overtaking them.

As he passed from sight and his frantic invectives died away in the distance, Plupy came forth from his hiding place, where he had been rolling in convulsions of sinful mirth, hunted up his withe, got a fresh supply of green apples and watched for new game.

An occasional shot at a dog or cat kept time from dragging too heavily, but was barren of result. At last, however, a glorious opportunity came. Old Si Smith's big white dog came trotting along the road. Now old Shep was a rather savage old brute and the boys gave him a wide berth. But this opportunity was too good to be lost, and Plupy, hastily impaling the hardest and best apple he had, took aim and let drive with all his strength, intending to give the unconscious animal a most tremendous thump.

Alas, the furious energy of the stroke dislodged the apple a thought too soon, and instead of striking the dog, it flew a bit high and went through the window of the blacksmith shop like a bullet from a gun, causing in the breast of the honest and well-meaning blacksmith sentiments of keen astonishment, profound sorrow and righteous indignation.

In a trice he had doffed his leather apron, rolled down his sleeves and sallied from his shop to lodge a complaint at the door of Plupy's house, to which citadel that prudent youth promptly retired at the first jingle of flying glass.

"Naou, Mrs. Shute," said this much-tried individual, "I don't think it jest right. This tarnal son of yours got me this mawnin' to fix him a stick for firin' apples 'n what duz he dew but go a firin' rocks right threw my winder. Naou I've got to jes go'n hire sum'un to mend that winder, 'n pay 'em fifteen cents jest likes not. Naou whaddier think on't?"

"Well, Mr. Dyer," said that matron kindly, "I am quite sure Harry did not intend to break your window, and especially after your kindness to him. I think if he was intending to break a window he would not do it quite so near home," she added. "Harry," she called, "come down here."

Plupy reappeared, having been leaning over the banisters listening with all his ears, and now began to justify his mother's confidence by vociferous explanation.

"Honest now, mother, I didn't mean to plug his window. I was jest letting ding at old Si Smith's dog, 'n it slipped, 'n went through Sam's window."

"Mr. Dyer," she corrected quietly.

"Yes 'um, Mister Dyer," hastily assented Plupy.

"W-a-a-a-l," said the mollified blacksmith, "I spusso. I seen that air cussed dog 'n I wuz agoin' to fire a rock at him myself. In course ye'll pay fer my winder, Mrs. Shute, slongs Harry broke it?"

"Oh, yes, of course, Mr. Dyer, how much will it be?"

"W-a-a-a-l," he drawled, making a mental calculation, "seems sough a feller had orter git 'bout twenty-five cents for getting mos' scart to death 'n hevin' a winder broke."

"That is certainly reasonable, Mr. Dyer," said Plupy's mother, handing him a ten- and fifteen-cent script. "It will of course, Harry, come out of your cornet money, and will, I hope, teach you to be more careful," she continued, whereat Plupy looked very much disgusted, as the accumulation of a fund sufficient to purchase a cornet had been the darling ambition of his young life.

All interest in life had now departed, and he listlessly dragged his shambling length to the front fence and slowly climbed upon the top rail where he sat moodily dangling his legs and musing upon the dreadful accumulation of disappointments and outrages to which he was peculiarly subject. Life was hard indeed. Other fellows have luck, he didn't.

As he sat there in moody silence, Pewt and Potter, returning from their fishing trip, jubilantly hailed him and held up each a string of kivers and small perch with a few undersized pickerel.

"Ya-ah, Plupy," roared Pewt derisively, "thotcher was going with us."

"Huh, couldn't, father made me stay in 'cause I didn't split my kindlins," said Plupy resentfully, glowering at the remembrance of his wrongs.

"That's too bad, Plupy," said Potter sympathetically.

"That so, Plupy, your old man's meaner'n tripe. I heard old man Collins say he cheated him and he had orter be hung."

Now Plupy, however indignant he might feel with his father in his own small bosom, did not allow his good name to be traduced, and he promptly called Pewt a liar, who instantly retorted that Plupy was another, and that his father was a bigger one. Plupy, although he might have passed over the personal application of the term, could not forgive it as applied to his father and flopped from his perch and assumed a ludicrous posture of offense, with one arm extended and one crossed over his chin, the middle joint of his third and little finger projecting beyond the others, which was supposed to give a cutting edge to his fists that nothing but brass knuckles could exceed.

Pewt promptly dropped his pole and string of fish and threw himself into an attitude of defense, doubling his fists more tightly than Plupy, but projecting the middle joint of the second finger, a proceeding which was popularly supposed to be very conducive to black eyes.

At these warlike demonstrations, several stable loafers and hostlers, who had been dozing in the sun in front of the stables, woke up and urged the boys, who were warily circling round each other, to sail in. As this encouragement did not precipitate matters, someone pushed Plupy violently into Pewt, who received him with vigorous punches. The fight was on. Plupy swung his arms like the spokes of a wheel. Pewt delivered sidewinders, rib-roasters and semi-circular digs. They clinched, writhed, twisted and fell, Pewt uppermost.

Plupy's legs wildly waved in the air vainly seeking purchase, then doubled under him. His stomach rose like a bow, there was a violent twist and Pewt was turned. But he squirmed out and they half rose, punching, pulling hair and twisting like eels, down they rolled off the sidewalk, Pewt again underneath, but they were pulled apart by more scientific bystanders and told to stand up like men.

At it they went, each one apparently trying to put in as many blows in a given time as he could, a clinch, a twist, and a fall. Again they grovel in the dust. Plupy tries to pull out every spear of Pewt's stringy and copious thatch; Pewt tries to obliterate all signs of humanity from Plupy's freckled countenance.

It looked as if both would be successful when suddenly there was an abrupt change of sentiment in the crowd, and old Mike Hartnett, who had been the most active in egging on hostilities, tore them apart with stern reproaches, just as Plupy's mother appeared, called from the duty of putting to sleep a wakeful baby by Keene's staccato shrieks of "Harry's a fightin', Harry's a fightin'," and took forcible possession of the most demoralized youth imaginable. His jacket was covered with dust and dragged over his head, one leg of his trousers pulled to his knee, his hair standing every way, his mouth swollen and his face scratched.

Pewt was also in the most astonishing condition possible, and looked as if he had been shaken up in a corncracker.

Plupy was hurried to the house by his horrified mother, notwithstanding his protestations and excuses, and sent to his room to spend the rest of the day in solitary confinement. He felt that this was unjust, but he recked not of injustice. He had played the man, and the deep and unspoken satisfaction that comes of a duty well done swelled up in his breast and filled him with a sweet elation.

But he soon began to be uneasy. He was imprisoned. The outside world never before seemed so beautiful, so alluring. It seemed as if he must get out. He would. He listened. Everything was quiet about the house. Keene and Cele had gone over to Lucy Watson's, Georgie was in Aunt Clark's side of the house, Frankie and Annie were taking their afternoon naps, and the soft creak of his mother's rocking-chair as she sung them to sleep was the only sound in the house.

Outside the rhythmic tink, tink of the blacksmith's hammer was heard. He rose and peered out of the window. Nobody in sight. If he could only get down the back way, but his mother would see him. The front stairway led by his aunt's room. If he only had a rope he could let himself out of the window like Tom Bailey in the "Story of a Bad Boy." There used to be a clothesline in the back closet. He tiptoed into the entry and back to the closet. Bully, it was there, two long pieces. He would take them both to be sure. Back he went to the chamber and stealthily let them out of the window. Either was long enough.

Hastily but quietly he tied one end of a rope to the bed post and tried it. It held. Then he carefully knotted the other end round his waist. He was not going to run the risk of warming his hands the way Tom Bailey did. He knew better than that. You bet he did.

Then he stuck his head out of the window. Nobody in sight. He drew it in and then slowly and carefully a long thin leg came over the window sill, then another, followed by a lanky body. There was a pause and then he cautiously grabbed the rope and let himself drop. There was a wild clutch for the window, a yell, and a tremendous splash, and the open rain-water hogshead, filled to the brim with tepid water, received him and charitably hid him from sight.

He had tied the wrong rope round his waist.

And when the bewildered mother came running to the door with her rudely awakened and blinking baby in her arms, she beheld her graceless and dripping son climbing out of the rain barrel, his hair plastered down on his scratched face, and his dripping garments clinging close to his skinny limbs and emphasizing the ludicrous lines of his figure.

Just what kind of settlement poor Plupy had with his father on his return from Boston that night is known only to Plupy and his father.

Before pitying the young man too much it would be well to remember that the elder Shute was more than locally famous for a keen sense of humor, and in his boyhood had done perhaps more than his fair share in turning the village of Exeter upside down. So it is fair to suppose that a graphic description of old Seth Tanner profanely chasing two wholly innocent but active boys, and the further portrayal of his son climbing dripping from the rain-water barrel would tend to put him in so cheerful a humor as practically to disarm hostility.

Whatever he thought or did in the matter, he made no objection when Plupy's mother, according to her custom in such cases, prepared a most appetizing meal and carried it up to the imprisoned youth.

Indeed, Plupy's father, as he sat that evening under the apple-tree smoking, laughed heartily now and then and indulged in sinful delight in reminiscences of his boyhood, which showed him to be in the most cheerful humor.

It was open to suspicion whether or not he was delighted beyond measure at the good account his son had rendered of himself in his fight with Pewt, as he was heard to remark that if he would only lick that Watson boy too he would be satisfied.

MARY E. WILKINS

(1862–1930)

Go far enough back in the ancestry of Mary E. Wilkins and you come upon a judge in the witchcraft trials, and her father was the first of the family to leave Salem. He was an architect, afterwards at intervals a small shopkeeper, sensitive and somewhat restless, who married one of the descendants of an old Massachusetts family. At Randolph, not far from Boston, their daughter Mary Eleanor was born, in the days of the Civil War.

Her health was delicate and her nervous system delicately organized; though they sent her to boarding-school she grew too ill to stay. Later she attended a day school, but such of her education as really mattered she gave herself at home, being a devoted and discriminating reader. Meanwhile the family had moved to Brattleboro, and Nature herself had taken a hand in the process.

Nature is likely to take a traveller somewhat by surprise in this neighborhood. If he has been going north for the first time by railroad along the Connecticut Valley, he may have had enough of its rich serenity to take his mind and eyes off the landscape. Then he hears a brakeman's warning cry, lifts his gaze, and beholds a wild loveliness so complete and unsuspected that to the end of his days he will recall the town. It has given him a dramatic introduction to Vermont. It seems to have helped to introduce Mary Wilkins to herself, for she speaks of the country thereabouts as if it acted upon her then as an incentive to create something worth creating. This at first was poetry, which she sent to various magazines for children, among them *St. Nicholas.* Then her only sister died, then, soon, her mother; then, not long after, her father, and she was quite alone and must work to live. She returned to her birthplace and went to work; also she wrote, but because poetry brought in so little, she now wrote stories. "Two Old Lovers" was taken by *Harper's Bazar,* and in 1884 *Harper's Magazine* printed "A Humble Romance." It rang through the reading public like the stroke of a bell, clear, pure and true. The bell was to strike often in the next few years; other stories came rapidly into print, and an audience was waiting for her first volume under the Harper imprint, "A Humble Romance and other Stories" (1887), and the second, "A New England Nun" (1891). Her vogue was even greater in England, and there it was due not to the eccentricity of the characters she favored, which had much to do with her reputation in this country, but to her recognition as a literary artist unmatched in her own *genre.* It was not to be expected that one who expressed herself so completely in the special technique of the short story should be equally successful under the different conditions of the novel, and some of hers are elongated short stories. Even her stories lose whenever they leave her special place and time—the New England village at its period of depletion from the emigration of native youth, and before foreigners came to raise families in their place. But time will take care of those: some of her stories will last as long as anything lasts in our literature.

This story, besides involving a first-class murder, centers upon a village agnostic, one of the old who by sheer spiritual vigor kept New England young when youth departed. No native son needs a description of the plant that gives its title to the tale. At the height of summer, life-everlasting lies along pasture slopes and in sunny hollows like patches of snow. Looking closely, the blossoms have a tidy look of artifice, clusters of miniature roses with petals of straw. They seem to demand that something be done with them: children used to twine the dry stalks into winter wreaths for the burying-ground, and women with a taste for home-doctoring clipped the blooms and filled little pillows; I have seen sweet-fern mingled with them. The pungent, spicy smell was supposed to have some healing power, but I never knew what it was supposed to heal.

LIFE-EVERLASTIN'

By Mary E. Wilkins

"Ain't that your sister goin' 'long the other side of the street, Mis' Ansel?"

Mrs. Ansel peered, scowling—the sun was in her face. "Yes, that's her."

"She's got a basket. I guess she's been somewheres."

"She's been somewheres after life-everlastin' blossoms. They keep forever, you know. She's goin' to make a pillow for old Oliver Weed's asthma; he's real bad off."

"So I've heard. I declare it makes me all out of patience, folks that have got as much money as them Weeds have, not havin' a doctor an' havin' something done. I don't believe his wife amounts to much in sickness either."

"I guess she don't either. I could tell a few things if it wa'n't for talkin' against my neighbors. I tell Luella if she's mind to be such a fool as to slave for folks that's got plenty to do for themselves with, she can. I want to know, now, Mis' Slate, if you think this bonnet is big enough for me. Does it set fur enough onto my head?"

"It sets jest as fur on as the fashion, Mis' Ansel, an' a good deal further on than some. I wish you could see some of 'em."

"Well, I s'pose this ain't a circumstance to some, but it looks dreadful odd to me."

"Of course it looks a little odd at first, you've wore your

293

bonnets so much further forward. You might twist up your hair a little higher if you was a mind to; that would tip it forward a little; but it ain't a mite too fur back for the fashion."

"Land! I can't do my hair any different from what I always do it, bonnet or no bonnet."

"You might friz your hair a little more in front; the hair ought to be real fluffy an' careless with this kind of a bonnet. Let me fix it a little."

Mrs. Ansel stood still before the glass while Mrs. Slate fixed her hair. She smiled a faint, foolish smile, and her homely face had the same expression as a pretty one on seeing itself in a new bonnet. Mrs. Ansel had never known that her face was homely. She was always pleased and satisfied with anything that was her own, and possession was to her the law of beauty.

Mrs. Slate, the milliner, was shorter than she. She stretched up, cocked her head, and twisted her mouth to one side with a superior air while she arranged her customer's thin front locks. Finally they lay tossed loosely over her flat, shiny forehead. "There," said the milliner; "that looks a good deal better. You see what you think."

Mrs. Ansel surveyed herself in the glass; her smile deepened. "Yes, it does look better, I guess."

"It's what I call a real stylish bonnet. You wouldn't be ashamed to wear it to meetin' anywhere, I don't care if it was in Boston or New York. I tell you what 'tis, Mis' Ansel, your sister would look nice in this kind of a bonnet." The milliner's prominent nose sloped her profile out sharply in the centre, like the beak of a bird; her little hands were skinny as claws, and restless; she always smiled, and her voice was subdued.

Mrs. Ansel still looked fondly at herself, but her tone changed; she sighed. "Yes, Luella would look good in it," said she. "I don't know as it would be quite so becomin' to her as it is to me; she never looked so well with anything that set back; but I guess she'd look pretty good in it. But I don't know when Luella's had a new bonnet, Mis' Slate. Of course she don't need any, not goin' to meetin' or anything."

"She don't ever go to meetin', does she?"

"No; she ain't been for twenty-five years. I feel bad 'nough about it. It seems to me sometimes if Luella would jest have a pretty new bonnet, an' go to meetin' Sabbath-days like other folks, I wouldn't ask for anything else."

"It must be a dreadful trial to you, Mis' Ansel."

"You don't know anything about it, Mis' Slate. You think there's bows enough on it, don't you?"

"Oh, plenty. I was speakin' to Jennie the other day about your sister—"

"An' the strings ain't too long?"

"Not a mite. You ain't never had a bonnet that become you any better than this does, Mis' Ansel. To tell the truth, I think you look a little better in it than you did in your summer one."

Mrs. Ansel began taking off the new bonnet, untying the crisp ribbon strings tenderly. "Well, I don't know but it's all right," said she.

"I'll get some paper an' do it up," said the milliner. "I ain't afraid but what you'll like it when you get used to it. You've always got to get used to anything new."

When Mrs. Ansel had gone down the street, delicately holding the new bonnet in its soft tissue wrapper, the milliner went into her little back room. There was one window in the room, and a grape-vine hung over it. A girl with fair hair and a delicately severe profile sat sewing by the window, with the grape-vine for a background.

"Well, I'm thankful that woman has gone," said the milliner. "I never saw such a fuss."

The girl said nothing. She nodded a little coldly, that was all.

"Are you puttin' in that linin' full enough?"

"It's all she brought."

"Oh, well, you can't do any better, then, of course. P'rhaps I hadn't ought to speak so about Mis' Ansel; she's a real nice woman; all is, she's kind of tryin' sometimes when anybody feels nervous. It's as hard work to get a bonnet onto her head that suits her as it would be if she was a queen; but after she once gets it she's settled on it, that's one comfort. She's a real nice woman, and I shouldn't want you to repeat what I said, Clara."

"I sha'n't say anything." There was a kind of mild hauteur about the girl that made the milliner color and twitch embarrassingly. She took a bonnet off the table and fell to work; but soon someone entered the shop, and she arose again.

Presently she was whispering over the counter to the customer that she had Clara Vinton working for her now;

that she was a nice girl, but she'd acted dreadful kind of stiff somehow ever since the minister had been going with her, and she wasn't much company for her; but she didn't want her to say anything about it, for she was a real nice girl.

"I see Mis' Ansel goin' home with her new bonnet," remarked the customer.

"Yes; she jest went out with it."

When she reached home she found her sister, Luella Norcross, sitting on the door-step.

Luella followed her sister into the house. It was quite a smart house. Mrs. Ansel loved to furbish it, and she had a little income of her own. There were no dull colors anywhere; the walls gleamed with gold paper, and the carpets were brilliant.

Luella sat in the sitting-room and waited, while her sister went for a sheet which she had promised her. The mantel-shelf was marble, and there were some tall gilded vases on it. The stove shone like a mirror; there was a bright rug before it, and over on the table stood a lamp, whose shade was decorated with roses.

Luella plunged her hand down into the mass of everlasting flowers in her basket; the soft, healing fragrance came up in her face. "They're packed pretty solid," she muttered. "I guess there's enough."

When Mrs. Ansel returned with the sheet she was frowning. "There," said she, "I can't hunt no more tonight. I've had every identical thing out of that red chist, an' that's all I can seem to see. I don't know whether there's any more or not; if there is, you'll have to wait till I ain't jest home from down street, and can hunt better'n I can to-night."

Luella unfolded the sheet and examined it. "Oh, well, this is pretty good; it'll make three, I guess. I'll wait, and maybe you'll come across the others some time."

"You'll have to wait if you have 'em. Did you see the lamp?"

"Well, no, I didn't notice it, as I know of. That it?"

"You ain't been sittin' right here an' never seen that new lamp?"

"I guess I must have been lookin' at somethin' else."

"I never see such a woman! Anything like that sittin' right there before your face an' eyes, an' you never pay attention to it! I s'pose if I had Bunker Hill Monument posted up here in the middle of the sittin'-room, you'd set right down under it an' think, an' never notice there was anything uncommon."

"It's a pretty lamp—ain't it?"

"It's real handsome."

Luella arose and gathered her shawl about her; she had laid the folded sheet over the top of her basket.

"Wait a minute," said Mrs. Ansel; "you ain't seen my new bonnet."

Luella rested her basket on the chair, and stood patiently while her sister took the bonnet out of the wrapper and adjusted it before the looking-glass.

"There!" said she, turning around, "what do you think of it?"

"I should think it was real pretty."

"You don't think it sets too far back, do you?"

"I shouldn't think it did."

"Shouldn't you rather have this changeable ribbon than plain?"

"Seems to me I should." Luella's voice had unmistakably an abstracted drawl.

Her sister turned on her. "You don't act no more as if you cared anything about my new bonnet than you would if I was the pump with a new tin dipper on the top of it," said she. "If I was you I'd act a little more like other folks, or I'd give up. It's bad enough for you to go 'round lookin' like a scarecrow yourself; you might take a little interest in what your own sister has to wear."

Luella said nothing; she gathered up her basket of everlasting blossoms again.

Her sister paused and eyed her fiercely for a second; then she continued: "For my part, I'm ashamed," said she— "mortified to death. It was only this afternoon that I heard somebody speakin' about it. Here you've been wearin' that old black bonnet, that you had when father died, all these years, an' never goin' to meetin'. If you'd only have a decent new bonnet—I don't know as you'd want one that sets quite so far back as this one—an' go to meetin' like other folks, there'd be some sense in it."

Luella, her basket on her arm, started for the door. Although her shoulders were round, she carried her handsome head in a stately fashion. "We've talked this over times enough," said she.

"Here you are roamin' the woods and pastures Sabbath-days in that old bonnet, an' jest as likely as not to meet all the folks goin' to meetin'. What do you s'pose I care about havin' a new bonnet if I meet you gettin' along in that old thing—my own sister?"

Luella marched out of the house. When she was nearly out of the yard her sister ran to the door and called after her.

"Luella," said she.

The stately figure paused, but did not turn around. "What is it?"

"Look here a minute," said Mrs. Ansel, mysteriously; "I want to tell you something."

Luella stepped back, her sister bent forward—she still had on the new bonnet— "I went into Mis' Plum's on my way down street," said she, "an' she said the minister wanted to marry the Vinton girl, but she won't have him, 'cause there ain't no parsonage, an' she don't think there's enough to live on. Mis' Plum says she thinks she shows her sense; he don't have but four hundred a year, an' there'd be a lot of children, the way there always is in poor ministers' families, an' nothin' to keep 'em on. Mis' Plum says she heard he applied to the church to see if they wouldn't give him a parsonage; he didn't know but they'd hire that house of yours that's next to the meetin'-house; but they wouldn't; they say they can't afford it."

"I shouldn't think four hundred dollars was much if preachin' was worth anything," remarked Luella.

"Oh, well, it does very well for you to talk when you don't give anything for preachin'."

Luella again went out of the yard. She was in the street when her sister called her again.

"Look 'round here a minute."

Luella looked.

"Do you think it sets too far back?"

"No, I don't think it does," Luella answered, loudly, then she kept on down the road. She had not far to go. The house where she lived stood at the turn of the road, on a gentle rise of ground; next to it was the large unoccupied cottage which she owned; next to that was the church. Luella lived in the old Norcross homestead; her grandfather had built it. It was one of those old buildings which aped the New England mansion-houses without once approaching their solid state. It settled unevenly down into its place. Its sparse front yard was full of evergreens, lilac bushes, and phlox; its windows, gleaming with green lights, were awry, and all its white clapboards were out of plumb.

Luella went around to the side door; the front one was never used—indeed, it was swollen and would not open —and the front walk was green. The side door opened into a little square entry. On one side was the sitting-room, on the other the kitchen. Luella went into the kitchen, and an old woman rose up from a chair by the stove. She was small as a child, but her muscles were large, her flaxen hair was braided lightly, her round blue eyes were filmy, and she grinned constantly without speaking.

"Got the cleanin' done, 'Liza?" asked Luella. The old woman nodded, and her grin widened. She was called foolish; her humble capacities could not diffuse themselves but were strong in only one direction; she could wash and scrub, and in that she took delight. Luella harbored her, fed and clothed her, and let her practise her one little note of work.

After Luella had taken off her bonnet and shawl, she went to work preparing supper. The old woman was not smart enough to do that. She sat watching her. When Luella set the tea-pot on the stove and cut the bread, she fairly crowed like a baby.

"Maria offered me a piece of her new apple-pie an' a piece of sage-cheese," remarked Luella, "but I wouldn't take it. If I'm a mind to stint myself and pay up Joe Perry's rent it's nobody's business, but I ain't goin' to be mean enough to live on other folks to do it."

The old woman grinned as she ate. Luella had fallen into the habit of talking quite confidentially to her, unreciprocative as she was.

After supper Luella put away the tea-things—that was too fine work for the old woman—then she lighted her sitting-room lamp, and sat down there to make the case for the life-everlasting pillow. The old woman crept in after her, and sat by the stove in a little chair, holding her sodden hands in her lap.

"I hope to goodness this pillow will help him some," said Luella. "They're real good for asthma. Mother used to use 'em." She sewed with strong jerks. The old man for whom she was making the pillow was rich in the village sense, and miserly. Ill as he sometimes was, he and his wife would not call in a doctor on account of the expense; they scarcely kept warm and fed themselves. Public opinion was strong against them; but Luella viewed it all with a broad charity which was quite past the daily horizon of the village people. "I don't care if they are rich an' able to buy things themselves, we hadn't ought to let 'em suffer," she argued. "Mebbe they can't help bein' close any more'n we can help somethin' we've got. It's a failin', and folks ought to help folks with failin's, I don't care what they are." So Luella Norcross made broth and gruel, and carried them in to old Oliver Weed, and even gave him some of her dry cedar-wood; and people said she was as foolish as old Eliza. All the burly whining tramps and beseeching pedlars of unsalable wares, who came to the village, flocked to her door, sure of a welcome.

On a summer's day the tramps sat on her door-step and ate their free lunches, in winter they ate them comfortably by the kitchen fire. Many a time her barn and warm haymow harbored them over a cold stormy night.

"Might jest as well stick out a sign, 'Tramps' Tavern,' on the barn, an' done with it," Mrs. Ansel said. "If you don't get set on fire some night by them miserable sneakin' tramps, I miss my guess."

But she never did, and the tramp slouched peaceably out of her yard, late in the frosty morning, after she had given him a good breakfast in the warm kitchen.

There was an old pedlar of essences who came regularly, and she always bought of him, although his essences were poor, and her cake scantily flavored in consequence. Him she often lodged in her nice spare chamber, although she distrusted his cleanliness, and she and old Eliza had much scrubbing to do thereafter.

Luella even traded faithfully with a sly-eyed Italian

woman, who went about, bent to one side by a great basket of vases and plaster images. "You'd ought to be ashamed of yourself encouragin' such folks," Mrs. Ansel remonstrated, "she's jest as miserable an' low as she can be."

"I don't care how low she is," said Luella. "She's keepin' one commandment sellin' plaster images to get her livin', an' I'm a-goin' to help her."

And Luella crowded the little plaster flower girls and fruit boys together on the sitting-room shelf, to make room for the new little shepherdess.

This very day she had been visited by an old broken-down minister, who often stood at her door, tall and tremulous in his shiny black broadcloth, with a heavy bag of undesirable books. There were some hanging-shelves in Luella's sitting-room which were filled with these books, but to-day she had bought another.

"There ain't room on the shelves for another one, but I s'pose I can stow it away somewhere," she told Eliza, after he had gone. "I've give away all I can seem to. The book ain't very interestin'."

Luella usually lodged the book agent over night, when he came to the village, although he also had his failings. Many a night she was awakened by the creaking of the cellar-stairs, when the old minister crept down stealthily, a lamp balanced unsteadily in his shaking hand, to the cider-barrel. She would listen anxiously until she heard him return to his room, then get up and look about and sniff for fire.

There was not a woman in the village who had so many

blessings, worth whatever they might be, offered to her. If she was not in full orthodox flavor among the respectable part of the town, her fame was bright among the poor and maybe lawless element, whom she befriended. They showed it by their shuffling footprints thick in her yard, and the frequency of their petitions at her door. It was the only way that they could show it. The poor can show their love and gratitude only by the continual outreaching of their hands.

This evening, while Luella sewed on her life-everlasting pillow, and the old woman sat grinning in the corner, there was a step in the yard. Luella laid down her work, and looked at Eliza, and listened. The step came steadily up the drive; the shoes squeaked. Luella took up her work again.

"I know who 'tis," said she. "It's the book man; his shoes squeak just that way, an' I told him he'd better come back here to-night an' stay over. It saves him payin' for lodgin'."

There came a sharp knock on the side door.

"You go let him in, 'Liza," said Luella.

The old woman patted out of the room. Presently she looked in again, and her grin was a broad laugh. "It's the minister," she chuckled.

Luella rose and went herself. There in the entry stood a young man, short and square-shouldered, with a pleasant boyish face. He looked bravely at Luella, and tried to speak with suave fluency, but his big hands twitched at the ends of his short coat sleeves.

"Good-evening, Miss Norcross, good-evening," said he.

"Oh, it's you, Mr. Sands!" said Luella. "Good-evenin'. Walk in an' be seated."

Luella herself was a little stiff. She pushed forward the big black-covered rocking-chair for the minister, then she sat down herself, and took up her sewing.

"It is a charming evening," remarked the minister.

"I thought it seemed real pleasant when I looked out after supper," said Luella.

She and the minister spoke about the conditions of several of the parish invalids, they spoke about a fire and a funeral which had taken place that week, and all the time there was a constraint in their manners. Finally there was a pause; then the minister burst out. A blush flamed out to the roots of his curly hair. He tried to make his voice casual, but it slipped into his benediction cadences.

"I don't see you at church very often, Miss Norcross," said he.

"You don't see me at all," returned Luella.

The minister tried to smile. "Well, maybe that is a little nearer the truth, Miss Norcross."

Luella sewed a few stitches on her life-everlasting pillow; then she laid it down in her lap, straightened herself, and looked at the minister. Her deep-set blue eyes seemed to see every atom of him; her noble forehead even, from which the gray hair was pulled well back, and which was scarcely lined, seemed to front him with a kind of visual power of its own.

"I may just as well tell you the truth, Mr. Sands," said she, "an' we may just as well come to the point at once.

I know what you've come for; my sister told me you was comin' to see about my not goin' to meetin'. Well, I'll tell you once for all, I'm just as much obliged to you, but it won't do any good. I've made up my mind I ain't goin' to meetin', an' I've got good reasons."

"Would you mind giving them, Miss Norcross?"

"I ain't goin' to argue."

"But just giving me a few of your reasons wouldn't be arguing." The young man had now acquired the tone which he wished. He smiled on Luella with an innocent patronage and crossed his legs. Luella thought he looked very young.

"The fact is," said she, "I'm not a believer, an' I won't be a hypocrite. That's all there is about it."

The minister looked at her. It was the first time he had encountered an outspoken doubter, and it was for a minute to him as if he faced one of the veritable mediaeval dragons of the church. This simple and untutored village agnostic filled him with amazement and terror. When he spoke it was not to take up the argument for the doctrine, but to turn its gold side, as it were, towards his opponent, in order to persuade belief. "Your soul's salvation—do you never think of that?" he queried, solemnly. "You know heaven and your soul's salvation depend upon it."

"I ain't never worried much about my soul's salvation," said Luella. "I've had too many other souls to think about. An' it seems to me I'd be dreadful piggish to make goin' to heaven any reason for believin' a thing that ain't reasonable."

The minister made a rally; he remembered one of the

things he had planned to say. "But you've read the New Testament, Miss Norcross," said he, "and you must admit that 'never man spake like this man.' When you read the words of Christ you must see that there was never any man like Him."

"I know there wa'n't," said Luella, "that's jest the reason why the whole story don't seem sensible."

The minister gave a kind of gasp. "But you believe in God, don't you, Miss Norcross?" said he.

"I ain't a fool," replied Luella. She arose with a decided air. "Do you like apples, Mr. Sands?" said she.

The minister gasped again, and assented.

"I've got some real nice sweet ones and some Porters," said Luella, in a cheerful tone, "an' I'm goin' to get you a plate of 'em, Mr. Sands."

Luella went out and got the plate of apples, and the minister began eating them. He felt uneasily that it was his duty to reopen the argument. "If you believe in God—" he began.

But Luella shook her head at him as if she were his mother. "I'd rather not argue any more," said she. "Try that big Porter; I guess it's meller." And the minister ate his apples with enjoyment. Luella filled his pockets with some when he went home. "He seems like a real good young man," she said to old Eliza after the minister had gone; "an' that Vinton girl would make him jest the kind of a wife he'd ought to have. She's real up an' comin', an' she'd prop him up firm on his feet. I s'pose if I let him have that house he'd be tickled 'most to death. I'd kind of 'lotted on the rent of it, but I s'pose I could get along."

The old woman grinned feebly. She had been asleep in her corner, and her blue eyes looked dimmer than ever. She comprehended not a word; but that did not matter to Luella, who had fallen into the habit of utilizing her as a sort of spiritual lay-figure upon which to drape her own ideas.

The next morning, about nine o'clock, she carried the pillow, which she had finished and stuffed with the life-everlasting blossoms, to old Oliver Weed's. The house stood in a wide field, and there were no other houses very near. The grass was wet with dew, and all the field was sweet in the morning freshness. Luella, carrying her life-everlasting pillow before her, went over the fragrant path to the back door. She noticed as she went that the great barn doors were closed.

"Queer the barn ain't open," she thought to herself. "I wonder what John Gleason's about, late as this is in the mornin'?"

John Gleason was old Oliver Weed's hired man. He had been a tramp. Luella herself had fed him, and let him sleep off a drunken debauch in her barn once. People had wondered at Oliver Weed's hiring him, but he had to pay him much less than the regular price for farm hands.

Luella heard the cows low in the barn as she opened the kitchen door. "Where—did all that—blood come from?" said she.

She began to breathe in quick gasps; she stood clutching her pillow, and looking. Then she called: "Mr. Weed! Mr. Weed! Where be you? Mis' Weed! Is anything the matter? Mis' Weed!" The silence seemed to beat against her ears. She went across the kitchen to the bedroom. Here and there she held back her dress. She reached the bedroom door, and looked in.

Luella pressed back across the kitchen into the yard. She went out into the road, and turned towards the village. She still carried the life-everlasting pillow, but she carried it as if her arms and that were all stone. She met a woman whom she knew, and the woman spoke; but Luella did not notice her; she kept on. The woman stopped and looked after her.

Luella went to the house where the sheriff lived, and knocked. The sheriff himself opened the door. He was a large, pleasant man. He began saying something facetious about her being out calling early, but Luella stopped him.

"You'd—better go up to the—Weed house," said she, in a dry voice. "There's some—trouble."

The sheriff started. "Why, what do you mean, Luella?"

"The old man an' his wife are—both killed. I went in there to carry this, an'—I saw them."

"My God!" said the sheriff. He caught up his hat, and started on a run to the barn for his horse.

The sheriff's wife and daughter pressed forward and plied Luella with horrified questions; they urged her to come in and rest, she looked so pale; but she said little, and turned towards home. Flying teams passed her on the road; men rushed up behind her and questioned her. When she reached the Weed house the field seemed black with people. When she got to her own house she went into the sitting-room and sat down. She felt faint. She did not think of lying down; she never did in the daytime. She leaned her head back in her chair and turned her face towards the yard. Everything out there, the trees, the grass, the crowding ranks of daisies, the next house, looked strange, as if another light than that of the sun was on them. But she somehow noticed even then how a blind on the second floor of the house was shut that had been open. "I wonder how that come about?" she muttered, feebly.

Pretty soon her sister, Mrs. Ansel, came hurrying in. She was wringing her hands. "Oh, ain't it awful? ain't it awful!" she cried. "Good land, Luella, how you look! You'll faint away. I'm going to mix you up some peppermint before I do another thing."

Mrs. Ansel made a cup of hot peppermint tea for her, and she drank it.

"Now tell me all about it," said Mrs. Ansel. "What did you see first? What was you goin' in there for?"

"To carry the pillow," said Luella, pointing to it. "I can't talk about it, Maria."

Mrs. Ansel went over to the lounge and took up the pillow. "Mercy sakes! what's that on it?" she cried, in horror.

"I —s'pose I—hit it against the wall somehow," replied Luella. "I can't talk about it, Maria."

Mrs. Ansel could not learn much from her sister. Presently she left, and lingered slowly past the Weed house, to which her curiosity attracted her, but which her terror and horror would not let her approach closely.

The peppermint revived Luella a little. After a while she got up and put on the potatoes for dinner. Old Eliza was scrubbing the floor. When dinner was ready she ate all the potatoes, and Luella sat back and looked at her,

All the afternoon people kept coming to the house and questioning her, and exclaiming with horror. It seemed to Luella that her own horror was beyond exclamations. There was no doubt in the public mind that the murderer was the hired man, John Gleason. He was nowhere to be found; the constables and detectives were searching fiercely for him.

That night when Luella went to bed she stood at her chamber window a minute, looking out. It was bright moonlight. Her window faced the unoccupied house, and she noticed again how the blind was shut.

"It's queer," she thought, "for that blind wouldn't stay shut; the fastenin' wa'n't good." As she looked, the blind swung slowly open. "The wind is jest swingin' it back and forth," she thought. Then she saw distinctly the chamber window open, a dark arm thrust out, and the blind closed again.

"*He's in there*," said Luella. She had put out her lamp. She went down-stairs in the dark, and made sure that all the doors and windows were securely fastened. She even put chairs and tables against them. Then she went back to her chamber, dressed herself, and watched the next house. She did not stir until morning. The next day there was a cold rain. The search for John Gleason continued, the whole village was out, and strange officials were driving through the streets. Everybody thought that the murderer had escaped to Canada, taking with him the money which he had stolen from the poor old man's strong-box under his bed.

All the day long Luella watched the next house through the gray drive of the rain. About sunset she packed a basket with food, stole across to the house, and set it in the corner of the door. She got back before a soul passed on the road. She had set Eliza at a task away from the windows.

The moon rose early. After supper Luella sat again in her chamber without any lamp and watched. About nine o'clock she saw the door of the next house swing open a little, and the basket was drawn in.

"*He's in there*," said Luella. She went down and fastened up the house as she had done the night before. Old Eliza went peacefully to bed, and she watched again. She put a coverlid over her shoulders, and sat, all huddled up, peering out. The rain had stopped; the wall of the next house shone like silver in the moonlight. She watched until the moon went down and until daylight came; then she went to bed, and slept an hour.

After breakfast that morning she set old Eliza at a task, and went up to her chamber again. She sank down on her knees beside the bed. "O God," said she, "have I got to give him up—have I? Have I got to give him up to be hung? What's goin' to become of him then? Where'll he go to when he's been so awful wicked? Oh, what shall I do? Here he is a-takin' my vittles, an' comin' to my house, an' a-trustin' me!" Luella lifted her arms; her face was all distorted. She seemed to see the whole crew of her pitiful dependents crowding around her, and pleading for the poor man who had thrown himself upon her mercy. She saw the old drunken essence man, the miserable china woman, all the wretched and vicious tramps and drunkards whom she had befriended, pressing up to her, and pleading her to keep faith with their poor brother.

The thought that John Gleason had trusted her, had taken that food when he knew that she might in consequence betray him to the gallows, filled her with a pity that was almost tenderness, and appealed strongly to her loyalty and honor.

On the other hand, she remembered what she had seen in the Weed house. The poor old man and woman seemed calling to her for help. She reflected upon what she had heard the day before; that the detectives were after John Gleason for another murder; this was not the first. She called to mind the danger that other helpless people would be in if this murderer were at large. Would not their blood be upon her hands? She called to mind the horrible details of what she had seen, the useless cruelty, and the horror of it.

Once she arose with a jerk, and got her bonnet out of the closet. Then she put it back, and threw herself down by the bed again. "Oh!" she groaned, "I don't know what to do!"

Luella shut herself in her own room nearly all day. She went down and got the meals, then returned. The sodden old woman did not notice anything unusual. At dusk she watched her chance, and carried over more food, and she watched and saw it taken in again.

This night she did not lock the house. All she fastened was old Eliza's bedroom door; that she locked securely, and hid the key. All the other doors and windows were unfastened, and when she went up-stairs she set the side door partly open. She set her lamp on the bureau, and looked at her face in the glass. It was white and drawn, and there was a desperate look in her deep-set eyes. "Mebbe it's the last time I shall ever see my face," said she. "I don't know but I'm awful wicked to give him the chance to do another murder, but I can't give him up. If he comes in an' kills me, I sha'n't have to, an' maybe he'll jest take the money an' go, an' then I sha'n't have to."

Luella had two or three hundred dollars in an old wallet between her feather-bed and the mattress. She took it out and opened it, spreading the bills. Then she laid it on the bureau. She took a gold ring off her finger, and unfastened her ear-rings and laid them beside it, and a silver watch that had belonged to her father. Down-stairs she had arranged the teaspoons and a little silver cream-jug in full sight on the kitchen table.

After the preparations were all made she blew out her lamp, folded back the bed-spread, lay down in her clothes, and pulled it over her smoothly. She folded her hands and lay there. There was not a bolt or a bar between her and the murderer next door. She closed her eyes and lay still. Every now and then she thought she heard him down-stairs; but the night wore on, and he did not come. At daylight Luella rose. She was so numb and weak that she could scarcely stand. She put away the money and the jewelry, then she went down-stairs and kindled the kitchen fire and got breakfast. The silver was on the table just as she had left it, the door half open, and the cold morning wind coming in. Luella gave one great sob when she shut the door. "He must have seen it," she said, "but he wouldn't do nothin' to hurt me, an' I've got to give him up."

She said no more after that; she was quite calm getting breakfast. After the meal was finished and the dishes cleared away she told old Eliza to put on her other dress and her bonnet and shawl. She had made up her mind to take the old creature with her; she was afraid to leave her alone in the house, with the murderer next door to spy out her own departure.

When the two women were ready they went out of the yard, and Luella felt the eyes of John Gleason upon her. They went down the road to the village, old Eliza keeping a little behind her mistress. Luella aimed straight for the sheriff's house. He drove into the yard as she entered; he had been out all night on a false scent. He stopped when he saw Luella, and she came up to him. "John Gleason is in that vacant house of mine," said she. He caught at the reins, but she stopped him. "You've got to wait long enough to give me time to get home, so I sha'n't be right in the midst of it, if you've got any mercy," said she, in a loud, strained voice. Then she turned and ran. She stopped only long enough to tell old Eliza to follow her straight home and go at once into the house. She ran through the village street like a girl. People came to the windows and stared after her. Every minute she fancied she heard wheels behind her; but the sheriff did not come until after she had been in the house fifteen minutes, and old Eliza also was at home.

Luella was crouching at her chamber window, peering

around the curtain, when the sheriff and six men came into the yard and surrounded the next house. She had a wild hope that John Gleason might not be there, that he might have escaped during the night. She watched. The men entered, there was the sound of a scuffle and loud voices, and then she saw John Gleason dragged out.

Presently Luella went down-stairs; she had to keep hold of the banister. Old Eliza was gaping at the kitchen window. "Come away from that window, 'Liza," said Luella, "and wash up the floor right away." Then Luella began cleaning potatoes and beets for dinner.

The next Sunday Luella went to church for the first time in twenty-five years. Old Eliza also went shuffling smilingly up the aisle behind her mistress. Everybody stared. Luella paused at her sister's pew, and her brother-in-law sat a little while looking at her before he arose to let her in.

Mrs. Ansel was quite flushed. She pulled her new bonnet farther on her head; she glanced with agitated hauteur across her sister at old Eliza; then her eyes rolled towards her sister's bonnet.

Presently she touched Luella. "What possessed you to bring her, an' come out lookin' so?" she whispered. "Why didn't you get a new bonnet before you came to meetin'?"

Luella looked at her in a bewildered fashion for a minute, then she set her face towards the pulpit. She listened to the sermon; it had in it some innocent youthful conceits, and also considerable honest belief and ardent feeling. The minister saw Luella, and thought with a flush of pride that his arguments had convinced her. The night before, he had

received a note from her tendering him the use of her
vacant house. After the service he pressed forward to
speak to her. He thanked her for her note, said that he
was glad to see her out to meeting, and shook her hand
vehemently. Then he joined Clara Vinton quite openly
and the two walked on together. There was quite a little
procession passing up the street. The way led between
pleasant cottages with the front yards full of autumn flowers—asters and pansies and prince's feathers. Presently
they passed a wide stretch of pasture-land where life-
everlasting flowers grew. Luella walked with an old
woman with a long, saintly face; old Eliza followed after.

Luella's face looked haggard and composed under her
flimsy black crêpe frillings. She kept her eyes, with a satisfied expression, upon the young minister and the tall girl
who walked beside him with a grave, stately air.

"I hear they're goin' to be married," whispered the old
woman.

"I guess they are," replied Luella.

Just then Clara turned her face, and her fine, stern profile showed.

"She'll make him a good wife, I guess," said the old
woman. She turned to Luella, and her voice had an inde-
scribably shy and caressing tone. "I was real glad to see
you to meetin' to-day," she whispered. "I knew you'd feel
like comin' some time; I always said you would." She
flushed all over her soft old face as she spoke.

Luella also flushed a little, but her voice was resolute.
"I ain't got much to say about it, Mis' Alden," said she,
"but I'm going to say this much—it ain't no more'n right

I should, though I don't believe in a lot of palaver about things like this—I've made up my mind that I'm goin' to believe in Jesus Christ. I ain't never, but I'm goin' to now, for"—Luella's voice turned shrill with passion—"*I don't see any other way out of it for John Gleason!*"

DOROTHY CANFIELD

There is bound to be something thrilling in the spectacle of a mere human being holding the tremendous at bay, a frail hero calling fate to come on. Everyone who lives long enough must hold at bay the fatal enemy old age, but if he lives in the deep country he may have to protect himself also against good-will. If he wants to live by himself he may have a hard time convincing a rural community that he is entitled to do so. A woman in New Hampshire well over the edge of the eighties told me she didn't propose to let anyone come to live with her: "I've lived by myself s'long, I've got used to good company," said she, and went on stubbornly keeping a tidy house. Here, taken from Dorothy Canfield's admirable collection of characters, "Raw Material," is an old man of Vermont who held off a community for the length of a lifetime. I do not wonder that so many Vermonters wrote to her about him from wherever in the wide world they happened now to be; he is—or was—to be found in more than one stronghold of the Green Mountains, a peaceful old warrior, standing the double siege of time and society. When he wins, what Vermonter could forbear to cheer!

I had already chosen for "Golden Tales of Our America" a Vermont story of Dorothy Canfield's about an artist who expressed herself in a bedquilt: could I have had a third chance I would have used it on "Almera Hawley Canfield," also from "Raw Material," the story which the hired man opens by telling

her, at the age of eight, that there's a look about her mouth
"sort o' like Aunt Almera, your grandmother—no—my sakes,
you must be her great-granddaughter!" In the course of
these recollections of eight men and women whose lives were in
some way influenced by this tiny tremendous creature, one notices
more than a look about the mouth in the way of family resemblance. That personality did not wear itself out in one generation.

Vermont, old or contemporaneous, is safe with Dorothy Canfield as interpreter; she has the state in her blood as well as in
her heart, and in her Vermont books it is present like a person.
She has lived in many other parts of the world but for years her
home has been there. The scenes of some of her best and best-
known novels and of that American classic of childhood, "Understood Betsy," are laid there. In 1931 she published a volume of
"Basque Stories," sympathetic studies of an ancient, self-sufficient
and self-respecting race. One of these quotes a saying of Henry
Quatre, who grew up alongside the Basques in the Pyrenees:
"There's no use in trying to do anything with a Basque. Once
they have settled that something ought to be done, they go ahead
and do it." Old Man Warner would have been no stranger to
Henry of Navarre.

OLD MAN WARNER

By Dorothy Canfield

I MUST warn you at the outset that unless you or some of your folks came from Vermont, it is hardly worth your while to read about Old Man Warner. You will not be able to see anything in his story except, as we say in Vermont, a "gape and swallow" about nothing. Well, I don't claim much dramatic action for the story of Old Man Warner, but I am setting it down on the chance that it may fall into the hands of some one brought up on Vermont stories as I was. I know that for him there will be something in Old Man Warner's life, something of Vermont, something we feel and cannot express, as we feel the incommunicable aura of a personality.

The old man has been a weight on the collective mind of our town ever since I was a little girl, and that is a long time ago. He was an old man even then. Year after year, as our Board of Selectmen planned the year's town budget they had this worry about Old Man Warner, and what to do with him. It was not that old Mr. Warner was a dangerous character, or anything but strictly honest and law-abiding. But he had his own way of bothering his fellow citizens.

In his young days he had inherited a farm from his father, back up in Arnold Hollow, where at that time, about 1850, there was a cozy little settlement of five or six farms with big families. He settled there, cultivated the farm, married, and brought up a family of three sons. When the Civil War came, he volunteered together with his oldest boy, and went off to fight in the second year of the war. He came back alone in 1864, the son having fallen in the Battle of the Wilderness. And he went back up to Arnold Hollow to live and there he stayed, although the rest of his world broke up and rearranged itself in a different pattern, mostly centering about the new railroad track in the main valley.

Only the older men returned to the Arnold Hollow settlement to go on cultivating their steep, rocky farms. The younger ones set off for the West, the two remaining Warner boys with the others. Their father and mother stayed, the man hardly ever leaving the farm now even to go to town. His wife said once he seemed to feel as though he never could get caught up on the years he had missed during the war. She said he always had thought the world of his own home.

The boys did pretty well out in Iowa, had the usual ups and downs of pioneer farmers, and by 1898, when their mother died, leaving their father alone at seventy-one, they were men of forty-eight and forty-six, who had comfortable homes to which to invite him to pass his old age.

Everybody in our town began to lay plans about what they would buy at the auction, when Old Man Warner would sell off his things, as the other Arnold Hollow families had. By this time, for one reason or another, the Warners were the only people left up there. The Selectmen planned to cut out the road up into Arnold Hollow, and put the tidy little sum saved from its upkeep into improvements on the main valley thoroughfare. But old Mr. Warner wrote his sons and told the Selectmen that he saw no reason for leaving his home to go and live in a strange place and be a burden to his children, with whom, having seen them at the rarest intervals during the last thirty years, he did not feel very well acquainted. And he always had liked his own home. Why should he leave it? It was pretty late in the day for him to get used to western ways. He'd just be a bother to his boys. He didn't want to be a bother to anybody, and he didn't propose to be!

There were a good many protests all round, but of course the Selectmen had not the faintest authority over him, and as quite probably his sons were at heart relieved, nothing was done. The town very grudgingly voted the money to keep up the Arnold Hollow road, but consoled itself by saying freely that the old cuss never had been so very bright and was worse now, evidently had no idea what he was trying to do, and would soon get tired of living alone and "doing for himself."

That was twenty-two years ago. Selectmen who were then vigorous and middle-aged, grew old, decrepit, died, and were buried. Boys who were learning their letters then, grew up, married, had children, and became Selectmen in their turn. Old Man Warner's sons grew old and died, and the names of most of his grand-children, scattered all over the West, were unknown to us. And still the old man lived alone in his home and "did for himself."

Every spring, when road work began, the Selectmen groaned over having to keep up the Arnold Hollow road, and every autumn they tried their best to persuade the old man to come down to a settlement where he could be taken care of. Our town is very poor, and taxes are a heavy item in our calculations. It is just all we can do to keep our schools and roads going, and we grudge every penny we are forced to spend on tramps, paupers, or the indigent sick. Selectmen in whose régime town expenses were high, are not only never reëlected to town office, but their name is a by-word and a reproach for years afterwards. We elect them, among other things, to see to it that town expenses are not high, and to lay their plans accordingly.

Decades of Selectmen, heavy with this responsibility, tried to lay their plans accordingly in regard to Old Man Warner, and ran their heads into a stone wall. One Board of Selectmen after another knew exactly what would happen; the old dumb-head would get a stroke of paralysis, or palsy, or softening of the brain, or something, and the town Treasury would bleed at every pore for expensive medical service, maybe an operation at a hospital, and after that, somebody paid to take care of him. If they could only ship him off to his family! One of the granddaughters, now a middle-aged woman, kept up a tenuous connection with the old man, and answered, after long intervals, anxious communications from the Selectmen. Or if not that, if only they could get him down out of there in the winter, so they would not be saddled with the perpetual worry about what was happening to him, with the perpetual need to break out the snow in the road and go up there to see that he was all right.

But Old Man Warner was still not bright enough to see any reason why he should lie down on his own folks, or why he should not live in his own home. When gentle expostulations were tried, he always answered mildly that he guessed he'd rather go on living the way he was for a while longer; and when blustering was tried, he straightened up, looked the blusterer in the eye, and said he guessed there wasn't no law in Vermont to turn a man off his own farm, s'long's he paid his debts, and he didn't owe any that he knew of.

That was the fact, too. He paid spot cash for what he bought in his semi-yearly trips to the village to "do trading," as our phrase goes. He bought very little, a couple of pairs of overalls a year, a bag apiece of sugar, and coffee, and rice, and salt, and flour, some raisins, and pepper. And once or twice during the long period of his hermit life, an overcoat and a new pair of trousers. What he brought down from his farm was more than enough to pay for such purchases, for he continued to cultivate his land, less and less of it, of course, each year, but still enough to feed his horse and cow and pig and hens, and to provide him with corn and potatoes and onions. He salted down and smoked a hog every fall and ate his hens when they got too old to lay.

And, of course, as long as he was actually economically independent, the town, groaning with apprehension over the danger to its treasury though it was, could not lay a finger on the cranky old codger. And yet, of course his economic independence couldn't last! From one day to the next, something was bound to happen to him, something that would cost the town money.

Each year the Selectmen, planning the town expenditures with the concentrated prudence born of hard necessity, cast an uneasy mental glance up Arnold Hollow way, and scringed at the thought that perhaps this was the year when money would have to be taken away from the road or the school fund to pay for Old Man Warner's doctoring and nursing and finally for his burial, because as the years went by, even the tenuous western granddaughter vanished; died, or moved, or something. Old Man Warner was now entirely alone in the world.

All during my childhood and youth he was a legendary figure of "sot" obstinacy and queerness. We children used to be sent up once in a while, to take our turn in seeing that the old man was all right. It was an expedition like no other. You turned off the main road and went up the steep, stony winding mountain road, dense with the shade of sugar-maples and oaks. At the top, when your blown horse stopped to rest, you saw before you the grassy lane leading across the little upland plateau where the Arnold Hollow settlement had been. The older people said they could almost hear faint echoes of whetting scythes, and barking dogs, and cheerful homely noises, as there had been in the old days. But for us children there was nothing but a breathlessly hushed, sunny glade of lush meadows, oppressively silent and spooky, with a few eyeless old wrecks of abandoned farm houses, drooping and gray. You went past the creepy place as fast as your horse could gallop, and clattered into the thicket of shivering white birches which grew close to the road like a screen; and then—there was no sensation in my childhood quite like the coming out into the ordered, inhabited, humanized little clearing, in front of Old Man Warner's home. There were portly hens crooning around on the close-cropped grass, and a pig grunting sociably from his pen at you, and shining milk-pans lying in the sun tilted against the white birch sticks of the wood-pile, and Old Man Warner himself, infinitely aged and stooped, in his faded, clean overalls, emerging from the barn-door to peer at you out of his bright old eyes and to give you a hearty, "Well, you're quite a long ways from home, don't you know it? Git off your horse, can't ye? I've got a new calf in here." Or perhaps if it were a Sunday, he sat in the sun on the front porch, with a clean shirt on, reading the weekly edition of the *New York Tribune*. He drove two miles every Saturday afternoon, down to his R.F.D. mail-box on the main road, to get this.

You heard so much talk about him down in the valley, so much fussing and stewing about his being so "sot," and so queer, that it always surprised you when you saw him, to find he was just like anybody else. You saw his calf, and had a drink of milk in his clean, well-scrubbed kitchen, and played with the latest kitten, and then you said good-by for that time, and got on your horse and went back through the birch thicket into the ghostly decay of the abandoned farms, back down the long, stony road to the valley where everybody was so cross with the unreasonable old man for causing them so much worry.

"How *could* he expect to go along like that, when other

old folks, so much younger than he, gave up and acted like other people, and settled down where you could take care of them! The house might burn down over his head, and he with it; or he might fall and break his hip and be there for days, yelling and fainting away till somebody happened to go by; or a cow might get ugly and hook him, and nobody to send for help." All these frightening possibilities and many others had been repeatedly presented to the old man himself with the elaborations and detail which came from heart-felt alarm about him. But he continued to say mildly that he guessed he'd go on living the way he was for a while yet.

"A *while!*" He was ninety years old.

And then he was ninety-one, and then ninety-two; and we were surer and surer he would "come on the town," before each fiscal year was over. At the beginning of last winter our Selectmen went up in a body to try to bully or coax the shrunken, wizened old man, now only half his former size, to go down to the valley. He remarked that he "guessed there wasn't no law in Vermont," and so forth, just as he had to their fathers. He was so old, that he could no longer straighten up as he said it, for his back was helplessly bent with rheumatism, and for lack of teeth he whistled and clucked and lisped a good deal as he pronounced his formula. But his meaning was as clear as it had been thirty years ago. They came sulkily away without him, knowing that they would both be laughed at and blamed, in the valley, because the cussed old crab had got the best of them, again.

Last February, a couple of men, crossing over to a

lumber-job on Hemlock Mountain, by way of the Arnold Hollow road, saw no smoke coming out of the chimney, knocked at the door, and getting no answer, opened it and stepped in. There lay Old Man Warner, dead on his kitchen floor in front of his well-blacked cook-stove. The tiny, crooked, old body was fully dressed, even to a fur cap and mittens, and in one hand was his sharp, well-ground ax. One stove-lid was off, and a charred stick of wood lay half in and half out of the fire box. Evidently the old man had stepped to the fire to put in a stick of wood before he went out to split some more, and had been stricken instantly, before he could move a step. His cold, white old face was composed and quiet, just as it had always been in life.

The two lumbermen fed the half-starved pig and hens and turned back to the valley with the news, driving the old man's cow and horse in front of them; and in a couple of hours we all knew that Old Man Warner had died, all alone, in his own kitchen.

Well, what do you think! We were as stirred up about it—! We turned out and gave him one of the best funerals the town ever saw. And we put up a good marble tomb-stone that told all about how he had lived. We found we were proud of him, as proud as could be, the darned old bull-dog, who had stuck it out all alone, in spite of us. We brag now about his single-handed victory over old age and loneliness, and we keep talking about him to the children, just as we brag about our grandfathers' victories in the Civil War, and talk to the children about the doings of the Green Mountain Boys. Old Man Warner has become history. We take as much satisfaction in the old fellow's spunk, as though he had been our own grandfather, and we spare our listeners no detail of his story: ". . . And there he stuck year after year, with the whole town plaguing at him to quit. And he earned his own living, and chopped his own wood, and kept himself and the house just as decent, and never got queer and frowzy and half-cracked, but stayed just like anybody, as nice an old man as ever you saw—all alone, all stark alone—beholden to nobody—asking no odds of anybody—yes, sir, and died with his boots on, at ninety-three, on a kitchen floor you could have et off of, 'twas so clean."

BLISS PERRY

Even summer boarders soon discover the part taken by cold weather in the life of northern farms. They see taller wood-piles the farther north they go. They get some notion of the importance of owning a wood lot. Perhaps they notice how the necessity of keeping a covered way from kitchen to stock has produced an architectural arrangement of house and farm-buildings described by the uninformed as "rambling." Perhaps one may find himself in Vermont on a brief business trip in one of those seasons when the thermometer lives up—or down—to its incredible reputation, reaching with no effort at all temperatures like thirty or thirty-five degrees below—Vermonters have learned not to quote veracious lower figures. Then he finds out what it does to your throat to do much talking in the open air, and may even ask himself whether this has anything to do with habits of laconic speech. But he will have to live in this part of the world over at least a series of winters to appreciate just how much the cold does get into everything, just how much of the social and even psychological structure of rural New England was involved in the process of keeping warm in winter.

Oliver Wendell Holmes, in that treatise on social distinction to which I have elsewhere referred, says with his usual acumen that one reason why two-story "genteel" residences were likely to be cheerless and unsatisfactory was that they were rarely kept at an agreeable temperature. "The mansion-house has large fire-places and generous chimneys, and is open to the sunshine. The farmhouse makes no pretensions, but it has a good warm kitchen, at any rate, and one can be comfortable there with the rest of the family, without fear and without reproach. These lesser country-houses of genteel aspirations are much given to patent subterfuges of one kind and another to get heat without combustion. The chilly parlor and the slippery hair-cloth seat take the life out of the warmest welcome. If one would make these places wholesome, happy and cheerful, the first precept would be, 'The dearest fuel, plenty of it, and let half the heat go up the chimney.' If you can't afford this, don't try to live in a 'genteel' fashion, but stick to the ways of the honest farmhouse."

Professor Perry's story brings out not only this striking truth, and its application to the length of time it took some suitors to bring their courtship to the proposing-point, but also an aspect of the fuel question even more poignant, the minister's coal bill under conditions, inside and outside the parsonage, that he is pathetically unable to control. If it also brings out a trait for which certain citizens of the North Atlantic States have been more famous than popular, it shows that this quality made its possessor unpopular in his own town and in his own house. Alvah Bayley is "near"; he has made money and will no doubt continue to make it squeal under his clutch after this episode is closed, but for once and in a righteous outburst of generosity, his own blood betrays him. Alvira, his daughter, brings her inherited business sense to bear on rescuing him from pulling his reputation down on his own head. A conflict of good and evil powers, each of them New England to the core, went on over the head of the bewildered and grateful parson when Alvira outsmarted Alvah for his benefit.

I read this story in *Scribner's Magazine* when it first came out, and it made such an impression on what was then my young mind that this year, looking for a cold-weather story, it came at once to the surface of memory though I had not meanwhile re-

read it in the collection, "The Powers at Play," in which, with seven other stories, it was published by Scribner in 1899. Bliss Perry deserves well of American literature, not only as author and as editor for years of the *Atlantic Monthly*, but as ornament of what he has called "a noble profession for the noble-hearted, and but a petty calling for a petty mind"—that of university professor. Two generations ago, as he records in "The Amateur Spirit," students were required to take off their hats when four rods from any professor—two rods being considered enough for a tutor. This form of respect has gone with the indiscriminating homage it symbolized, but Bliss Perry is one of the professors to whom one who loves America takes off his hat.

BY THE COMMITTEE

By BLISS PERRY

THE town of Whiteridge, N. H., was cursed with a bene-factress. She was a little old non-resident widow, with granite insides, a native of Whiteridge, married early to a Boston merchant, and now desirous of linking her name perpetually with that of her birthplace. She had presented the township with the Martha J. Torringford town-hall, the village with the Martha J. Torringford drinking-fountain, and the Congregational Church with the Martha J. Torringford parsonage, all upon conditions stated by herself. The hall was fine to look upon, but the use of tobacco was forbidden in or about the building, with the result that the voters of Whiteridge seriously thought of holding the March meeting, as usual, in the old hall above Alvah Bayley's general store, where the genial sawdust covered the floor at town-meeting time, and the women-folk had nothing to say about anything. The drinking-fountain was just too low for a horse, unless he were un-checked—the donor took this means of combating the pernicious check-rein—and just too high for a dog. How-ever, this was immaterial, as the town had refused to bond itself for a water system, and the dust of two summers lay thick in the great marble bowl.

The Congregational parsonage was the earliest and the most immediately useful of the widow Torringford's gifts, but it was far too large, even for the Reverend Mr. Chippendale's family, and there was no fund for furnishing it, or for paying the running expenses. It was a broad, low building, of yellow, glazed brick, with plate-glass windows, and two outside chimneys, and a cast-iron stag in the front yard. The farmers from miles around stopped their teams in the middle of the street to gaze at it. When Mr Chippendale first entered the parsonage he rubbed his hands with delight on observing the big hot-air registers. Born in India, he had been dreading the New Hampshire winters. It was in September. The minister and his sharp-faced wife nailed their "God-bless-our-home" motto to the Lincrusta-Walton wall of the sitting-room, draped some pressed palm-leaves from India along the brocaded frieze of the dining-room, and decided to leave the parlor unfurnished for the present. Their happiness seemed complete.

Early in October, Mr. Chippendale inquired the price of coal. Whiteridge was six miles up-hill from the railroad, and Alvah Bayley informed him that, seeing it was for the parsonage, his coal would be eight dollars and a quarter a ton. The minister ordered ten tons, and figured out the cost thoughtfully as he walked home. That winter was singularly mild, for Whiteridge, but before spring he ordered eight tons more. Daily, while he shovelled the precious stuff with his own hands into that yawning hot-air furnace, his figuring became more interesting. His salary was thirteen hundred dollars. The next winter there was another Chippendale baby, and the necessity of keeping the nursery at seventy meant twenty-one tons of coal ordered from Alvah Bayley between October and May. That winter was considered mild also, by the weather-wise, but what with the baby, and clothes for the three older children, and the cost of hiring a cutter for calls in the out-districts, and a few necessary books, the spring found an unpaid account of a hundred dollars upon Alvah Bayley's ledgers. It worried Mr. Chippendale, but autumn came, and he had not been able to pay it off. Winter settled itself upon Whiteridge with an iron grip early in November, and before January was over the furnace of the Martha J. Torringford parsonage had eaten another hundred dollars' worth of coal—at nine dollars a ton—and there was the rest of January, February, March, and April still to come.

Mr. Chippendale's blond hair grew gray that winter, though Alvira Bayley, who sat directly behind him in the front seat of the choir, was the only person besides Mrs. Chippendale to notice it. Alvira admired Mr. Chippendale more than any minister she had ever heard, and the faraway look in his blue eyes—as if he were addressing a very remote gallery—thrilled her to a kind of ecstasy. She was sure that Mrs. Chippendale did not quite appreciate him. Once she ventured timidly to address her father upon the subject of Mr. Chippendale's salary, Alvah Bayley being Chairman of the parish committee though not a member of the church.

"Father," she said, as Alvah was warming his feet against the side of the great soapstone stove in the Bayley sitting-room, preparatory to going to bed, "don't you suppose the parish would raise Mr. Chippendale's salary, if you favored it?"

The store-keeper snorted angrily, and his lower jaw closed. There was a fringe of beard all along the under edges of it, like sea-weed clinging to a rock. "I guess not! We're paying two hundred more now than we ever paid before."

"But he's worth more than any minister we ever had," retorted the daughter. "He's a real saintly man. And I believe they find it hard work to get along. His Sunday coat is getting terrible shiny; you can't help but see it when you sit in the choir."

"Guess his coat's as good as mine," growled Alvah. "It ain't any harder for him to get along than for other folks; or oughtn't to be. He ain't a saver—that's what's the matter with him—he ain't a saver."

"I should like to know how a minister can save anything in that great big house," persisted the girl. "They don't pretend to use the parlor, as it is. Folks say the furnace takes an awful sight of coal; it's some new kind, that you can't burn wood in. And you say we can't afford to burn coal."

She glanced toward the closed parlor-door, meaningly. There was a bright new base-burner in there, and she would have so liked to light it for the nights when Orton Ranney, the cashier of the Whiteridge bank, and for years a patient admirer of hers, came to call upon her. But her father would not allow the extravagance, and Orton always had to sit by the soapstone stove in the sitting-room, constrained and chafing in Alvah's presence. Yet he had told Alvira once that her father was the richest man in town.

"And we can't," affirmed the store-keeper, doggedly, as he rose and started for his bedroom. "I hope we ain't going to have that parlor stove all over again to-night, Alviry."

"No, father," said the girl. But tears of vexation started to her eyes.

Alvah Bayley was reminded of this conversation the next day, when the minister entered the store and made his way to the back corner where Mr. Bayley sat over his day-book. The store-keeper nodded, not appearing to notice Mr. Chippendale's half-outstretched hand. In fact, he disliked shaking hands with anybody. Natives of White-ridge understood his peculiarities, and his face was not of a kind to tempt strangers into demonstrations of regard. But Mr. Chippendale felt a trifle disconcerted.

"Cold enough for you?" inquired Alvah. He had put this query to every customer that morning, and the minister felt that it was somewhat depersonalized. Nevertheless he answered with a brave jocoseness that he could stand a few more degrees of heat. The store-keeper gazed at him impassively. Mr. Chippendale fidgeted. "In fact," he continued, weakening, "I came in to see about some more coal."

"Humph!" muttered Alvah, turning to his ledger. "All out so soon, eh?" He ran his pencil down a line of figures. "October 10th, twelve tons. How many more will take you through?"

"Ten, I hope," said Mr. Chippendale. He had made this calculation in the night watches.

Alvah wrote down the order. Then he looked up suddenly, with a glance that seemed to penetrate quite through the minister. He lowered his voice a little. "You ain't going to make it go, are you!" he demanded, brusquely.

Mr. Chippendale divined his meaning, and flushed. But he was talking to the chairman of the parish committee, and he remembered the sharp-faced wife and the babies. "No," he said, "on thirteen hundred dollars, and obliged as I am to live in that expensive parsonage, I'm afraid I can't make it go."

Alvah nodded grimly. "I thought so."

"I was told when I came here," continued the minister, flushing more deeply still, "that Mrs. Torringford contemplated setting apart a fund to defray the necessary expense of taking care of such a large house. If it were not for the heating—"

Alvah broke in savagely. "That's her business. She's changed her mind. She's always changing her mind. She's worried the life out of us over that town-hall. But that ain't the point, Mr. Chippendale. The point is, we're afraid you ain't a saver. We can't have a minister here who don't pay his bills."

The blood went out of Mr. Chippendale's face. He turned up the collar of his worn ulster. "How much do I owe you, Mr. Bayley?" he inquired dryly.

The store-keeper took a newly written bill from a pile. "$284.30," he answered, as if quite unconscious of the wound he had given to the shabbily dressed gentleman before him. "That don't include this last order for coal."

"You may make that order one ton instead of ten," said the minister.

"Just as you say," replied Alvah. "That'll be $293.30, then. Coal has come up again."

Mr. Chippendale turned on his heel and went out. He felt a trifle faint, and was glad, for once, of the stinging January wind. Of course, they must leave Whiteridge; that was what Alvah Bayley, as chairman of the parish committee, had meant him to understand. But how could they go? And whither could they go? And what would Mrs. Chippendale say?

He found the thin-faced wife crying, as often, with the babies playing unconcernedly around her, but this time the tears were from pure joy. She had opened her husband's mail; and the unhoped-for "call" had come—hinted at months before, then given up, just as the Chippendales had given up so many things, but now indubitably at hand —a call to a church in southern California, where the salary was two thousand dollars and the temperature averaged 68° Fahrenheit every month in the year! She thrust the letter into his hand, and caught it from him half read, to wave it frantically in the air. Then she pretended to kiss away every gray hair he had. She made the babies join hands and dance to a waltz which she dashed somehow out of the wheezy little parsonage melodeon. Thereupon she began all over again, by kissing Mr. Chippendale, and it is to be said for him that by this time he was looking very much less far away than usual.

Before the celebration was over Alvah Bayley's hired man drove up with the ton of coal. " 'Twon't last long, in this spell of weather," he volunteered, but Mr. Chippendale answered "Long enough" with a recklessness that

surprised himself. Before night he had placed his resignation in the hands of the chairman of the parish committee,
and he even left the furnace drafts open when he went
to bed.

The next morning, however, he began to think of the
$293.30. That must be paid before he left Whiteridge. The
California church had offered to reimburse him for the
expense of moving, but he could not take that money to
pay Alvah Bayley, and even if he did there would be nothing left with which to buy tickets for California. Again
and again he took account of the financial standing of all
his relations, but, so far back as he could remember, there
had never been a Chippendale who had at any one time
$300 to lend. He thought once, timorously, of applying
to Mrs. Martha J. Torringford, but recalled the fact that
she was spending that winter on the Nile. A week went
by. Alvah Bayley issued the call for a parish meeting
to act upon the minister's resignation, and Mr. Chippendale
began to work upon his farewell sermon, but day and night,
in spite of his happy prospect for the future, he was burdened and harassed by the thought of that unpaid bill.

He was not alone in his anxiety. Alvah Bayley rumi-
nated nightly over the $293.30, as he sat warming his
stockings against the soapstone stove in his sitting-room.
Alvira wondered what ailed him, but the close-fisted old
store-keeper was not in the habit of taking counsel with
her, or with anyone. No one in Whiteridge knew of Mr.
Chippendale's debt; Alvah had spoken simply for himself
when he had mentioned the public dissatisfaction with a

minister who was not a saver. Though the pastor had never been altogether liked by the out-districts—not having enough "nat'ral how d'ye do" about him, it was thought— the announcement of his resignation was received with genuine regret in the village. The choir was cast down, and Alvira Bayley in particular alternated in her feelings, from deep wrath against the California church for stealing away her pastor, to a self-sacrificing joy that he was going to a milder climate and a greater income. She agitated herself by schemes for a farewell oyster-supper and donation-party for the Chippendales, and hesitated to propose it only because she feared her father's disapproval. Yet her affection for the departing minister grew with every hour, and one night she had opened her lips flutteringly, to propose her plan, when Alvah brought all four legs of his chair down with a thump, and stuck his feet into his slippers with pleasurable animation. He had just thought of a way to get hold of that $293.30.

Alvira looked up inquiringly. "What's the matter, father?"

"Nothing," said the store-keeper. "Except that I was just thinking about the minister. Seems to be 'twould look better if Whiteridge folks gave him a kind of send-off, you know, just to show that there ain't any hard feelings on either side."

Alvira's breath quickened. She bent lower over the splasher she was embroidering for the Chippendales' best bed-room set. "A sort of donation-party, father?" she ventured.

"No!" he exclaimed. "Land sakes, no! They don't want a lot of cord-wood and maple sugar to take with 'em. What Mr. Chippendale needs is spot cash."

"I think so too," cried Alvira, boldly.

"The question is," said Alvah, meditatively, running his fingers through his fringe of beard, "what's the quickest and best way to raise it? Someone ought to start a subscription paper. Suppose you take the cutter and old Tom tomorrow and try the out-districts, and I'll take the Street. We can do this a good deal better ourselves, Alviry, than to get a lot more into it. I'll draw up a couple of subscription papers now."

He shuffled over to the desk in the corner of the sitting-room, and for some minutes Alvira listened in a tumult of pleasure to the scratching of his pen. She even half forgave him for that matter of the parlor base-burner. When he handed one of the papers to her, she gave a little cry of delight. Alvah Bayley's name headed each list with a subscription of $25.

"Father!" she exclaimed. "Why, father!"

Alvah busied himself with putting a huge rock-maple log into the soapstone stove, to last through the night. He seemed to make more noise about it than usual.

"How much money do you think we can raise?" asked his daughter, folding up the splasher as if it had suddenly become a thing of no value.

"Well," said Alvah, "that depends. But I should think we'd ought to raise close on to three hundred dollars."

"My!" said the girl, "wouldn't that be nice!"

"I guess it would!" replied Alvah Bayley.

At noon upon the second day thereafter the canvass of the town was completed. By dint of his position as chairman of the parish committee, his own generous subscription, and his intimate knowledge of the financial status of each member of the congregation, the store-keeper secured more money in the Street than anyone else would have thought possible, though it fell a trifle short of his own calculations. But the out-districts more than made up the deficiency. Under the spell of Alvira's enthusiasm, the "spot cash" slipped out of tea-pots and secret "high-boy" drawers with magical readiness, and the donors gazed after the girl's disappearing cutter in stupid wonder at their unwonted affection for the Chippendales.

Only one thing occurred to mar Alvira's unthinking pleasure in her mission. At the very last house upon the list, Aunt 'Lindy Waters, gazing at her suspiciously as the girl wrote "Miss Belinda Waters, fifty cents," asked for a receipt. Alvira wrote one, signing it "By the Committee," and drew on her mittens.

"I s'pose it's all right," said Aunt 'Lindy, concessively; "I didn't know but the minister might be owing your father a little something—that was all."

Alvira colored. "That's a real mean thing to say, Aunt 'Lindy. You can have your fifty cents back again, there!" But Belinda scornfully refused.

All the way home that little arrow of the spinster rankled in Alvira's innocent bosom. Shamefully mean had it been to say it, and yet— She hung her head. Was it really this, after all, that had put the idea of the collection into her father's mind? If it were she could never hold up her face in Whiteridge any more. To think of sitting in the front seat of the choir Sunday after Sunday, confronting those stern, reproachful farmer-folk from the out-districts, whose slowly won money she had begged from them, only to make her father richer than before!

Half a dozen times during the noon-meal her lips parted to ask Alvah the question whose answer she dreaded to hear, but each time her courage failed her. Alvah was in high spirits over the completion of their self-appointed task, and after dinner father and daughter sat down to count the money. The desk was quite covered with the crumpled bills: fives and twos and ones and a great deal of silver. Alvira's fingers shook as she sorted and counted.

"Well," announced the store-keeper, finally, "it's $271.74. I guess I might as well make it seventy-five." He took a penny from his pocket, and added it to the pile before him. "I struck it pretty close, didn't I?" he added, reflectively. "How do the subscription papers foot up, Alviry?"

"Three hundred and twenty-one dollars and seventy-four cents," she replied. "Why, there ought to be fifty dollars more."

He ran his eye over the columns, and handed them back with a hard chuckle. "You've counted my subscription twice, Alviry, that's all."

"But it ought anyway to be there once, father," she said, nervously.

"It's going to be," answered Alvah, and opening the drawer where the receipt blanks were kept, took out one and began to fill in the name of Rev. Enoch Chippendale upon the upper left-hand corner.

"Father," demanded Alvira, "does Mr. Chippendale owe you any money?"

He wrote on without heeding her.

"Alvah Bayley," cried the girl, "how much does he owe you?" She seized his right hand, making his pen sprawl. "It isn't much, is it?" she added, plaintively, frightened at her own temerity.

He shook off her hand angrily, and wrote: "*Received payment, Alvah Bayley.*" "He owes me that," he said, doggedly, pushing the receipt toward her. "Two hundred and ninety three dollars and thirty cents. We make him a present of it. That counts in my twenty-five dollars and leaves him three dollars and forty-five cents over, in cash. If it wa'n't for you and me, he couldn't have got a cent of it."

The girl's face grew white. "But what do you suppose folks'll say about us?" she exclaimed. "It seems to me it would kill me, father. You can afford to let him have that money just as well as not. It isn't *right.*"

"You set down and stop shaking!" thundered Alvah. "There! Now you set still. This is my money, every cent on't, except three dollars and forty-five cents. I could have the law on to the minister to-day for it, if I was a mind to. Don't you say another word. I'm going in there now to give him this receipt and the balance in cash, and he'll be glad enough to get it, too. You set still!"

But she leaped to her feet again, in spite of his command.

For six years, ever since she was nineteen, she had kept house for her father and had never dared to assert herself against his wishes until now. But her affection for her pastor, and pride in the Bayley good name, swept her out of herself.

"I won't sit down, Alvah Bayley," she flashed back, "unless I want to!"

The moment she had said it she felt clear-headed and cool, for all her white heat of anger. He caught a look in her eye that reminded him somewhat uncomfortably of her mother.

"It may be right, and it may be wrong," she went on, bitterly, "but whichever it is, it's *mean*. I didn't believe you would do such a thing, father. And you're not going to do such a thing, either!"

"I ain't, am I?" shouted the store-keeper. "I guess we'll see about that this very minute!" He snatched three dollar bills from the pile before him, and forty-five cents in silver. Then he grasped his hat, and stamped out noisily, without looking at his daughter, who stood motionless by the desk. The Chippendales lived only two doors away, and in a moment he was standing on the elaborate porch of the Martha J. Torringford parsonage, pressing the electric bell. An untidy maid-of-all-work ushered him through the big barren hall—unheated, for economy's sake—and into the family sitting-room. There was no one there but two of the babies, who toddled over to show the stranger their picture-books, but drew off again upon a nearer view. The dining-room door was ajar, and from the appearance of the uncleaned table the Chippendales could not have had an elaborate meal. Already the store-keeper wished the interview well over. A door opened, and Mr. Chippendale hurried in from his farewell sermon, not having taken time to change his frayed study gown. His eyes looked anxious, and his heart sank as he gazed upon Alvah Bayley's immovable lower jaw.

"Good-afternoon, Mr. Bayley," he exclaimed, as hospitably as he could. "I—I hope you are enjoying good health."

"Tol'able," replied the store-keeper, absently. He fumbled in his pocket and brought out the receipt. Mr. Chippendale took it for the bill, and began to grow crimson.

"The fact is, Mr. Chippendale," said Alvah, "folks up and down the Street and in the out-districts have kind of wanted to give you a testimonial before you left town. The committee in charge thought you might be feeling a little worried about that bill with me, and so we arranged to make you a present of this receipted bill—and the balance of the subscription in cash."

He peered up at the minister's face as he held out the receipt. Mr. Chippendale's lips were moving, but his emotion was such that no sound escaped them. Bayley fumbled in his pocket for the pitiful little balance in cash, but his courage failed him. His nerves had been more shaken by the scene with Alvira than he had supposed. He fingered the money a moment and then blurted out: "That balance, Mr. Chippendale—well, you'll find that deposited to your credit at the bank. That'll do just as well," he added, mainly to himself.

The minister put out both hands rapturously: the revulsion of feeling was still so strong that he could not trust himself to speak. But Alvah Bayley made no response to this mute demonstration of gratitude. He simply reached for his hat and got out of the house as best he could.

It had been an uncomfortable five minutes for him, but he had put the thing through. Some people up and down the Street might call it rather sharp, perhaps, and of course Alviry would feel sore about it, but it was every man's duty to look out for himself. Charity began at home, every time! He was tempted, nevertheless, to keep straight on to the store, and to let Alvira cool off a little before he faced her. But he had rushed out without his overcoat, and was already shivering. So he turned in at his own gate, went around to the side-door, as usual, and entered the sitting-room. He determined to get the first word, if there was to be any further argument, and his mouth was open to pronounce it when he became aware that the room was empty. The desk was swept bare of its bills and silver, and Alvira was nowhere to be found.

"Alviry!" he screamed. "Alviry!"

But there was no answer. Her cloak and hat were gone from the hook in the hall. Had he so angered her that she had left him? Her mother had threatened to do that once. Fear and shame overmastered him, and he ran out to the barn, hatless, to hitch up the cutter and old Tom.

.   .   .   .

She had stood by the desk, with her eyes closed, until the door had slammed behind him. Then she glanced desperately at the money. It was the minister's, every penny of it! Her father and she would be disgraced forever, if people found out what he had done. He had no right to take it, and what was more, she had collected fully half of it herself! What could she do with it? Suddenly she thought of Orton Ranney. Orton would help her if he dared, she knew. And she would make him dare!

Catching a napkin from the table, she swept into it the silver and the piles of bills. Then she flung on her cloak and hat, and hurried down to the bank. She would have run if she had not known that people were watching her from their windows. Orton Ranney, a mild-eyed, pink-faced, bashful little man of forty, posting his books all alone in the tiny bank building, happened to catch sight of her, as she crossed the street toward him. His bachelor heart fluttered a little, as usual, but he did not dream of her coming in.

"Orton Ranney," she panted, as she entered, "do you want to help me more than anyone ever helped me yet?" Her eyes were flashing with excitement.

The flattered cashier rubbed his hands. "I guess I do, Alvira," he murmured, gallantly. "Come right in here." He opened the iron gate, and let her in behind his own desk. "What is it, Alvira?" he asked, astonished at his own boldness with her.

"It's this," she exclaimed, untying a napkin, and spreading out the money on the desk. "Father and I have raised all this money for Mr. Chippendale. There's pretty nearly three hundred dollars."

The cashier nodded. He had given five dollars himself, all for the sake of getting on the right side of the girl's father. "Well?" he smiled.

"Well, I want Mr. Chippendale to *have* it," she cried, with a bitter energy that amazed him. "It's his by rights, but he owes father two hundred and ninety-three dollars, and father has gone over to give him a receipt for that, and is going to keep this himself. He took out three dollars and forty-five cents to give Mr. Chippendale, and that was every cent there was left. I helped count it."

The cashier whistled softly.

"Don't you ever say a word," she commanded. "Nobody in Whiteridge knows that he owes father anything like that. Now I want you to give this money to the minister right away. Will you?"

"But what will your father say, Alvira?" he ventured, cautiously.

She turned on him. "Orton Ranney, if you want to choose between Alvah Bayley and Alvira Bayley, you can't choose any too quick. I expect father'll be here any minute." Her face was within a foot of his own, and it would have fired a less susceptible man than her admirer into heroic rashness.

"If it comes to that, Alvira," he gasped, choking a little, "why, I guess you know where to find me. Don't you, Alvira?"

"Then what's the best way to get this to the minister?" she demanded, inexorably.

"You might deposit it to his credit," he suggested, trying to call back his routed instinct for business. "Then nobody else could touch it, and he could come and get it when he wanted to."

"Of course!" she cried. "I don't know why I didn't think of that. I just thought of coming here to—to you." It was Alvira's turn to look embarrassed.

"How much did you say it was?" he asked.

"Two hundred and seventy-one dollars and seventy-five cents, less three dollars and forty-five cents."

He reached for a desposit blank and filled it out. "You sign it," said he.

"How? Alvira Bayley?"

"Oh, any way. 'By the Committee,' I guess. Now let me count that cash."

"I'll help you," she volunteered.

Side by side they stood at the desk, sorting the bills and putting the silver in little piles. Never had it taken the cashier so long to count that amount of money, and when the task was completed he wondered why he had not been bright enough to make a mistake, so as to have the delicious pleasure of counting it all over again. Reluctantly he turned away, and posted the $268.30 to the minister's credit. Mr. Chippendale's previous status at the White ridge bank had been represented by an over-drawn account of forty-five cents, which sum the tender-hearted cashier, unwilling to remind the minister of his insolvency, had himself placed to Mr. Chippendale's credit in order to balance the books.

He returned to Alvira, who still stood leaning against the desk. Now that her great object was accomplished, she began to be fearful again, and to wonder if she had not seemed too forward.

"Orton," she said, playing with one of his pens, "I don't know what you'll think of me, coming in like this."

"Don't you, Alvira?" he questioned, in his softest second-tenor notes. For how many years those tones had entranced her, as she and Orton had stood up together in the choir! They seemed now to wrap themselves about her heart. "Don't you really know what I think of you?" His right hand slipped off the desk, fell innocently to his side, and then began to rise surreptitiously, tremblingly, toward her waist. "I—I guess, Alvira—"

"Sh!" said the girl.

The bank-door opened. Alvira faced around toward it with a sudden defiance. But it was not her father; it was only the Rev. Enoch Chippendale.

His overcoat was unbuttoned, and the frayed study gown showed beneath it. In marked agitation he advanced to the cashier's grated window; then he caught sight of Alvira Bayley, and took off his hat. Her presence seemed to disconcert him.

"A most unexpected occurrence has just taken place, Mr. Ranney," he began. "A most undeserved and yet a most welcome generosity has been evinced toward us. If I understood your father aright, Miss Alvira—and yet Mrs. Chippendale was sure there must be some mistake—you know Mrs. Chippendale is not very well and is therefore somewhat over-inclined to be apprehensive—and to tell the truth I was not altogether sure that I understood your father myself—but—" here he hesitated and pulled out the receipt which Alvah Bayley had signed—"he conveyed the impression that the good-will of the parish had succeeded in liquidating my indebtedness to him, and that there was a balance credited to me here besides, Mr. Ranney. That is what I scarcely can believe. It seems such unprecedented—"

"It's all right," interrupted the cashier, blandly.

"Yes, it's all right," echoed Alvira.

"May—may I ask how much it is, Mr. Ranney?"

The cashier stepped gravely over to his books. "Two hundred and sixty-eight dollars and thirty cents," he replied. "Will you have that in cash, Mr. Chippendale?"

The minister drew a long, astonished breath. "Is it possible!" he cried. "Why, yes, I think it would please Mrs. Chippendale if I were to take it in cash." His eyes were wet.

"Kindly draw a check for it, then," suggested the cashier, pushing a blank check through the window, and swiftly counting out the bills.

"I believe *you* were at the bottom of this, Miss Alvira," hazarded the minister, affectionately, as he buttoned his study gown carefully over his undreamed-of wealth.

"She was on the committee," said the cashier, proudly.

At that instant a cutter was pulled up outside, and the alarmed features of Alvah Bayley appeared in the doorway. He was accompanied by the postmaster, who was certain that he had seen Alvira enter the bank, and was at a loss to understand the reason for Alvah's agitated inquiries about her. No sooner did Mr. Chippendale catch sight of the store-keeper, than he made a rush for him, with beatific face and outstretched hands.

"You see, Mr. Bayley," he cried, "we were so delighted that we could scarcely wait, and so I hurried right down here for the balance."

"To be sure," stammered the store-keeper, in confusion. "You got ahead of me a little. Here it is." He drew out the three dollars and forty-five cents, shamefacedly, and presented it to the minister. As he did so his eyes met Alvira's; the bronzed grating and the cashier's desk were between them, but the girl's look seemed to scorch him; she was at that moment the very image of her mother, the one person before whose slowly roused intensity of passion his own will-power had been as tow to fire. For a minute father and daughter faced each other. Then she saw his eyes quail and sink, and she knew who was master.

The Reverend Mr. Chippendale gazed in perplexity at the latest addition to his earthly treasure. "I don't understand this," he exclaimed; "Mr. Ranney has already given me two hundred and sixty-eight dollars and thirty cents. There must be some mistake."

"No, there isn't," interrupted the clear, crisp tones of Alvira Bayley, as distinctly as if she were giving out the number of a hymn at prayer-meeting. "It's all right. Father means to make you a present of that receipted bill he spoke of, and the committee raised two hundred and seventy-one dollars and seventy-five cents besides. We deposited it all here except three dollars and forty-five cents that Father had in his pocket. You mustn't say another word; I wish 't was twice as much as it is. But don't you thing we've done pretty well, Mr. Johnson?"

The postmaster had been glancing stealthily from father

to daughter, conscious of some mystery which baffled his omniscience. But he betrayed no curiosity, as he answered, with a cheerful alacrity, "Strikes me it's a pretty slick job, Miss Alviry, all around. Credit to everybody concerned. It ain't going to be a secret, is it?"

"Oh, no!" exclaimed the girl. "I want everyone to know it. Be sure you get the figures just right, Mr. Johnson."

The minister was wringing Alvah Bayley's nerveless hand. "I can never forget your thoughtfulness, never!" he murmured.

"Are you going home, father?" said Alvira, coolly, while the blushing cashier held the iron gate wide open for her. "I guess I'll go along with you in the cutter. Mr. Chippendale, tell Mrs. Chippendale I'm coming in to see her right away. Oh, by the way, Orton, we ought to practice those hymns to-night. I'll have the coal fire started in the parlor, so that we can use the piano. It'll be real comfortable in there; will you come?"

JAMES BRENDAN CONNOLLY

The heart of old Massachusetts, like the conch-shells on her mantelpieces, held the sound of the sea. Her history began with a ship, and for generations her sea-faring men brought into her life the exotic features of Canton shawls and Smyrna silks, preserved foreign fruits, cocoanuts, parrots and carved ivories. My mother and her younger sister were never in China, but in my childhood there hung on our wall their portraits with slanting eyes and complexions pearly as the lady's in "Java Head"; their sailor-uncle had given their daguerreotypes to an artist in Hong-Kong, who had copied them according to his Chinese lights.

But Massachusetts' real sea-treasure was fish. "Nothing is here to be had which fishing doth hinder, but further us to obtain," said Captain John Smith, who had New England's future always on his mind. The first settlers of Gloucester in 1623 came there to fish. James Brendan Connolly says that when a divine of that early day came among them and said, "Remember, brethren, that you journeyed here to save your souls," one of the brethren is reported to have risen to remark: "And to ketch fish." Boston reached out for the fresh fish market; Gloucester devoted herself to the salt fish trade and now, they say, leads the world in it. No one has given the world a better idea of the life of Gloucestermen on deep-sea fishing-grounds than the author of this story.

"My sea experience," he says, "began with my being washed out of my cabin bunk in my uncle's fishing schooner when I was seven years old. . . . I came ashore from that trip with the clear notion that great waves breaking over a vessel was the regular thing out to sea." Since then he has sailed as cattleman on the North Atlantic, on an oil-ship in the Gulf of Mexico, a river-boat on the Mississippi, a whaler and a submarine, not to speak of battle-ships, cruisers, destroyers, patrols, flying-boats and airships. Having left Harvard to go to the Olympic Games in Athens in 1896, where he won the first Olympic championship of modern times, he distinguished himself in various strenuous sports, as a marine at Santiago, and as a war correspondent in Mexico, in Europe during the Great War and in Ireland during the time of the Black and Tans. For the purpose of this collection the important feature of his crowded career is that he sailed again and again with Gloucester fishermen, and was one of the crew of the fishing schooner *Esperanto* when she won the First International Fisherman's Race. All this and more one may learn in "The Book of the Gloucester Fishermen," his account of the experiences out of which came stories that brought salt air and strong wind into contemporary American fiction.

"I drove her and I drove her and I drove her," said one of these men, "and she suffered and she suffered and she suffered, and could I make her quit? The man never lived who could make her quit!" his "inflection of pride and pity bearing his testimony to her unconquerable soul." Such a man lives in this story, and such a ship. She is worthy to sail with that craft of whom he sings

> "For she's the Lucy Foster,
>   She's a seiner out of Gloucester,
>   She's an able, handsome lady
>   And she's go-o-ing home."

FROM REYKJAVIK TO GLOUCESTER

By James Brendan Connolly

ELEVATED above the head of a deep wharf-slip, low flanked by a ship-chandler's shop to one side and a sail-maker's loft to another, commanding a fine view of the docks and harbor beneath, and of the bay beyond, perched up where nothing coming or going past Eastern Point will fail to be noticed—this is the look-out tower of the Great Eastern Fish Company of the port of Gloucester, which, be it known, is the first fish mart of our country. In the official bulletins of the company this place is known as the "Observatory," but in the every-day speech of the fishermen of Gloucester it is better and more fittingly described as the "Crow's Nest."

To attain this aerie it is needful to go round and round long flights of steps, that creak to your weight and sway to the wind as you climb. After you get there, you find a room of three flat walls and a rounded front of which the rear or west side is blocked off by the staircase whereby you came. Coast charts, bank soundings, world maps, and magazine illustrations of a nautical and sporting nature are tacked to the wall on your left. On the wall at your right—the southerly—are several pairs of marine glasses, a long telescope, and an aneroid barometer, hung from nails driven here and there, wherever space is to be found among the relief models of what all men know to be fast-sailing fishermen. A fresh varnished but much dented spar, an old topmast most likely, butts through the centre of the ceiling and is braced to the floor.

The east side is all of glass. This is the side that opens on to a little quarter-deck balcony, and looks out to sea. This balcony may be entirely closed in by an arrangement of shutters that work over and down like companion hatches, although you find out later that you have to climb to the upper deck by way of an outside rope ladder to make them work. In the centre of one of the hatches, when you come to look, is a brass-bound port-hole, plainly intended for stormy weather. A realistic bit of railing, really the taffrail of a fisherman wrecked off Thatcher's, is there to guard the unwary—once over the low rail and you are down to the waters of the dock. There is a row of scuppers along the balcony's deck, and under the rail are a couple of cleats, to which are made fast the halyards that run to the flag at the masthead.

Only one chair is in this place, after the fashion of up-to-date fishermen, which always carry a hinged chair in the cabin for the captain's use. This chair is for the look-out on duty. All others must sit on the lockers against the walls, or squat on the stair-landing at the rear, or content themselves with leaning over the stern of the quarter-deck. All this goes to make up the famous "Crow's Nest," of that abode of modern vikings, the fishing port of Gloucester.

It is the business of the look-out on duty to take his station in front of the window and watch for incoming vessels. If it is a fine day, like this one, he will hoist the window-sashes back to the pulleys, push forward his chair, and rest his feet on the rail. When he sights an inbound fisherman, he will identify her at the earliest possible moment, and make immediate report of the same to the office.

Two men are paid for this work, each standing watch in his turn. Being keen of eye and acquainted with the minute peculiarities of every schooner in the fleet, these men can name vessels at incredible distances. In some cases, where neither knowledge nor eyesight could possibly avail, they make marvellous guesses—for which they do not attempt to account. It may be a sixth sense that enables them to pick out and identify a vessel while she is yet but a blur in the haze to most of us.

Their business, as has been said, is to make early report of incoming vessels. They do that very well, and it is for that they are paid; but their pleasure and their most arduous occupation lies in the absorbing art of conversation. In the skilful development of this faculty they are aided by a volunteer staff of regular callers, who much prefer to put in time at this congenial observatory than to attend to any fatiguing business that might arise to meet them were they to stroll incautiously along the wharves.

What subject might suggest itself to the council of Crow's Nest at any particular lull, no prophet could say with certainty; but on a day like this, a beautiful summer morning, with a gentle easterly sighing in over the rail, and the docks and the harbor below alive with the loading and outfitting of many seiners, it could not very well get far away from the doings of the mackerel fleet.

Fourteen of the seining fleet were in, and this favorable easterly would be sure to bring in more. It had been an extraordinary season for the seiners. There was plenty of mackerel to be had, and they were bringing great prices. Stocks of three and four thousand dollars were getting common for vessels, and men no longer boasted of sharing anything under a hundred dollars for a short trip. It promised to be an unprecedented season altogether, and the watchers in the tower, when next they resumed the conversation, were disposed to rejoice.

"It's a good thing for Gloucester, it's a fine thing for the men," observed the look-out in the chair. "Won't be so many have to go to Georges or the big banks this winter to find grub and rent for the wife and children. Here's a lad coming in now—wait, till I make sure with the glass—yes, the Lucy Foster. Bill, report the Lucy Foster, Captain Marrs, to the office, will you? Ten days she's been gone. This lad'll be glad enough for a good mackerel season, for he does hate haddockin' in winter. He went last winter, and he says he's had enough of that kind of fishin'."

"Shouldn't think he'd have to—the money he's made, Petie."

"No, he oughtn't to, but Wesley's been a spender. But this spring, before he went on the southern mackerel cruise, he gave it out that he was going to save. I don't know myself what's drivin' him—he's close-mouthed enough for all he's so reckless some ways. But I wouldn't be surprised if he was stowin' away something against getting married this fall. He's certainly piling up a stock and hustlin' as if he intended to have a little salvage to draw on when he made up his mind to stop ashore a winter and start housekeeping. And if he does get married, I s'pose that ends the Lucy for carryin' the broom. I don't expect we'll hear of any more piling on sail to see how much she really can stand up under, or layin' her over to see how far she'll go without capsizing."

"Why?" put in one of those slow-witted ones, who must always have things explained in detail.

"Why? why?" snorted the man in the chair. "Did y'ever see any of the drivers keep it up long after gettin' married? Don't it tame the wildest of 'em when they get to thinkin' that p'raps the wife and children's waitin' for them at the end of the trip?"

"Well, I dunno. I don't see as Archie Nichols slacked any since he got married."

"Archie Nichols? Good Lord! does he count? Married a no-use woman that's druv him to drink and worse things than he ever took up with before. Leave Archie out. And look at the others. There's Tommy Bolton now. What do his crew tell you about him now? Do you hear of him pullin' the spars out of his vessel since he settled down to a home of his own? Can't you see him any afternoon now between trips walking down Main Street abreast of his little woman and the latest fat baby on his arm? Ever hear of Billie Simms in this year o' grace havin' to go on the railway 'bout every other trip or so to have the Henry Clay Parker overhauled for strained seams for'ard? I guess not. Nor Wesley Marrs, nowadays; and he's only engaged, at the worst—tryin' to see what he can do with the Lucy without getting her hove down. I guess not."

"I say, Peter," inserted a subtle one, who measured exactly the temper of the sage in the chair, and was eager to forward the psychological moment, "was Wesley Marrs such a devil for driving, after all?"

"Devil? He was all the devils, when it came to carryin' sail. Now I was with him three years. My last trip, when I fell from the masthead in among the gurry kids and broke my knee-cap, I was with Wesley Marrs in the Lucy Foster. I'm telling you this man'd spread a whole mains'l to a gale as quick as your wife or mine'd hang out a bed-sheet to the sun. When a sail went into the air—busted—Wesley used to follow it with his eyes and then say, surprised-like: 'Don't it beat hell—the rotten canvas they puts on vessels these days?' "

"You must have been with him, Peter, when that record run was made from Iceland—when the Lucy and the English yacht had their big race."

"Was I? Twenty-eight hundred miles, they call it, from Rikievik to Gloucester, and the Lucy came down in nine days and ten hours. That's going, people, for any vessel; but this one that time had her hold full of fletched halibut."

"What was it brought him along so fast?"

"Well—I guess wind had as much to do with it as anything. Just plain wind, out of the bosom of the North Atlantic, and p'raps a little, just a little, of Wesley Marrs' drivin' her."

"Who beat?" interjected a voice that should never have been allowed to disturb the silence of this generally well-posted company.

The man in the chair looked around with much curiosity to discover the inquirer. It was a young fellow, plainly not long in Gloucester, one of those lads who so frequently come there to try fishing—and quite often make good fishermen—but who are sometimes a great trial to their friends while acquiring the rudiments.

"Who beat?" echoed Peter in scorn. "And *when'd* you get in and *where'd* you get your fish?"

"I say, Peter," put in the subtle questioner on whom devolved the duty of holding the story to its course, "were you there when the match was made?"

"Was I? Warn't the skipper and me and Joe Lane gittin' down to a little table over a glass—you don't stand up to a bar there generally—and the skipper was pretty well pleased. You see he'd only bought out the Wild Irishman's half of the Lucy late that spring and this was his first trip. He paid $5,000 cash for the Irishman's half—our firm owned the other half same as now. And the last thing the Irishman said when he signed the papers and took the money was: 'Now, Wesley, b'y, you're gettin' a great vessel —fourteen thousand to build, but we'll say nothing of that. You're gettin' a vessel that nothing of her tonnage anywhere can sail away from. While I owned her she was the jewel of the fleet. Don't let anything cross her bow, Wesley, b'y.' The Irishman went to the Pacific Coast that time to look up seals Behring Sea way.

"Well, Wesley was telling us about that very talk with the Irishman and saying how the Lucy could sail and everything like that. You know how he'd be likely to carry on talkin' 'bout his vessel. This swell-dressed Englishman was takin' it all in. We didn't know who he was, though we suspicioned he was English every time we looked at him. At last he mixes in. He says:

" 'Excuse me, but I gather you are fishermen up here for halibut?'

" 'You're right,' says Wesley.

" 'From the States?'

" 'From America? Yes—from Gloucester,' says Wesley.

" 'Ah, from Gloucester. Fine, able fishermen from there, I hear,'—he kind of drawed his words out—'hardy, courageous, fine, able seamen—'

" 'And fine able vessels,' says Wesley, warmin' up right away. We guessed easy enough what was in Wesley's mind. Somebody or other'd been writing stories 'bout Gloucester fishermen 'bout that time and putting them in the old style pinkies and square-ended tubs that was the fashion when some of your fathers and mine went to sea. I never yet went among strangers in any of the new vessels that they didn't seem to be surprised at the build of our vessels, and, of course, the Lucy Foster and a few others of that model struck 'em dumb. Anyway, to get along with the story, the Englishman was surprised to hear that the Lucy was a fisherman—he'd an eye for fine vessels, y'see—and had noticed her in the harbor. But he didn't know much about our kind of people and Wesley kind of explained some things to him.

"Then the Englishman told his story. He owned the big schooner yacht, the all-white fellow with the varnished top-rails and yellow stripe along the run. We'd had an eye on her, by the way, and a handsome craft she was. That was his cruiser. He'd come in the day before from some queer place on the coast of Norway and he didn't see anything in Rikievik to hold him. He was bound for America next by way of Boston, Newport, New York, Baltimore, and so on down, so's to be among the West Indies for the winter.

"Well, he was a pretty hot sport, this one, and you all know the kind of a boy Wesley used to be when anybody spoke against his Lucy. They had an argument, back to the days of the old America and all that. Finally, they 'greed to race to Gloucester. The Englishman said he'd just as leave run into Gloucester so long as it was so handy to Boston.

"This Englishman was all right. He says about the money: 'Your word is sufficient for me, Captain. Men that look like you will pay up. If you lose, you pay over a thousand dollars. If I lose, I pay over to you a thousand, to settle as soon as both boats get into Gloucester. And in the matter of time allowance—the Bounding Billow, you must have noticed, is half as big again as you are. She isn't loaded down like you, and I can afford to give it. She has never been beaten at ocean racing, by the way, and I am willing to give you time allowance for our larger measurement.'

"'To hell with time allowance,' says Wesley. 'When fishermen race, they all start together. And first vessel home wins. You're a little longer and more beam and draught—let it go. And's for being loaded down—the Lucy could stow away half as many more halibut, and I wish she had it, the way halibut's been this summer. Don't worry about the Lucy. Those couple of hundred thousand of fletched halibut down below'll just give her a grip on things—sort o' stiffen her up and keep her from layin' over too much when it comes to blow—and it's coming to blow or I don't know. There'll be wind stirrin' before you or me see Eastern Point, and the vessel that'll carry the sail'll be the lad for the trip. I tell you, man, with all of these September gales coming our way, you won't think you're yachting off Cowes. I hope your gear's been overhauled lately,' says Wesley, and with that they left to get things ready.

"There was a gentle gale stirrin' from the no'th'ard when we sailed out of Rikievik next day, Friday. Wesley liked the look o' things pretty well. We put out behind the Englishman, him under two-reefed mains'l and the Lucy under a single reef—two jibs and whole fores'l, both of us. That was along 'bout dark. Wesley didn't make any attempt to push by the yacht—just laid to wind'ard of her. He did love to get to wind'ard of a vessel—lay off her quarter and watch her. And for most of the rest of that night, we stayed there so.

"When the sun ought to have been pretty near to showin' up again, Wesley says: 'Boys, I can't see but what the Lucy's holdin' her own, and I guess we'll wear off to the east'ard just a little. We might's well get out of sight of this fellow quick's we can now. I've a notion, too, this breeze'll be coming from that quarter before a great while, and there's nothing the Lucy likes quite so well as to take it just a tri-i-fle slanting when it blows.'

"I don't know whether the Bounding Billow people saw us get away or not—p'r'aps they didn't care. Anyway, they didn't come after us. We sunk their port light down afore daylight, and by good sun-up there wasn't a sail of her in sight.

"Well, it didn't come to blow same's Wesley thought it would and, nacherally, he was roarin' 'round fine. We shook out the reef in the mains'l before noon-time of that first day, and later we set both tops'ls and that whoppin' gauze balloon of the Lucy's. And she carried 'em easy, too. We warn't loafing altogether; we was makin' nine knots right straight along. But that wasn't pleasing Wesley.

"Next day and the next it was the same story, and part of the next day it was lighter yet. We hove the log, and got only eight knots for twenty-four hours hand-runnin'. Then, almost all at once, from a nice summer breeze it jumped to a gale. And it was a gale—one of those healthy, able zephyrs that makes up north there and gets a good runnin' start afore it tears things loose in the forties.

"Whoo-o-ish it whistled! A regular old buster of a no'theaster—whoo-o-ish!—and Wesley dancin' on and off the break while he watched it comin' on. 'I'm thinkin',' he says, 'we can stow some of those summer kites for a while. Might put the tops'ls in gaskets, boys, and that balloon in stops. We won't be likely to need them any more this trip. This is the breeze I've been waiting for—struck in a little late, but it'll make up for lost time soon.'

"And it sure was making up for lost time. The mains'l pretty soon had to be tucked up, and on the next day tucked again. And before another day we had to take it in altogether, get the trys'l out the hold and fit that on. Now you know it was blowing some when Wesley Marrs had the Lucy under a trys'l and a yachtin' fellow somewhere 'round racing him for a thousand dollars a side; and, what was more, the name of the thing after they got into Gloucester.

"We went that way for thirty-odd hours, and Wesley was almost satisfied. 'Maybe,' says he, 'if this fine breeze holds, we'll make up for those yachtin' days in the fifties. What kind of weather, fellows, do you s'pose the Bounding Billow's making of it? Think now she's handling it like the Lucy, hay? I'd give something to know if she's carryin' a whole fores'l and both jibs right now. Boys,' he says, 'but this is fine weather. In forty-eight hours, and this fine breeze holds, we'll be raisin' Thatcher's twin lights!' Wesley was mighty well satisfied with the way things was lookin' just then.

"That was Friday night late. After midnight it was, for I went on watch at twelve o'clock. I remember well Wesley and Murdie Greenlaw at the wheel when I came out of the cabin door to go for'ard. We was driving through it and she layin' over. Man, but she was layin' over. I'll tell you how she was layin' over. That very afternoon it was that Billie Henderson had walked along her weather run from her stern to her fore-rigging. You've heard of that trick, some of you. Yes, sir—we had a line on him in case he slipped—that's the truth.

"Well, it must have been getting on toward one o'clock, for I was figuring on being called aft to take the wheel for my second hour; and then in one more hour a fellow could go below and dry off and have a good sleep. We were driving through it—two jibs, fores'l and trys'l. We hadn't seen the top of her port-rail for more than two days; and this was one of those nights when the water gets full of phosphorus. It'd been a new moon gone down, and rain that morning, and you all know how the water fires after rain and a new moon. It was fair afire now. And the Lucy! she was leapin' from the top of one sea to the top of another. We made a lane you could see for a cable length behind, and there was blue smoke, I swear, coming from each side.

"Her nose would poke under and we would get it all over. I had my elbow crooked in the fore-rigging so I wouldn't wash off. When she'd rise, she'd throw the water over her shoulder, and it'd run the whole length of her deck and race over the taffrail. That was only the spray, mind you. She was taking it over the rail all the time, besides, as if she had no rail at all. The skipper and Murdie at the wheel must've been pulp. Three or four others were in the waist—five or six men besides the skipper had to be on deck all the time. We was all in oilskins and red-jacks, of course, and we was all properly soaked.

"Well, we was whoopin' along; we'd just shot by some lumberin' old tramp steamer that was making awful bad weather of it, and somebody in the waist'd just called out, 'We're this far, anyway, thank the Lord.' The cook had his head out the fo'c's'le gangway—just a narrow slit to sing out to us on deck—when we saw the skipper jump into the main riggin' and look ahead, and then jump back on deck again as if he saw a ghost. He hollers:

" 'If there ain't the Englishman ahead, and carryin' a two-reefed mains'l! A two-reefed mains'l! And goin' like a liner! I'll be damned if I'll stand on the deck of the Lucy Foster and see the Bounding Billow beat her home. I'll bust the Lucy's spars, but I'll beat him. Bend on the stays'l. I guess the Lucy can carry as much sail as that window-frame boat. Bend on that stays'l.'

"You can bet that shook the boys up. A stays'l! And her planks rattlin' then! Dan Ross—most of you know Dan—big Dan, that was lost on the Fredonia afterward—Dan was nearest me under the weather rail. He says, 'I'll fix that stays'l.' And he did fix her, as he thought. He yanks the halyards loose and they goes flyin' aloft. We could just make them out slinging between the fore and main rigging —like long devils, with the block on the end.

"Dan hollers out: 'Stays'l halyard-ends loose and can't get hold of 'em—they're aloft.'

"The skipper says: 'Go after them.'

"Dan roars back: 'What do you take me for?'

" 'For a man,' hollers the skipper; 'but I guess I was mistaken.'

" 'Show me a man crazy enough to go after them,' says Dan.

" 'Here's one,' roars the skipper, and so help me, if he didn't start aloft. Blowing! My blessed soul, we needed cotton-hooks to hang on by. The boys was curled up under the wind'ard rail with their fingers in the ringbolts. And up went Wesley Marrs—to looard, mind you. And however he managed it—we couldn't half make out what he was doing up there—but he got hold of them.

"Down he comes with the ends fast round his waist. 'Here,' he says to Dan, 'take hold of that.' He unwound about two fathoms of it. 'That's one end of the stays'l halyards you run aloft a little while back. That snaps into the after upper corner of the stays'l, so long as we got to make things plain to you. And this'—he gave him the other end—'this is what you haul on. Is that plain enough? Then see if you can hang on to it, so's better men than yourself won't have to go aloft in a gale to get them down again. Now then, up with that stays'l. Call all hands for'ard there, cook—and call all hands aft there, Murdie—and up with that stays'l! Up with it.'

"And up she went. Such a slattin' afore we got her up! But she got there—and then! If she was leapin' before she was high-divin' now. The water was firing like I was telling you, firing like an ocean of diamonds and white sulphur mixed; and there was that blue smoke you could almost smell coming out from both sides of her wake. I misdoubted if we'd ever get her home. If I'd had a knife handy, you'd have seen the stays'l go into the sky. But I didn't have a knife, nor nobody else on deck, and all we could do was to hope we'd get in to walk down Main Street just once again, and swearin' we'd never ship another trip with that crazy Wesley Marrs, so long's we lived again. Yes, sir, that was an awful run home. We carried our stays'l past the Point. And that's the same Lucy and the same Wesley Marrs coming in the dock there now."

"And what happened to the Bounding Billow? Did you pass her?"

"The Bounding Billow? Hell, no. We got in Monday morning at five o'clock. There warn't any Bounding Billow in sight that night—just one of them ghost dreams of Wesley's. The Englishman didn't get along till about the middle of the week."

"And what did he have to say?"

"The English? Oh, that was funny, too—but hold up a second and see what that telephone wants, one of you."

"It's the office, Petie. They want to know what Captain Marrs got."

"Oh, all right. He'll make fast and be up the wharf in a minute, tell them. He's getting ready to step ashore now."

It was a man of medium height and easy swing who came up the dock with half his crew in tow. He had the sunburned skin of a healthy boy and the vigorous jaw of a man of action. He spat tobacco-juice as he rolled along, but his teeth showed white and unconquerable when he grinned up at the look-out. It was the voice of a moderate blow, a summer gale at play, that answered the hail from Crow's Nest.

"Hulloh, Peter," it roared. "Any signs of fish up there, boy?"

"Hulloh, skipper. What you got?"

"Four hundred barrels."

"Good. Where'd you get 'em."

"Off Monhegan mostly. One school off Middle Bank on the way down. All medium schools. How's the market?"

"Fourteen and a half to-day."

"Good. Report me to the office, will you?—four hundred barrels. Come along down, Peter, and wash the gurry out of your throat. Tell 'em all up there to come."

"In a minute. Here, Johnnie"— Peter lit on a boy of tender years, a boy of an age that ordinarily would not have been allowed to breathe this smoky atmosphere, but in this case a boy who was sometimes suffered to skirt the edge of the blessed circle because of his tractable ways and certain useful connections. He was a purveyor of supplies and a nephew of the firm, a willing boy and not too obtrusive. "Here, Johnnie, telephone the office that the Lucy Foster hails for four hundred barrels, small schools and fine fish—and take charge while we're gone. We'll be at the Anchorage—if anything heaves in sight. But make sure before you disturb us, don't get worried by any coasters or yachts, mind. Do a good job now, and I'll tell your uncle about you, and maybe some day he'll let you have a vessel of your own. Come along, fellows, and p'r'aps we can get it out of Wesley himself just what the Englishman did say after he got in and found the Lucy three days before him. And p'r'aps we c'n get a word out him about his marriage—if it *is* comin' off this fall."

And down the winding stairs the chief look-out and his staff worked their way. It was tack and jibe, until they reached the street below; then it was wear off and a straight run of it, in the wake of Wesley to the Anchorage.

Up in the Crow's Nest the flag went to the mast-head for the Lucy Foster, arrived with four hundred barrels of fine mackerel. And Johnnie, a born hero-worshipper, looked out to sea for incoming fishermen, bravely singing all the while:

> "I'll bust her spars,"
> Says Wesley Marrs,
> "But I'll beat the Bounding Billow."

AN INDEX FOR EXILES

Ready access to a variety of subjects dear to New Englanders may be obtained by this informal and unprecedented index. The mere mention will sometimes be enough; extended treatment is indicated by *italic* figures.

For *Elms,* look in Holmes's "Elsie Venner"; for *Lilacs,* in Amy Lowell's poems; I could not find a *Snowstorm* in a short story to match the one in Whittier's "Snow-Bound" or the one in the seventeenth chapter of Sylvester Judd's novel "Margaret."